ADVANCES IN LONG-TERM CARE

Volume 1

Advances in
LONG-TERM CARE

Volume 1

Paul R. Katz, MD
Robert L. Kane, MD
Mathy D. Mezey, RN, Ed D

Editors

SPRINGER PUBLISHING COMPANY
New York

Springer Publishing Company, Inc.
536 Broadway
New York, NY 10012

91 92 93 94 95 / 5 4 3 2 1

ISBN 0-8261-6830-2
ISSN 1053-0606

Printed in the United States of America

Contents

Contributors

VOLUME EDITORS

Paul R. Katz, MD, has a longstanding interest in issues related to long-term care. He is currently coordinator of the Geriatric Medicine fellowship in the Division of Geriatrics at the State University of New York at Buffalo. He also serves as Director of Long-Term Care Services at the Buffalo Veterans Administration Medical Center and as medical director of University affiliated teaching nursing homes. His research interests have focused on physician practice patterns in long-term care and on medical education; he is co-editor of *Principles and Practice of Nursing Home Care*—also published by Springer. He is active in the American Geriatrics Society and the American Medical Directors Association and serves as chairman of an annual national conference on medical care in the nursing home.

Robert L. Kane, MD, is the holder of the Minnesota Endowed Chair in Long-Term Care and Aging at the University of Minnesota School of Public Health. He has studied and written widely in the areas of geriatrics and long-term care with special attention to issues of quality assurance, functional assessment, and international comparisons of care. Most recently he has co-edited a volume on international perspectives on care of the elderly, *Improving the Health of Older Persons*, and, with Rosalie Kane, has written *Long-Term Care: Principles, Programs and Policies*. His co-authored text, *Essentials of Clinical Geriatrics*, has recently been issued in its second edition.

Mathy D. Mezey, RN, EdD, FAAN, is Professor of Gerontological Nursing at the University of Pennsylvania, School of Nursing, and Associate Director of the Ralston-Penn Center for Care-Education, and Research for the Older Adult. She has a long-standing involvement in the preparation of nurses to work with the elderly. She is former Director of the Robert Wood Johnson Foundation Teaching Nursing Home Program and has recently co-edited a volume on the teaching nursing home entitled *Nursing Homes and Nursing Care*.

AUTHORS

Ruby Abrahams, MA, MSW
Research Associate
Bigel Institute for Health Policy
Brandeis University
415 South Street
Waltham, MA

Joan L. Buchanan, PhD
Senior Researcher and Associate Department Head
System Sciences Department
The RAND Corporation
1700 Main Street
Santa Monica, CA

Kathleen Coen Buckwalter, PhD, RN
Professor and Associate Director
Office of Nursing Research Development & Utilization
University of Iowa
College of Nursing
Iowa City, IA

John A. Capitman, PhD
Associate Research Professor
Bigel Institute for Health Policy
Heller School
Brandeis University
415 South Street
Waltham, MA

Lois K. Evans, DNSc, RN, FAAN
Assistant Professor and Director
Geropsychiatric Nursing
University of Pennsylvania
School of Nursing
420 Service Drive
Philadelphia, PA

Judith Garrard, PhD
Professor
Division of Health Services Research & Policy
School of Public Health
University of Minnesota
Box 729 Mayo Building
420 Delaware Street, S.E.
Minneapolis, MN

Catherine Hawes, PhD
Program Director
Program on Aging and Long-Term Care
Research Triangle Institute
P.O. Box 12194
Research Triangle Park, NC

Karen R. Josephson, MPH
Research Associate
VA Medical Center (11E), 16111 Plummer Street
Sepulveda, CA

Robert L. Kane, MD
Dean
School of Public Health
University of Minnesota
A-304 Mayo (Box 197)
420 Delaware Street, S.E.
Minneapolis, MN

Marshall B. Kapp, JD, MPH
Professor,
Department of Community Health
Director,
Office of Geriatric Medicine and Gerontology
Wright State University
School of Medicine
Box 927
Dayton, OH

Jurgis Karuza, PhD
Multidisciplinary Center on Aging
State University of New York at Buffalo
Department of Psychology
State University College at Buffalo
1300 Elmwood Avenue
Buffalo, NY

Paul R. Katz, M.D.
Assistant Professor of Medicine
Division of Geriatrics
State University of New York at Buffalo
Director of Long Term Care
VA Medical Center (111-T)
3495 Bailey Avenue
Buffalo, NY

Margaret A. MacAdam, PhD
Senior Research Associate
Bigel Institute for Health Policy
Brandeis University
415 South Street
Waltham, MA

Joseph G. Ouslander, MD
Medical Director, Victory Village
Jewish Homes for the Aging of Greater
  Los Angeles
Associate Professor
Multicampus Division of Geriatric Medi-
  cine and Gerontology
UCLA School of Medicine
18855 Victory Blvd.
Reseda, CA

Edward R. Ratner, MD
Instructor
Department of Medicine
420 Delaware Street, S.E.
Minneapolis, MN

Alan S. Robbins, MD
Chief of Staff
VA Medical Center (11)
16111 Plummer Street
Sepulveda, CA

Laurence Z. Rubenstein, MD
Clinical Director, GRECC, and Asso-
  ciate Professor of Medicine UCLA
VA Medical Center (11E)
16111 Plummer Street
Sepulveda, CA

Neville E. Strumpf, PhD, RNC, FAAN
Associate Professor and
Director, Gerontological Nurse Clini-
  cian Program
School of Nursing
University of Pennsylvania
Philadelphia, PA

William G. Weissert, PhD
Professor, Health Services Management
  & Policy
Research Scientist, Institute of Geron-
  tology
School of Public Health II
The University of Michigan
1420 Washington Heights
Ann Arbor, MI

Carter Catlett Williams, MSW, ACSW
Social Work Consultant in Aging
5202 West Cedar Lane
Bethesda, MD

Foreword

We applaud the goals and efforts of the editors and authors of this first volume of a series addressing the special challenges and advances in long-term care. From both the social and medical perspectives we (along with others) have seen the growing burdens faced by chronically ill frail persons (mostly but not only older persons), their families, and society; fortunately there have also been increasing commitments to understanding and dealing effectively with these facts. It is indeed timely that a series like this undertakes to present in a systematic way the advances that have been and are continuing to be documented.

This first volume addresses a number of the major issues affecting long-term care in nursing homes as well as care at home, particularly in the areas of clinical care and organization of care. Topics covered range from practical approaches to falls, urinary incontinence, psychosocial interventions, and living settings for cognitively impaired persons, to efforts to achieve higher levels of quality of care through new laws and regulations and through attention to restorative and individualized care as alternatives to the practice of physical restraint. New contributions to long-term care resources are discussed, including care- or case-management and the roles of geriatric nurse practitioners, as well as methodological issues of assessing success in home care. The importance of understanding the legal basis for decisions about long-term care is imaginatively presented.

There are also other aspects of long-term care, at both the clinical and policy levels, in which advances are being made; we anticipate that these will be addressed in future volumes in this series. In addition to home care and nursing-home care there are other important settings in which care is provided: day programs, group homes, foster homes, and life care communities. Furthermore, it is essential in our view that long-term care be approached in the context of the full range of care, as needed by persons with chronic physical and/or psychosocial disabilities. This may include primary and continuing care; and temporary acute care. The interrelationships between long-term care factors and the rest of the life of a frail person are just beginning to receive the attention they deserve; we have much to learn, to demonstrate, and to report about truly comprehensive care in which the choices and autonomy of the individual are kept paramount.

Other dimensions of life should also come into the purview of long-term care knowledge and research: the role of art and the humanities (in relation to long-term care), and the *experience* of long-term care as it is known by the recipients. Such studies are essential in order that we may all hear the voices of the persons whose fabric of daily life is at stake, and provide the wholeness of approach that a more narrowly defined agenda would miss. The persons most directly involved (patients and families) must participate in molding long-term care research.

As we learn more about the causes and characteristics of the problems that lead to long-term care we can certainly hope to prevent and minimize them and through rehabilitative approaches restore degrees of independence. Attention for these aspects too is promised in this series. For some time to come there will clearly be the continuing need to advance our understanding of the explicit features of long-term care itself, which this volume is effectively undertaking.

T. FRANKLIN WILLIAMS, M.D.
CARTER CATLETT WILLIAMS, M.S.W., A.C.S.W.

Bethesda, Maryland

Preface

This volume, the first in a series to be published biennially, attests to the prominent position long-term care now occupies within the nation's health care system. This so-called "coming of age" is surprising not because long-term care is unworthy of attention but rather for the time it has taken to capture the interest and imagination of key health care professionals including physicians, nurses, researchers, and policymakers.

Such inattention is based, at least in part, on the difficulty in clearly defining long-term care. Long-term care involves many disciplines including physical and mental health care, and health and social care, and formal and informal services. Although long-term care does, in fact, have a time dimension, usually measured in months or years, not everyone agrees when it begins or when and if it ever actually ends. Long-term care is further obscured as a result of the frequent transitions to and from acute care and the resultant overlap in services and clientele.

Long-term care has remained unappealing for other less compelling reasons, one of which relates to the slow and oftentimes undramatic nature of change affecting those receiving its services. Acute care, in contrast, is characterized by rather dramatic and rapid changes providing both the practitioner and investigator short, well circumscribed episodes in which to treat illness or conduct research. Long-term care, typified by chronic disease and disability, dependence on a largely nonprofessional work force, and a low level of technology, is no match for acute care when it comes to the "glamour quotient." No wonder so many health care professionals graduate without ever having had adequate exposure to long-term care. This is particularly true for physicians. Medical students and residents infrequently participate in home care or manage patients in more formalized institutional settings. Such a lack of experience may help explain the many indifferent or denigrating attitudes exhibited toward long-term care. Finally, as most entitlements have been directed to acute care over the past two to three decades, long-term care has taken on the appearance of a "welfare program" and with that has come all of the attendant biases and neglect.

The shift in focus toward long-term care over the past several years can be attributed, in large part, to a better appreciation for changing demographics. Although the elderly population continues to burgeon as a result of increased life expectancy and an aging baby boom generation, little evidence exists that supports the notion that those attaining old age in the future will be any less chronically ill or disabled than preceding cohorts. As the number of persons with limitations in activity due to chronic conditions increases significantly into the next century, hospital, physician, nursing home, and home care services will rise proportionately as of course will costs. Not surprisingly, finding the means in which to deliver needed services in an efficient and cost-effective manner will be one of the major quests in the decade of the nineties.

With this mandate clearly in mind, plus the realization that there are few, if any, recurring publications devoted exclusively to long-term care issues (save for trade publications), the *Advances in Long-Term Care* series was conceived. The focus of *Advances*, although varying somewhat from volume to volume, will remain along three major areas; (1) interdisciplinary perspectives in clinical practice, (2) health policy, and (3) epidemiology. Those health care professionals involved in direct patient care and, secondarily, those involved in the formulation of policy affecting such care should derive substantial benefit from this series. We also anticipate that many of the articles in *Advances* will find their way into the classroom setting and be of significant use to students in a wide range of disciplines.

Although the word "advances" may, to many, appear out of place juxtaposed with "long-term care" we believe the title accurately reflects the current state of affairs. Whether one defines advances as "forward movement," "improvement" or "progress," examples abound. The issue of physical restraints reviewed by Evans and colleagues in this volume is one such example. Whereas restraints were seen just a few years ago as necessary and accepted as good medical care in nursing homes and hospitals, patients, families, and providers are now questioning the role of restraints in patient management. Restraint free institutions have in fact become the norm, a truly phenomenal change over a mere 24 months!

In keeping with the broad nature of long-term care the contents of this volume cover a wide spectrum spanning medicine, nursing, psychology, law, and health and social policy. We hope that the issues raised, of which many will be controversial, will not only assist the reader in the more effective and efficient delivery of services but also highlight those areas in which further research is needed.

We would like to thank the distinguished panel of scholars comprising the Advisory Board who not only shared our vision at the conception of this project but who assisted greatly in the selection of topics and contributors and in the review of manuscripts. Thanks are also extended to the editorial staff at Springer Publishing Company whose commitment to long-term care education remains unmatched. Finally, much appreciation is extended to Arlene Peters whose organizational skills helped keep this entire project on schedule.

PRK, RLK, MDM

Forthcoming

ADVANCES IN LONG-TERM CARE, Volume 2

1

Psychosocial Interventions in Long-Term Care: A Critical Overview

Jurgis Karuza
Paul R. Katz

INTRODUCTION

This chapter presents a critical overview of psychosocial interventions currently advocated for use in institutionalized long-term care settings. Unfortunately, no clear consensus exists on when and why various interventions work, a problem compounded by the largely anecdotal empirical literature. Even so, changes in regulations and philosophy of care, and the increase in complexity of care nursing homes are expected to provide define a situation where psychosocial interventions will play an increasingly prominent role. A review of some of the empirical literature suggests that psychosocial interventions have the potential to play an important adjunct role in patient care. Further, they can serve as a vehicle for job enrichment for nursing staff, especially nurses aides, and lead to positive effects for staff. A major question that remains unanswered is the extent to which these benefits are due to the intervention or to more generic "non-specific therapeutic" effects. It is necessary for nursing home administrators and staff to commit to a programmatic and rigorous approach in developing, conducting, and evaluating psychosocial interventions and in training staff to deliver them.

PSYCHOSOCIAL INTERVENTIONS

We begin by drawing a distinction between clinical psychological, psychiatric, or formal counseling treatments, and psychosocial interventions. The former therapeutic efforts address acute pathological emotional and

1

behavioral problems. While these treatments vary in their views of underlying cause of problems, for example, metabolic imbalance, environmental stress, and how to treat them (e.g., drug therapy, psychotherapy), they typically share a "medical model" approach to the delivery of care (Karuza, et al., 1990; Rabinowitz, Zevon, & Karuza, 1988). Trained and recognized health or allied health professionals are given the responsibility and authority to diagnose the problem and to implement a treatment plan. The goal of the treatment is the amelioration or control of the pathological behavior and the treatment itself is specialized, e.g., drug therapy, and in many ways is discontinuous from the normal everyday programming of the nursing home. In contrast, the latter psychosocial interventions address less dramatic "problems of adjustment" to nursing home life and/or functional impairments. These problems may be chronic, such as those associated with progressive dementia, or acute episodes of maladjustment, such as coping with a nursing home transfer. In any case, nursing home residents play a more active and central role in the intervention, with the nursing home staff members, possibly nurses aides or activities coordinators, taking on a more facilitating role. The goal of these interventions is not to "cure a problem" but to enhance or maintain the functioning level of the residents, with the interventions themselves frequently becoming a part of the daily routine of nursing home life.

Need for Nursing Home-Based Psychosocial Interventions

Psychosocial interventions are assumed to be good and useful. While there is an abundance of anecdotal published testimonials for using psychosocial interventions, reviews of the empirical research (e.g., Burckhardt, 1987) indicate a mixed pattern of effectiveness. The case remains to be made among administrators and health professionals for implementing psychosocial interventions within the nursing home.

Demographic and Epidemiological Trends

Democraphic trends create an environment that encourages the development and use of psychosocial interventions. The current and future nursing home resident population is at risk for emotional and behavioral problems. Estimates in the literature indicate a prevalence of mental health needs in 50–80% of nursing home residents (e.g., Newman et al., 1989; Rovner, et al., 1986). A study by Zimmer, Watson, and Treat (1984) indicates behavioral problems are present in 64.2% of New York nursing home residents. Of those residents, 66.5% had a diagnosis of organic brain syndrome and only 14% had a psychiatric diagnosis or a diagnosis of depression. This trend will accelerate as nursing home residents become older. Currently, 1.4 million

(22%) of those 85 years of age or older are institutionalized and this will balloon to 4.6 million in the year 2040 (U.S. Senate, 1987). This is significant, given the increased prevalence of mental health and cognitive disorders in later life. Another factor is the long-standing and continuing commitment to deinstitutionalization of psychiatric hospital patients. In the future, the nursing home industry will be serving a majority of clients with emotional and behavioral problems, many of whom will not have a primary psychiatric diagnosis.

Complicating these trends are various financial and regulatory pressures that are pushing nursing homes to admit and treat elderly clients who are either more incapacitated or who have more complex medical conditions. Newman, et al. (1989), recently reported a statewide study of Utah nursing home residents. They discovered that among those who were considered appropriate for nursing home placement according to Health Care Financing Administration (HCFA) criteria, 79.6% of the residents had moderate to intense needs for mental health care. Intense medical and physical problems were significantly related to more intense psychosocial needs and, interestingly, primary psychiatric diagnosis was not predictive of the psychosocial problem intensity. Emerging data suggest that residents' mental health is associated with health care utilization (e.g., Koenig et al., 1989). To the extent that this data is reliable, resident mental health and behavioral problems can have an impact on the cost of care, not to mention the residents' quality of life. Controlling these costs by addressing residents' mental health care at all levels presents a promising direction to explore.

Holding aside psychiatric problems, nursing home residents with mental health needs fall into two general categories. First, are those residents who have chronic behavioral problems which are associated with dementia. Second, are residents that have acute problems of adjustment and coping, such as those arising from the stress of adjustment to a novel environment (e.g., Stein, Linn, & Stein, 1985) family conflicts (Brody, 1985), relocation trauma (Schulz & Brenner, 1977) or adaptation to changes in functional level. Psychosocial interventions can be especially well suited for these residents.

Rise of Geriatric-based Models of Nursing Home Care

Concurrently, nursing home care is being redefined by health care policymakers and health professionals in geriatrics. Approaches based on a geriatric medicine primary care model (e.g., Association of American Medical Colleges, 1983; Calkins, 1987; Katz & Calkins, 1989), are moving away from the medicalization of the nursing home and are increasingly sensitive to issues such as maintenance of functioning, enhancement of quality of life, and the role social and environmental factors play in normal aging and pathological processes. This can be seen in preliminary data from a recent survey of New York State nursing homes we conducted ($n = 530$ with a response rate of 60%). Nursing home administrators endorsed a medical care model of nursing homes significantly less than models which stressed promotion of resident independence or protecting residents ($p < .001$). Focusing on mental health and behavioral problems, a "non toxic" approach, which features psychosocial interventions rather than medical model–based drug therapies, is seriously advocated by an increasingly larger number of geriatricians and geriatric nurses. While these trends are encouraging, support for a primary care approach in geriatrics is far from universal and strong pressures to medicalize aging processes still exists (Kane, 1989; Estes & Binney, 1989). The interdisciplinary approach, ideally a central component of the geriatric model in practice (Calkins, 1987; Calkins & Karuza, 1988), can facilitate the contributions of other disciplines such as psychology and social work in the diagnosis and treatment of mental health problems in the nursing home.

Legislative Mandates

Perhaps the most forceful impetus comes from recent legislative mandates, in particular, the Omnibus Budget Reconciliation Act of 1987 (OBRA). This federal legislation was in direct response to the report issued by the National Academy of Sciences. The report (Institute of Medicine, 1986), which was part of a study commissioned by the Department of Health and Human Services, found that nursing home care needed improvement and that regulatory reform offered a mechanism to achieve better care. The OBRA legislation specifically recognized the mental health problems in nursing home residents and has several key provisions dealing specifically with these issues. Among them is the requirement for preadmission screening of nursing home residents. For new residents, if there is a primary or secondary diagnosis of a mental disorder (other than dementia) or mental retardation, they must be referred to another site for "active treatment." If a resident is in a nursing home less than 30 months and develops a primary or secondary diagnosis of a mental disorder (other than dementia), he or she must be referred to another site for "active treatment." If the resident is in nursing home more than 30 months and has a mental disorder, he or she has a choice of seeking treatment in the nursing home or at another site.

In view of these changes, nursing homes will have to be more sensitive to mental health issues. At the very least, they must develop adequate screening of residents prior to admission. Further, they must develop an adequate mental health treatment response to those individuals who are residents for over 30 months. Administrators need to develop appropriate and effective clinical psychological and psychiatric treatment options for acute episodes. At the very least, this requires exploring the cost effectiveness of a variety of therapeutic approaches, both pharmacological and psychotherapeutic, and the building of a responsive referral network. It is imperative that the administrator not stop here. Given the costs of paying for those therapeutic treatments, and the low levels of reimbursement currently available, the nursing home administrator would be wise also to examine psychosocial interventions *as primary prevention strategies.*

A second relevant facet of the legislation is concerned with staff training. All nurse's aides are required to undergo 75 hours of training in basic nursing skills, personal care skills, basic restorative services, residents' rights, and *recognition of mental health needs.*

The importance of addressing mental health needs of the residents in the training can be seen in the following clarification from HCFA (1988):

> Mental health and social service needs: The nurse's aide will demonstrate basic skills by modifying his/her own behavior in response to residents' behavior; identifying developmental tasks associated with the aging process, and using task analysis and segmenting of those tasks to increase independence; providing training in and the opportunity for self care according to residents' capabilities; demonstrating principles of behavior modification by reinforcing appropriate behavior and causing inappropriate behavior to be reduced or eliminated; demonstrating skills supporting age-appropriate behavior by allowing the resident to make personal choices; providing and reinforcing other behavior consistent with residents' dignity; and, utilizing residents' family as a source of emotional support. (HCFA, 1988, pp. 11–12)

The implication of this aspect of the legislation is that nursing homes will be required to train staff in psychosocial interventions and rely on them to conduct those interventions. Realistically speaking, this mandated regulation is leading to the "professionalization" of nurse's aides, traditionally lowest ranking members of the nursing staff hierarchy.

REVIEW OF SOME TYPICAL PSYCHOSOCIAL INTERVENTIONS

This section will review several of the prevalent and accepted psychosocial intervention strategies that are used in nursing home settings. The following review is not a comprehensive critique of the literature, but is designed to provide a working overview of some of the more common psychosocial interventions reported in the literature.

Disciplinary based therapies and interventions with formal certification, such as art therapy, are not included. Other reviews that may be of some interest include Burckhardt (1987) and Gugel (1989). Before starting, we would like to focus on some general issues in implementing any psychosocial intervention in a nursing home.

First, on basis of several research reviews, there is no single universally optimal psychosocial intervention (e.g., Burckhardt, 1987). The task before the administrator and staff is effectively to develop flexible psychosocial programming for the residents.

Second, effective psychosocial programming must be sensitive to the individual differences in skills and interests of residents. In several evaluations of psychosocial interventions it is clear that residents' characteristics such as mental competence (e.g., Goldwasser, Auerbach, & Harkines, 1987), attitudes toward the nursing home (e.g., Berghorn & Schafer, 1986), and age (e.g., Fallot, 1979) can moderate the effectiveness of the intervention.

Third, nursing homes also vary in characteristics, such as, staffing levels, the case mix of residents, and the physical layout (Maas, 1988), which may make some psychosocial interventions more or less practical.

This leads to a fourth point, that the development of psychosocial interventions requires the satisfactory matching of interventions to residents. Lawton and Nahemow's (1973) discussion of person-environment transactions offers a useful model to adopt in charting a psychosocial intervention program. As seen in Figure 1.1, adaptive functioning of a resident is the product of two factors, his or her competence level and the environmental pressures or demands. Maladaptive behavior and emotional reactions occur when the environmental demands are *too strong*, or *too weak* relative to the abilities and competencies of the individual. Adaptive functioning occurs when there is a match of competence to demands with maximal performance occurring when the demands of the situation are slightly challenging to the individual. There is an implicit recognition in the psychosocial intervention literature that interventions vary in the demands they place on individuals. In selecting psychosocial programming an individual should be matched to the psychosocial intervention's demands. An important corollary of this model, is that providing too simple a psychosocial intervention to a more competent resident can be just as deleterious as providing too demanding and stressful an intervention to a less competent resident.

A fifth point to consider is that adequate assessments of residents are essential in the effective psychosocial programming, even if a psychiatric primary diagnosis is excluded. In keeping with the person-environmental transaction model, these assessments must provide sufficient information to determine the competency levels and should be multidimensional. The purpose of these assessments is not so much to provide a diagnosis of a mental or behavioral problem but to determine the applicability of the intervention to the resident. The dynamics of most of these interventions is not to actively prescribe a treatment for the residents, but to allow ongoing opportunities for residents to maximize their functioning and to better adjust to their lives. Assessments should include evaluations of cognitive functioning, perceptual acuity, linguistic ability, and functional level. Since many of these inter-

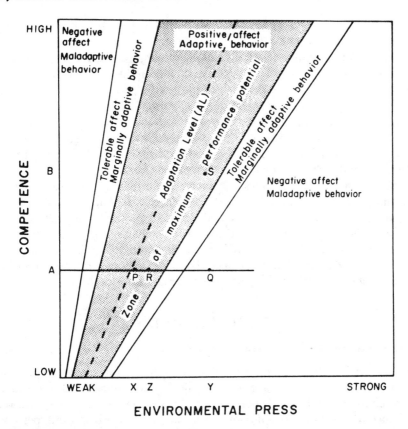

ENVIRONMENTAL PRESS

FIGURE 1.1 Diagrammatic representation of the behavioral and affective outcomes of person–environment transactions (from Lawton and Nahemow, 1973. Copyright 1973 by the American Psychological Association. Reprinted by permission.)

ventions make use of group sessions, social skill level and desire for socialization should also be assessed.

Sixth, the facilitators of these interventions, the nurse's aides, the activities directors, and the nurses, need to be trained in the intervention. These interventions, for the most part, are not complex therapeutic systems and do not need extensive certification. Still, to be effective, the facilitators need to be familiar with the rationale and methods of each intervention. It is interesting to note that in evaluations of various psychosocial interventions there typically is no measure of the extent to which the staff facilitators were knowledgeable of the intervention methods or effective in the application of the methodology (Gropper-Katz, 1987). This is an important factor when attempting to interpret results when they do not show the intervention having an effect on residents. Was the technique ineffective? Or was the technique ineffectively applied?

Finally, follow-through and evaluation of the impact of the intervention is critical. In a dramatic follow-up study by Schulz and Hanusa (1978), nursing home residents who initially significantly benefitted by an intervention (visitation by students) exhibited steep declines in their well-being after the intervention was suddenly terminated, compared to a control group who did not receive the intervention. Administrators and staff need to insure a commitment to a psychosocial intervention, otherwise, undesirable negative effects from the termination of the intervention may be seen in the residents. As the extant literature reviews frequently note, more rigorous evaluations of psychosocial interventions are needed. To guard against negative effects, and to create an organizational expectation that psychosocial interventions are useful tools, a commitment to a systematic evaluation of the impact psychosocial interventions have on residents and staff is indispensable. Establishing a documented track record can help incorporate psychosocial interventions as a respected part of the nursing home culture.

Reality Orientation

Intervention's Goals and Assumptions

Reality orientation has been defined as an active participatory program for demented residents to reorient them to their current situation. It is assumed that reinforcing residents' contact with reality can counteract their confusion, enhance personal responsibility over behavior, and foster better interpersonal communication (cf., Folsom, 1968; Hogstel, 1979; Campos, 1984). It assumes some plasticity in cognitive functioning and that by creating a more stimulating environment, the resident can practice and better use existing cognitive skills. The expectation is that the rate of cognitive decline and associated functional loss found in demented residents can be decelerated, if not reversed. Some versions of reality orientation therapies include an "attitude therapy" component which seeks to communicate to the resident a feeling of friendliness, calmness, consistency and security.

Description of Technique

There are two basic approaches to reality orientation, a 24-hour a day approach and a more formal classroom approach. Frequently the approaches are combined. In the 24-hour a day approach, staff continually reorient residents to time, place, and person by asking residents questions and reinforcing correct responses. Environmental props, such as clocks, calendars, name tags, and reality orientation boards are used as cues. Staff are expected to engage residents in their environment, provide clear instructions, ask simple questions of residents, and provide a friendly atmosphere. In the 24-hour approach the staff as a whole are responsible for the implementation and conduct of the reality orientation intervention.

In the classroom approach 5–6 residents meet in a group that is led by a facilitator, a trained staff member. Classes are held frequently, either daily or 4–5 times a week and typically last 30 minutes. In the classroom setting environmental props, such as clocks, calendars, name tags, and reality orientation boards are also used as cues. Classroom techniques focus on group rehearsal of orientation information and reinforcement for correct responses. They have also included more varied group activities, such as bingo (Woods, 1979). The mixture of activities dilutes the character of reality orientation and causes the sessions to more resemble other nursing home activities. In addition, some approaches advocate the combination of reality orientation with other techniques such as exercise programs or validation therapy (e.g., Bleathman, 1988). This creates difficulties in interpreting the effectiveness of the intervention.

Target Population

Reality orientation is primarily aimed at those residents who exhibit behaviors considered confused or disoriented in respect to space and time. In practice, the primary targets of reality orientation are often residents with moderate levels of dementia.

Evaluation

The results of various studies indicate a mixed picture of effectiveness. Reality orientation has been found effective in several studies. Predominantly, the effects of reality orientation have been found on cognitive measures (Citrin & Dixon, 1977; Hanley, McGuire, & Boyd, 1981; Nodhturft & Sweeney, 1982; Woods, 1979; Zepelin, Wolfe, & Kleinplatz, 1981). Reeves and Ivinson (1985) found reality orientation coupled with environmental manipulation produced behavioral changes, but most studies do not report statistically significant behavioral changes.

Most of the evaluation studies examined the short-term impact of reality orientation, 6–12 weeks (e.g., Citrin & Dixon, 1977; Reeves & Ivinson, 1985). One study, Zepelin, Wolfe, & Kleinplatz (1981), did examine the impact of reality orientation over a yearlong period. Residents in the reality orientation group compared to a control group had improvements in cognitive measures 6 months posttreatment. At 12 months the differences between groups, while in the correct direction, fell short of statistical significance. Johnson, McLaren, and McPherson (1981) found no differences in the effectiveness of classroom-based and 24-hour-based reality orientation.

Other studies find no effects of reality orientation (e.g., Barnes, 1974;

Letcher, Peterson, & Scarbrough, 1974; Voelkel, 1978). A major gap in the literature is that the medical and cognitive status of the residents is not adequately taken into account. Whether reality orientation is effective among more demented residents is not clear, with some evidence (Brook, Degun, & Mather, 1975) suggesting less cognitively impaired residents may benefit more. Several case studies and anecdotal reports suggest adverse effects associated with reality orientation (e.g., Dietch, Hewett, & Jones, 1989).

Perhaps the most critical response to reality orientation comes from those who advocate specialized care units for demented residents (Cleary, et al., 1988; Maas, 1988). Reality orientation can overstimulate the demented resident, placing too many demands on the resident and, in effect, create a more confusing and distracting environment. This more stressful environment can result in negative effects on the part of the residents. Contrary to reality orientation's implicit logic, specialized care units strive to reduce the cognitive strain of the environment to better match the lower threshold levels of the demented resident (see Chapter 3, this volume).

Validation Therapy

Intervention's Goals and Assumptions

Validation therapy is a humanistically based approach originated by Feil (1982) and based upon principles of Carl Roger's client-centered therapy. It is designed to give disoriented residents a sense of self and dignity by validating their feelings. A major premise of validation therapy is that many residents of nursing homes are in a state of despair (Erikson, 1950). The withdrawal, isolation, and disorientation of residents are seen as defense or coping mechanisms that the residents use to defend against anxiety associated with unresolved existential conflicts. These tendencies are further exacerbated by the intellectual, social, and sensory deprivation that can be found in nursing homes (Babins, 1988; Babins, Dillon, & Merovitz, 1988). Validation therapy strives to humanize the relationships between the residents and their caregivers.

Description of Technique

Validation therapy involves 5–10 residents who meet in a group to discuss unresolved personal conflicts (see Babins, 1988; Babins, Dillon, & Merovitz, 1988; Bleathman, 1988). A trained staff member leads the group. Topics for discussion typically focus on death, loneliness, or loss, and are picked by the group. Sing-alongs, role playing, and playing with objects are techniques to enhance resident self-expression. Asking of questions and validating resident feelings without interpretation are key elements in the sessions. The groups typically meet weekly or semi weekly for about one hour.

Target Population

Validation therapy is targeted at confused and withdrawn elderly. The approach may be especially appropriate for very old (over 85 years of age) residents. The approach is not considered appropriate for severely demented, vegetative, or psychotic residents (Babins, 1988).

Evaluation

Some evidence in the literature suggests that validation therapy may be effective (Babins, Dillon, & Merovitz, 1988; Peoples, 1982), however, the lack of control group designs, and absence of statistical analysis makes this literature equivocal.

Reminiscence Therapy

Intervention's Goals and Assumptions

Reminiscence therapy is based on a developmental approach (Erikson, 1950). The normal and adaptive task before elderly individuals is to engage in life review and the goal is the achievement of ego integrity, that is, a sense that life lived has been worthwhile and without regrets (Butler, 1980; Lo Gerfo, 1980; Osborn, 1989). To that extent it overlaps with some of the assumptions underlying validation therapy. The two approaches can be seen as differing in the emphasis placed on life review and validation of feelings. Several authors have distinguished between different types of reminiscence (e.g., Lo Gerfo, 1980; Osborn, 1989). Informative reminiscing stresses review of factual material. The opportunity to engage effective remembrance provides pleasure and self-esteem enhancement. Evaluative reminiscence stresses life review as a developmental task which can allow an individual to come to terms with old conflicts and defeats and to work through the meaning and acceptance of one's life. The possibility of obsessive and maladaptive reminiscence is noted among those elderly adults who are unable to accept their past and are despairing. It is assumed that the benefits of reminiscence are far-reaching and include improvement in self-esteem, acceptance of losses, increased life satisfaction, and decreased depression. A mechanism of how reminiscences can cause some of these adaptive effects is not clearly specified (Osborn, 1989).

Description of Technique

Reminiscence techniques are quite varied. Both individual-based and group-based interventions have been used (cf., Coleman, 1974; Goldwasser, Auerbach, & Harkines, 1987; Perrotta & Meacham, 1981). Interventions also vary in the extent to which they were structured (e.g., Fry, 1983). In group-based approaches the technique can change with the type of reminiscence, that is, factual or evaluative. In evaluative approaches the group members and group facilitator may need to take a more active role in guiding the reminiscence and avoid destructive obsessive reviews (Lo Gerfo, 1980). In evaluative reviews the reminiscences tend to be more personal, dealing with one's own life or non-personal dealing than factual reviews, which focus on recalling less personal historical events. Several authors comment on the importance of this latter type of review in fostering intergenerational links (Perschbacher, 1984). Frequently, aids such as music, photographs, old newspapers, or movies are used to facilitate the reminiscence.

The group approach consists of 5–10 residents and a trained staff facilitator who meet for 30 minutes to one hour once or twice a week. The length of the therapy typically ranges from 5 to 12 weeks (cf., Goldwasser, Auerbach, & Harkines, 1987; Berghorn & Schafer, 1986). The function of the group is to provide the resident with an atmosphere that stimulates and heightens the reminiscence activity. In the conduct of these sessions it is important to make sure reminiscence time given each resident allows adequate time to share his or her memories with the group, and to facilitate group discussion and interpretation of the memories in a positive way. Ensuring continuity within and between sessions is desirable.

Target Population

Reminiscence therapy requires residents who are verbal, and are cognitively functioning. The applicability of this kind of approach with confused and demented residents is open to question but a study did find evidence for the effectiveness of this approach with more demented residents (Goldwasser, Auerbach, & Harkines, 1987).

Evaluation

Early studies of a correlational nature found greater adjustment and happiness among residents who showed a higher frequency of reminiscing (e.g., Boylin, Gordon, & Nehrke, 1976). Among community-based residents experimental evidence for the effectiveness of reminiscence therapy relative to control groups varies (cf., Fallot, 1979; Perrotta & Meacham, 1981). Specific to nursing home residents, Goldwasser, Auerbach, & Harkines (1987) found positive effects of reminiscence on affective processes, but in general, the impact on cognitive, and behavioral processes is not clear (Burckhardt, 1987; Merriam, 1980). There is evidence that individual differences, such as the extent to which the residents hold values incongruent with the social structure of the nursing home (Berghorn & Schafer, 1986), may affect the effectiveness of the intervention.

Behavior Modification

Intervention's Goals and Assumptions

Behavior modification is based on the well established tradition of behavior-ism in psychology (Kazdin, 1975). It assumes behavior is lawful and objec-tively caused, and not a product of some unconscious mental process. Some of the current social learning theories (e.g., Bandura, 1977) are less radical and admit to the importance of cognitive processes in causing behavior. From a behavior modification perspective, the behavior of an individual is elicited by environmental causes that can be determined and changed. Specifically, the frequency and strength of a behavior are assumed to be functions of the consequences it produces, that is the resulting reinforcement. Reinforcers consist of those environmental stimuli which increase the probability of a response being made. They can be very concrete, such as food, or more symbolic, such as praise or attention. Cues are those stimuli in the environ-ment that signal to the individual that reinforcement is imminent, if a particular behavior is performed. Changing behavior is accomplished by changing the reinforcements in the environment, either stopping reinforce-ment for an unwanted behavior (extinction) or giving reinforcements when the individual performs a desired alternative behavior. Punishment, that is, actively doing something unpleasant to the individual as a consequence of his or her behavior, is not seen as effectively changing behavior.*

Description of Technique

The classical behavior modification technique in applied settings is described in full by Kazdin (1975) and in geriatrics by Burgio and Burgio (1986). The section below is designed to give a brief summary of the process. Behavior modification depends on a complete behavioral analysis. First, the unwanted behavior is designated and desirable alternative target behaviors are defined. In the case of complex behavioral change, for example increased socializa-tion, the global behavior is broken up into specific molecular behaviors. Next, the overt behavioral referents need to be determined, that is, isolating the maintaining conditions—the antecedents and consequences of the be-havior. This requires a rigorous observation period where the responses of the resident are systematically recorded. Third, the staff changes the reinforcement patterns in the environment. Frequently the staff's behavior when interacting with residents may be the reinforcement and so staff behavior must be changed (Baltes et al., 1983). To eliminate an unwanted

---

*Negative reinforcement is frequently confused with punishment. Negative reinforcement is different in that it removes something unpleasant in the environment as a consequence of the individual performing a behavior. Unlike punishment, negative reinforcement is a very effective way of changing behavior.

behavior, reinforcement that was previously obtained is eliminated. To develop new desired behaviors, the staff prompts the resident and reinforces the resident when the new behavior is performed. Attention is paid to the frequency of reinforcement, that is, the schedules of reinforcement. Behavior that is reinforced continuously is learned the quickest, but is the least long lasting. Behavior that is reinforced variably takes longer to learn but is longest lasting. Frequently, to develop novel behaviors, behavioral shaping is required where desired behavior is obtained through a process of successive approximations.

Target Population

Behavior modification can be used with all residents. In fact, some of the more dramatic examples of behavior modification success can be seen in more impaired subjects (Burgio & Burgio, 1986). Since intense cognitive involvement is not required for behavior modification, it is especially suited for demented patients. But, there is some evidence that individual differences, such as cognitive functioning (e.g., Hu et al., 1989) may moderate the effectiveness of the intervention. Unlike the other interventions, the staff member is the primary agent of change. This raises ethical issues, especially with impaired elderly. While the behavior modification can be done without an individual being aware of the intervention, behavior modification frequently involves and enlists the cooperation of the individual in helping define the unwanted and desired behaviors. Involving cognitively functioning residents in the behavior modification process is possible and may be desired, since the elderly residents themselves may be important sources of reinforcement in the nursing home environment, for example, socialization patterns.

Evaluation

Geriatric-based behavior modification literature, while not vast, documents the power and effectiveness of behavior modification in geriatric settings (Burgio & Burgio, 1986). Behavior modification techniques have been used to increase walking and exercise patterns of elderly residents (Burgio et al., 1986; MacDonald & Butler, 1974; Sperbeck & Whitbourne, 1981). Gains in verbal behavior and socialization skills among nursing home residents have been demonstrated by Balleseros et al. (1988); Blackman, Howe, and Pinkston (1976); Carsensen and Erickson (1986), Kletsch, Witman, and Santos (1983); and Praders and MacDonald (1986). Behavior modification principles have been used with some success in developing problem solving and memory skills in nursing home residents (Hussain & Lawrence, 1981; Langer et al., 1978). A large body of literature demonstrates the effectiveness of behavioral therapy on incontinence (e.g., Burgio & Burgio, 1986; Hadley, 1986; Hu et al., 1989; Ouslander, 1986; Resnick & Yalla, 1985).

While the evidence shows that behavior modification works, it is important to note that it requires a trained staff to monitor the intervention and an absolute commitment to the program over the long term. Without continuous monitoring, the reinforcement patterns may slip, resulting in the extinguishing of the desired behavior or unwanted behaviors being reinforced. The costs involved in staff time may not be worth the effects the intervention produces. For example the cost of a behavior modification program in controlling incontinence may be more expensive compared to laundering wet clothing and bed sheets (Schnelle et al., 1983).

A common problem is the generalizability of the behavior modification effects across time or place. The benefits of behavior modification obtained in one shift may not generalize to the next shift, if the next shift does not continue the intervention. Cross-shift cooperation is essential. So too environmental cues may be so strong that behavior changes found in one nursing home environment, e.g., the activities room, may not generalize to other environments, such as the dining area.

Some Additional Interventions

Aside from the more systematic and widely used psychosocial interventions described above, there is a constellation of additional interventions that have demonstrated effects. Some examples follow. Sensory training and sensory stimulation programs (e.g., Lowe & Silverstone, 1971) are aimed at increasing the mental and physical stimulation of nursing home residents who are regressed and who are not aware of or are unable to interact with their nursing home environment. These programs share some of the same assumptions of reality orientation, namely that by creating a more stimulating environment, the resident can practice and better use existing cognitive skills. In some cases these approaches are combined with reality orientation (Tolbert, 1983). As with reality orientation approaches, the effectiveness of these approaches with more severely demented and disoriented residents is equivocal (see Chapter 3, this volume).

Several clinicians have developed orienting/socialization approaches. For example, Moran and Gatz (1987) developed welcoming groups to orient new nursing home residents. This orienting intervention led to increased feelings of control and life satisfaction among the residents who participated relative to controls.

A number of interventions aimed at enhancing the perceived control residents have over their lives have proven to be effective (Langer & Rodin, 1976; Schulz, 1976). What is striking in these studies is that the positive effects are due to a relatively modest intervention, e.g., giving a resident a choice of whether he or she wished to water a plant, or when to see a visitor.

Formal exercise programs and interventions that encourage movement among elderly adults have been shown to be beneficial in improving cognitive performance (Diesfeldt & Diesfeldt-Groenendijk, 1977) and morale (Goldberg & Fitzpatrick, 1980). More research on the effectiveness of these and other innovative approaches is called for.

SOME UNANSWERED QUESTIONS AND NEW DIRECTIONS

The review of the various psychosocial interventions indicates a mixed picture of their effectiveness. But overall it is reasonable to say that the literature points to positive effects associated with the use of psychosocial interventions. Still, this literature as a whole can be criticized on several fronts, which makes scientifically based statements about psychosocial interventions premature and equivocal.

Internal Validity Concerns

The internal validity of much of the literature is suspect, making it hard to state conclusively the effects are due to the intervention, not to some confounding variable. A large portion of the literature consists of anecdotal articles, which, while dramatic, do not provide a source of incontrovertible support. Among the empirical studies, a frequent weakness is underutilization of experimentally based randomized control group designs. A potentially confounding element is the self-selection of residents into the intervention group and control group.

Assessments of psychosocial interventions should consist of repeated measures over time of a wide range of behaviors. Typically, however, no long-term follow-up of residents is reported. Another significant omission is measurement of possible moderating variables, such as residents' depression or health status, which may impact on the intervention's effectiveness. There is also a lack of process measures which could chart the flow of the intervention and its effects. Questions such as the optimal length of the intervention, the optimal number of participants in group-based interventions, or the optimal duration of a session are, for the most part, unanswered.

The measures used are often specific to that study. In the literature far-reaching effects of the psychosocial intervention are theoretically claimed, (e.g., changes in self-care behaviors), but empirically these more removed effects are not measured. Some studies rely on general ratings of staff who are frequently not blind to the treatment condition of the residents. While a few studies report preliminary evidence of reliability and validity of the scales, many do not. In her meta-analysis of mental health interventions in nursing homes, Burckhardt (1987) found only 9 studies reporting reliability estimates. Paralleling this is the Rabins et al. (1987) review of published nursing home articles. They found that out of 106 measures of mental functioning or behavioral disorders, only 23 were reliable. The development of reliable and valid measures are critical, if compelling evaluations of psychosocial intervention effects are to be done.

External Validity Concerns

Putting aside for a moment questions of the studies' internal validity, there are some questions about the generalizability of the effects of the different interventions, that is the external validity of the findings. Borrowing the logic of the person-environment transaction model, the role of individual differences and environmental determinants in the effectiveness of organized psychosocial interventions needs to be examined. Relatively little emphasis is placed on determining how individuals' competencies moderate the effectiveness of the psychosocial interventions. The issue of the generalizability of psychosocial interventions across residents' cognitive levels is not yet satisfactorily answered. Systematic research which examines effectiveness of psychosocial interventions as a specific function of resident competence level is called for.

Psychosocial interventions do not take place in a vacuum but are situated within the larger nursing home environment and are affected by the community culture and expectations. Distinguishing between the intervention and the effects of the larger environmental structure may not be easy. A recent study by Lemke and Moos (1989) illustrates this point. In their study of 1428 residents of 42 congregate residential settings (including nursing homes and domiciliaries) they found that residents' activity levels were dependent on their functional level and the demands of the facility. Less able residents were more likely to participate in facility-organized activities when the program was more structured and the staffing level was higher. However, they also found higher functioning residents were more active in environments that were larger, had lower settings, and stressed greater resident autonomy. The formality of psychosocial programming, and the staff involvement in the interventions may be additional critical ingredients which may enhance or detract from the overall efficacy of the intervention.

Specific and Nonspecific "Therapeutic Effects"

There are basic unanswered questions about why these therapies work. A major concern is the presence of a "Hawthorne Effect," namely, the residents' effects are due not to the psychosocial intervention alone but due to a combination of the psychosocial intervention and other dynamics nonspecific to the intervention, e.g., increased attention levels given residents by staff. In the clinical literature a distinction is frequently made between specific and nonspecific therapeutic effects. The former refers to therapeutic effects caused by the dynamics specific to the therapeutic model and the latter refers to effects caused by generic factors, such as a therapist's empathy, nonspecific to the therapeutic model. In the clinical psychological literature an interesting pattern is found where over time the therapeutic style of therapists from different theoretical models converge (Fiedler, 1950). In reviewing the literature on psychosocial interventions, the stated practice guidelines converge on several common principles, such as reinforcement of resident involvement. The training of staff and the systematic implementation and monitoring of the intervention in a nursing home setting may be a very potent intervention in its own right (Linn et al., 1989).

Each of the psychosocial approaches attempts to provide a theoretical base to explain its effectiveness. The empirical literature, however, is not predominantly theoretically based. In general, the research focuses on evaluating the outcomes of the interventions, but does not test whether the theoretically proposed dynamics do in fact produce the expected therapeutic effects. Notably absent are studies which systematically manipulate the key active elements of the psychosocial intervention.

Several potent nonspecific effects can be derived from the gerontology literature. First, the implementing and regularly scheduling of therapeutic sessions can create a more predictable environment for residents (Schulz, 1976). Second, inherent in many psychosocial interventions is the opportunity for socialization with other residents and staff. This can lead to many positive effects associated with enhanced socialization and social support (Cohen & Syme, 1985), such as, self-affirmation, an opportunity to vent feelings and to engage in positive social comparisons. Third, among the higher cognitively functioning residents, the intervention can provide residents with opportunities to master a part of their lives and their environment. These opportunities can affect residents' feelings of efficacy (Bandura, 1977), control (Langer & Rodin, 1976) and self-responsibility for solving their problems (Karuza et al., 1990). Fourth, in a related vein, the introduction of interventions can induce in residents greater "mindfulness" in which they actively engage in a cognitive restructuring of their environment (Alexander et al., 1989). Fifth, from a behavioral perspective, the attention of staff can be a reinforcer for the residents, increasing their activity levels and cognitive involvement (Langer et al., 1978). Sixth, the interventions can increase the professional involvement of staff and lead to more individualized resident care (McMahon, 1988).

The need is clear for more theoretically derived research that can help identify key critical mechanisms which produce the desired effects. In this way, more tailored psychosocial interventions can be created which can maximize effectiveness.

Psychosocial Interventions as Job Enrichment:
Impact on Staff

The role of staff as important nonspecific therapeutic agents must be recognized in the nursing home setting (Karuza & Feather, 1989). Involving staff, especially nurse's aides, in psychosocial interventions does increase the "professionalism" of the staff. A commitment to systematic psychosocial intervention programming can have an unanticipated, but no less powerful, impact on staff morale and quality of care. The training in psychosocial interventions should, ideally, lead nursing staff to be more aware of behavioral dynamics in nursing home environments. The responsibility of staff to implement and monitor the psychosocial interventions should further invigorate attention paid to quality of care issues.

Several nursing professionals have remarked on staff problems when caring for dependent residents and individuals with behavioral problems (e.g., Armstrong-Esther & Brown, 1986; Heine, 1986). Reviews of nursing home staff indicate that turnover and absenteeism are costly problems for administrators (e.g., Malany, 1979; Stryker-Gordon, 1981). Low pay is certainly a factor in turnover and morale problems of nursing staff, especially nurse's aides, but it is not a sufficient explanation of staff dynamics in nursing homes. There is evidence that factors such as feeling one's work is intrinsically rewarding, personal achievement, and interpersonal relations are associated with job satisfaction and organizational effectiveness in nursing homes (cf., Donovan, 1989; Holtz, 1982).

As several critics have noted (cf., Brannon et al., 1988; Karuza & Feather, 1989), nursing home staff, such as nursing home aides, can benefit from job redesign that enriches their job. This view is built on the premise that nursing staff, including nurse's aides, can be motivated intrinsically by the job itself. The notion of job enrichment (Hackman & Oldham, 1980) argues that five key job characteristics affect the motivating potential of any job. These job characteristics are skill variety, task identity, task significance, autonomy, and feedback on the job (both from the work itself and from supervisors). Specifically, redesigning the nursing home staff's jobs focuses on maximizing the number of skills the nursing staff is required to use, the extent to which they identify with the nursing care given, the extent to which they feel their efforts are important to the residents, the extent to which they have a say in what and when to do tasks, and the amount of information they receive about the results of their activities.

In a variety of work settings, both inside and outside the health care industry, job enrichment strategies have led to gains in employee satisfaction and productivity (Kopelman, 1985). As Hackman and Oldham (1980) point out, the usefulness of enrichment strategies depends on having a work force that is accepting challenges on the job. In some situations, the nursing staff may not benefit from job enrichment exercises because of their low need for challenge and personal growth on the job, but this may be the exception rather than the rule (Brannon et al., 1988).

A strong case can be made to specifically target nurse's aides as the lead persons implementing, facilitating, and monitoring psychosocial interventions. Traditionally, nurse's aides positions are not enriched. They are routine, repetitive, physically demanding, and closely regulated. The nature of the care-giving requirements for debilitated residents, and regulations can set definite barriers to some job enrichment strategies. But the involvement of nursing staff, especially nurse's aides, in different psychosocial interventions serves as a practical and powerful means to enrich their jobs. Since the interventions are not invasive treatments and do not require formal licensing or disciplinary certification, it is feasible to turn to nurse's aides as resource persons to implement and facilitate psychosocial interventions. Since nurse's aides positions are traditionally the lowest paid, the cost of psychosocial intervention programing should be less than if other higher paid staff were used. An anticipated bonus for the administrator should be the promise of reduced costs associated with lower nurse's aide turnover, and improved quality of care.

Using a nurse's aide as the lead person in psychosocial intervention programming can enrich his or her job in many ways. In conducting the interventions, e.g., scheduling, preparing material, fostering group interactions, collecting behavioral measures, implementing and monitoring reinforcement schedules, the nurse's aide is given new tasks, ones that capitalize on emotional and intellectual resources and not on physical strength. Training the nurse's aide and relying on him or her to conduct the interventions promotes the identification with the total nursing care given. The responsibility of implementing and following through on the psychosocial interventions fosters greater autonomy and enhances the significance of the nurse's aide's position within the nursing home context. By the nature of the intervention, the daily contact, the monitoring of the effects of the intervention on the residents, will open up feedback channels for the nurse's aide. He or she will be able to see in a more direct way the links between one's activities and resident's outcomes.

Some Benefits and Caveats

Weaving together the various themes of this chapter, implementing psychosocial interventions in nursing homes has the potential of benefitting both residents and staff. Psychosocial interventions can positively impact on residents directly and indirectly. To the extent to which the psychosocial intervention's specific therapeutic and nonspecific therapeutic ingredients are activated, the intervention can directly help residents learn new skills, practice old ones and validate their sense of self. This should result in behavioral, cognitive and affective changes which would lead the resident to be more adaptive in the nursing home environment. The nursing staff, especially nurse's aides, should benefit from increased morale as a result of the psychosocial intervention enriching their job.

A major issue that needs to be addressed is how many of the benefits of psychosocial interventions are due to the programming and how many are due to the nonspecific therapeutic dynamics that are present. Practically speaking it is of little concern why psychosocial interventions work, as long as they work. From another perspective, the long-term task is to develop cost-effective improvements in quality of care in nursing homes. Whether techniques specific to a psychosocial intervention or nonspecific ingredients are important has implications for future policy and regulation. If nonspecific therapeutic dynamics are the active ingredients, then the psychosocial intervention is not per se critical. The intervention becomes merely a convenient context in which the nonspecific therapeutic dynamics are expressed. If that is the case, the emphasis should not be on prescribing specific psychosocial interventions but developing training and structural changes in staffing and administration that capitalize on the nonspecific therapeutic dynamics. It is critical that nursing home administrators and researchers develop a systematic evaluation of psychosocial interventions' impacts on residents and staff and of factors that can enhance their effectiveness.

Some caveats should be sounded before embracing psychosocial interventions as the answer to all nursing home problems. First, is that using a nurse's aide as the lead person in psychosocial intervention programming requires nurse's aides who have the necessary communication and interpersonal skills which are essential in implementing and conducting the intervention. This can create new demands in the personnel selection process.

Second, if the psychosocial intervention programming is perceived by the nursing staff as unfairly enlarging the amount of work expected, then staff cooperation will be poor.

Third, if the nursing home environment is understaffed, then implementation of the psychosocial intervention will be jeopardized. Under conditions of staff shortage, the priority will be given to addressing basic functional and health needs, not psychosocial ones.

Fourth is the fact that, even though the OBRA legislation mandates training and delivery of mental health interventions, it does not mandate funding. Simply put, the administrator will not find a convenient revenue stream to subsidize the implementation of these psychosocial interventions. An advantage of using nurse's aides as psychosocial intervention facilitators is that their wage levels are much lower than health and allied health professionals. Administrators must take a larger perspective and consider the savings in personnel and health care utilization costs that are theoretically possible with implementing systematic psychosocial intervention programming. In keeping with this "bottom line" approach, it is important to make sure cost/benefit data are rigorously collected on both resident and staff outcomes.

Fifth is the danger of staff rivalries developing when designating nurse's aides as lead persons. Care must be given in developing a workable wage structure and in assigning duties and responsibilities so that they are in keeping with the organizational hierarchy. Since psychosocial interventions are not psychotherapeutic or psychiatric treatments, the danger of disciplinary turf issues is minimized. Even so, efforts should be made to actively integrate the nurse's aide and the psychosocial intervention into the interdisciplinary networks and continuity of care mechanisms that are in place.

Sixth is the importance of instituting adequate training in the specific and nonspecific therapeutic dynamics involved in the psychosocial interventions, not only to satisfy the OBRA regulations, but to ensure quality interventions. Trained geriatric psychologists, psychiatrists, and other health and allied health professionals are important resources for such training. Unfortunately, the number of health and allied health professionals with a background in geriatrics who can provide the training is still low for the need (Smyer, 1989).

Seventh is recognizing that the effective systematic implementation of psychosocial interventions requires a nursing home climate that is receptive and responsive to the intervention. If the administration and supervisory staff do not support the intervention efforts they will not succeed. Clear, objective, and scientifically based data on the efficacy of psychosocial interventions can be instrumental in ensuring a salubrious environment for the interventions.

REFERENCES

Alexander, C., Chandler, H., Langer, E., et al. (1989). Transcendental meditation, mindfulness, and longevity: An experimental study with the elderly. *Journal of Personality and Social Psychology, 57,* 950–964.

Armstrong-Esther C. & Brown, K. (1986). The influence of elderly patients' mental impairment on nurse-patient interaction. *Journal of Advanced Nursing, 11,* 379–387.

Association of American Medical Colleges. (1983). *Proceedings of the regional institutes on geriatrics and medical education.* Washington, DC: Association of American Medical Colleges.

Babins, L. (1988). Conceptual analysis of validation therapy. *International Journal of Aging and Human Development, 28,* 161–168.

Babins, L., Dillon, J., & Merovitz, S. (1988). The effects of validation therapy on disoriented elderly. *Activities, Adaptation & Aging, 12,* 73–86.

Balleseros, F., Izal, M., Diaz, P., et al. (1988). Training of conversational skills with institutionalized elderly: A preliminary study. *Perceptual and Motor Skills, 66,* 923–926.

Baltes, M., Honn, S., Barton, E., et al. (1983). On the social ecology of dependence and independence in elderly nursing home residents: A replication and extension. *Journal of Gerontology, 38*, 556–564.

Bandura, A. (1977). Self-efficacy: Toward a unifying theory of behavioral change. *Psychological Review, 84*, 191–215.

Barnes, J. (1974). The effects of reality orientation classroom on memory loss, confusion and disorientation in geriatric patients. *Gerontologist, 14*, 138–142.

Berghorn, F., & Schafer, D. (1986). Reminiscence intervention in nursing homes: What and who changes? *International Journal of Aging and Human Development, 24*, 113–127.

Blackman, D., Howe, M., & Pinkston, E. (1976). Increasing participation in social interaction of the institutionalized elderly. *Gerontologist, 16*, 69–76.

Bleathman, C. (1988). Validation therapy with the demented elderly. *Journal of Advanced Nursing, 13*, 511–514.

Boylin, W., Gordon, S., & Nehrke, M. (1976). Reminiscing and ego integrity in institutionalized males. *Gerontologist, 16*, 69–76.

Brannon, D., Smyer, M., Cohn, M., et al. (1988). A job diagnostic survey of nursing home caregivers: Implications for job redesign. *Gerontologist, 28*, 246–252.

Brody, E. (1985). Parent care as a normative family stress. *Gerontologist, 25*, 19–29.

Brook, P. Degun, G., & Mather, M. (1975). Reality orientation, a therapy for psychogeriatric patients: A controlled study. *British Journal of Psychiatry, 127*, 42–45.

Burckhardt, C. (1987). The effect of therapy on the mental health of the elderly. *Research in Nursing & Health, 10*, 277–285.

Burgio, L. & Burgio, K. (1986). Behavioral gerontology: Application of behavioral methods to the problems of older adults. *Journal of Applied Behavior Analysis, 19*, 321–328.

Burgio, L., Burgio, K., Engel, B., et al. (1986). Increasing distance and independence of ambulation in elderly nursing home residents. *Journal of Applied Behavior Analysis, 19*, 357–366.

Butler, R. (1980). The life review: An unrecognized bonanza. *International Journal of Aging and Human Development, 12*, 35–38.

Calkins, E. & Karuza, J. (1988). The relationship of geriatrics and gerontology: On forging links between curing and caring. In Osgood, N. & Belzer, A. (Eds.), *The research and practice of gerontology*. Hillsdale, NJ: Greenwood Press.

Calkins, E. (1987). Geriatrics and the health care revolution. *Journal of the American Geriatric Society, 35*, 669–699.

Campos, R. G. (1984). Does reality orientation work? *Journal of Gerontological Nursing, 10*, 53–64.

Carsensen, L. & Erickson, R. (1986). Enhancing the social environments of elderly nursing home residents: Are high rates of interaction enough? *Journal of Applied Behavior Analysis, 19*, 349–355.

Citrin, R. & Dixon, D. (1977). Reality orientation: A milieu therapy used in an institution for the aged. *Gerontologist, 17*, 39–43.

Cleary, A., Clamon, C., Price, P., et al. (1988). A reduced stimulation unit: Effects on patients with Alzheimer's Disease and related disorders. *Gerontologist, 28*, 511–514.

Cohen S. & Syme, S. L. (1985). *Social support and health*. Orlando, FL: Academic Press.

Coleman, P. (1974). Measuring reminiscence characteristics from conversation as adaptive features of old age. *International Journal of Aging and Human Development, 5*, 281–294.

Diesfeldt, H. & Diesfeldt-Groenendijk, H. (1977). Improving cognitive performance in psychogeriatric patients: The influence of physical exercise. *Age and Ageing, 6*, 58–64.

Dietch, J., Hewett, L., & Jones, S. (1989). Adverse effects of reality orientation. *Journal of the American Geriatric Society, 37*, 974–976.

Donovan, R. (1989). Work stress and job satisfaction: A study of home care workers in New York City. *Home Health Care Services Quarterly, 10*, 97–114.

Erikson, E. (1950). *Childhood and Society*. NY: Norton.

Estes, C. & Binney, E. (1989). The biomedicalization of aging: Dangers and Dilemmas. *Gerontologist, 29*, 587–596.

Fallot, R. (1979). The impact on mood of verbal reminiscing in later adulthood. *International Journal of Aging and Human Development, 10*, 385–400.

Feil, N. (1982). *Validation: The Feil method*. Cleveland: Edward Feil Productions.

Fiedler, F. (1950). A comparison of therapeutic relationships in psychoanalytic, non-directive and Adlerian therapy. *Journal of Consulting Psychology, 14*, 436–445.

Folsom, J. (1968). Reality orientation for the elderly mental patient. *Journal of Geriatric Psychiatry, 1*, 291–307.

Fry, P. (1983). Structured and unstructured reminiscence training and depression among the elderly. *Clinical Gerontologist, 1*, 15–37.

Goldberg, W. & Fitzpatrick, J. (1980). Movement therapy with the aged. *Nursing Research, 29*, 339–346.

Goldwasser, N., Auerbach, S., & Harkines, S. (1987). Cognitive, affective, and behavioral effects of reminiscence group therapy on demented elderly. *International Journal of Aging and Human Development, 25*, 209–222.

Gropper-Katz, E. (1987). Reality orientation research. *Journal of Gerontological Nursing, 13*, 13–18.

Gugel, R. (1989). Psychosocial interventions in the nursing home. In Katz, P. & Calkins, E. (Eds.), *Principles and Practice of Nursing Home Care* (pp. 212–224). New York: Springer Publishing Co.

Hackman, J. & Oldham, G. (1980). *Work Redesign*. Reading, MA: Addison-Wesley.

Hadley, E. (1986). Bladder training and related therapies for urinary incontinence in older people. *Journal of the American Medical Association 256*, 372–379.

Hanley, I., McGuire, R., & Boyd, W. (1981). Reality orientation and dementia: A controlled trial of two approaches. *British Journal of Psychiatry 138*, 10–14.

Health Care Financing Administration. (1988, June 9). Nurse's aide training and competency evaluation program: Draft document. Baltimore, MD: HCFA.

Heine, C. (1986). Burnout among nursing personnel. *Journal of Gerontological Nursing 12*, 14–18.

Hogstel, M. (1979). Use of reality orientation with aging confused patients. *Nursing Research 28*, 161–165.

Holtz, G. (1982). Nurse's aides in nursing homes: Why are they satisfied? *Journal of Gerontological Nursing 8*, 265–271.

Hu, T., Igou, J., Kaltrider, L., et al. (1989). A clinical trial of a behavioral therapy to reduce urinary incontinence in nursing homes. *Journal of the American Medical Association 261*, 2656–2662.

Hussain, R. & Lawrence, S. (1981). Social reinforcement of activity and problem-solving training in the treatment of depressed institutionalized elderly patients. *Cognitive Therapy and Research, 5*, 57–69.

Institute of Medicine. (1986). *Improving the quality of care in nursing homes*. Washington, DC: National Academy Press.

Johnson, C., McLaren, S., & McPherson, F. (1981). The comparative effectiveness of three versions of 'classroom' reality orientation. *Age and Ageing, 10*, 33–35.

Kane, R. (1989). The biomedical blues. *Gerontologist, 29*, 583.

Karuza, J. & Feather, J. (1989). Staff dynamics. In Katz, P. R. & Calkins, E., (Eds.), *Principles and Practice of Nursing Home Care*. New York: Springer Publishing Co.

Karuza, J., Zevon, M. A., Gleason, T., et al. (1990). Models of helping and coping, responsibility attributions and well being in community elderly and their helpers. *Psychology and Aging, 5*, 194–208.

Katz, P. & Calkins, E. (Eds.). (1989). *Principles and Practice of Nursing Home Care*. New York: Springer Publishing Co.

Kazdin, A. (1975). *Behavior Modification in Applied Settings*. Homewood, IL: Dorsey Press.

Kletsch, E., Witman, T., & Santos, J. (1983). Increasing verbal interaction among elderly socially isolated mentally retarded adults: A group language training procedure. *Journal of Applied Behavior Analysis, 16*, 217–233.

Koenig, H., Shelp, F., Goli, V., et al. (1989). Survival and health care utilization in elderly medical inpatients with major depression. *Journal of the American Geriatrics Society, 37*, 599–606.

Kopelman, R. (1985). Job redesign and productivity: A review of the evidence. *National Productivity Review, 4*, 237–255.

Langer, E. & Rodin, J. (1976). The effects of a control relevant intervention with the institutionalized aged. *Journal of Personality and Social Psychology, 34*, 191–198.

Langer, E., Rodin, J., Beck, P., et al. (1978). Environmental determinants of memory improvement in late adulthood. *Journal of Personality and Social Psychology, 37*, 2003–2013.

Lawton, M. P. & Nahemow, L. (1973). Ecology and the aging process. In Eisdorfer, C. & Lawton, M. P. (Eds.), *The psychology of adult development and aging* (pp. 619–674). Washington, DC: American Psychological Association.

Lemke, S. & Moos, R. (1989). Personal and environmental determinants of activity involvement among elderly residents of congregate facilities. *Journal of Gerontology, 44*, S139–148.

Letcher, P., Peterson, L., & Scarbrough, D. (1974). Reality orientation: A historical study of patient progress. *Hospital Community Psychiatry 25*, 801–803.

Linn, M., Linn, B., Stein, E., et al. (1989). Effect of nursing home staff training on quality of patient survival. *International Journal of Aging and Human Development, 28*, 305–315.

Lo Gerfo, M. (1980). Three ways of reminiscence in theory and practice. *International Journal of Aging and Human Development, 12*, 39–48.

Lowe, C. A. & Silverstone, B. M. (1971). A program of intensified stimulation and response facilitation for the senile aged. *Gerontologist, 11*, 341–347.

Maas, M. (1988). Management of patients with Alzheimer's Disease in long-term care facilities. *Nursing Clinics of North America, 23*, 57–68.

MacDonald, M. & Butler, A. (1974). Reversal of helplessness: Producing walking behavior in nursing home wheelchair residents using behavior modification procedures. *Journal of Gerontology, 29*, 97–101.

Malany, R. (1979). Supplemental Staffing: Coping with personnel turnover. *Nursing Homes, 28*, 20–23.

McMahon, R. (1988). The '24-hour reality orientation' type of approach to the confused elderly: A minimum standard for care. *Journal of Advanced Nursing, 13*, 693–700.

Merriam, S. (1980). The concept and function of reminiscence: Review of the research. *Gerontologist, 20,* 604–608.

Moran, J. & Gatz, M. (1987). Group therapies for nursing home adults: An evaluation of two treatment approaches. *Gerontologist, 27,* 588–591.

Newman, F., Griffin, B., Black, R., et al. (1989). Linking level of care to level of need: Assessing the need for mental health care for nursing home residents. *American Psychologist, 44,* 1315–1324.

Nodhturft, V. & Sweeney, N. (1982). Reality orientation therapy for the institutionalized elderly. *Journal of Gerontological Nursing, 8,* 396–401.

Osborn, C. (1989). Reminiscence: When the past eases the present. *Journal of Gerontological Nursing, 15,* 6–12.

Ouslander, J. (1986). Diagnostic evaluation of geriatric urinary incontinence. *Clinics in Geriatric Medicine, 2,* 715–730.

Peoples, M. (1982). Validation therapy versus reality orientation as treatment for the institutionalized disoriented elderly. Unpublished master's thesis, College of Nursing, University of Akron (OH).

Perrotta, P & Meacham, J. (1981). Can a reminiscing intervention alter depression and self-esteem? *International Journal of Aging and Human Development, 14,* 23–30.

Perschbacher, R. (1984). An application of reminiscence in an activity setting. *Gerontologist, 24,* 343–345.

Praders, K. & MacDonald, M. (1986). Telephone conversational skills training with socially isolated, impaired nursing home residents. *Journal of Applied Behavior Analysis, 19,* 337–348.

Rabinowitz, V. C., Zevon, M. A., & Karuza, J. (1988). Psychotherapy as helping: An attributional analysis. In Abramson, L. (Ed.). *Attribution processes and clinical psychology.* New York: Guilford Press.

Rabins, P., Rovner, B., Larson, D., et al. (1987). The use of mental health measures in nursing home research. *Journal of the American Geriatrics Society, 35,* 431–434.

Resnick, N. & Yalla, S. (1985). Management of urinary incontinence in the elderly. *The New England Journal of Medicine, 318,* 800–805.

Reeves, W. & Ivinson, D. (1985). Use of environmental manipulation and classroom and modified informal reality orientation with institutionalized, confused elderly patients. *Age and Ageing, 14,* 119–121.

Richman, L. (1969). Sensory training for geriatric patients. *American Journal of Occupational Therapy, 23,* 254–257.

Rovner, B., Kafonek, S., Filipp, L., et al. (1986). Prevalence of mental illness in a community nursing home. *American Journal of Psychiatry, 143,* 1446–1449.

Schnelle, J., Traughber, B., Morgan, D., et al. (1983). Management of geriatric incontinence in nursing homes. *Journal of Applied Behavior Analysis, 16,* 235–241.

Schulz, R. & Brenner, G. (1977). Relocation of the aged: A review and theoretical analysis. *Journal of Gerontology, 32,* 323–333.

Schulz, R. & Hanusa, B. (1978). Long-term effects of control and predictability-enhancing interventions: Findings and ethical issues. *Journal of Personality and Social Psychology, 36,* 1194–1201.

Schulz, R. (1976). The effect of control and predictability on the physical and psychological well-being of the institutionalized aged. *Journal of Personality and Social Psychology, 33,* 563–573.

Smyer, M. (1989). Nursing home as a setting for psychological practice. *American Psychologist 44,* 1307–1314.

Sperbeck, D. & Whitbourne, S. (1981). Dependency in the institutional setting: A behavioral training program for geriatric staff. *Gerontologist, 21,* 268–275.

Stein, S., Linn, M., & Stein, E. (1985). Patients anticipation of stress in nursing home care. *Gerontologist, 25*, 88–94.

Stryker-Gordon, R. (1981). *How to Reduce Employee Turnover in Nursing Homes.* Springfield, IL: Charles C Thomas.

Tolbert, B. M. (1983, January) Reality orientation and remotivation in a long-term care facility. *Nursing & Health Care*, 40–44.

U.S. Senate, Special Committee on Aging. (1987). *Developments in Aging: 1986* (Vols 1–3). Washington, DC: U.S. Government Printing Office.

Voelkel, D. (1978). A study of reality orientation and resocialization groups with confused elderly. *Journal of Gerontological Nursing, 4*, 13–18.

Woods, R. (1979). Reality orientation and staff attention: A controlled study. *British Journal of Psychiatry, 134*, 502–507.

Zepelin, H., Wolfe, C., & Kleinplatz, F. (1981). Evaluation of a year long reality orientation program. *Journal of Gerontology, 36*, 70–77.

Zimmer, J., Watson, N., & Treat, A. (1984). Behavioral problems among patients in skilled nursing facilities. *American Journal of Public Health, 74*, 1118–1121.

2
Falls in the Nursing-Home Setting: Causes and Preventive Approaches

Laurence Z. Rubenstein
Alan S. Robbins
Karen R. Josephson

Falls are a major cause of morbidity, immobility, and mortality among older persons, especially among those living in nursing homes. Many etiologies and risk factors predispose to falls. If falls are to be prevented, there needs to be a systematic and individualized diagnostic and therapeutic approach to patients who have fallen. Attention should also be paid to identifying and reducing risk factors for falls among frail older persons who have not yet fallen. This chapter presents a systematic approach for determining why an elderly person falls and for minimizing the chances of recurrence in the nursing home setting.

EPIDEMIOLOGIC CONSIDERATIONS

Both the incidence of falls in adults and the severity of complications rise steadily after middle age. Accidents are the fifth leading cause of death in people over age 65, and falls constitute two-thirds of these accidental deaths. About three-fourths of deaths due to falls in the United States occur in the 12% of the population age 65 and older (Hogue, 1982). Approximately a third of elderly persons living at home will fall each year, about 5% will sustain a fracture, and 1 in 40 will be hospitalized (Campbell et al., 1981). Of those admitted to hospital after a fall, only about half will be alive a year later.

Among institutionalized populations the risk and consequences of falling are even greater. Studies performed in institutional settings have reported annual incidence rates of falls between 0.6 and 3.6 falls per bed (mean rate

1.7 falls/bed), with 10 to 25% of falls resulting in a serious complication, such as a fracture or laceration (Rubenstein et al., 1988). Each year about 1800 fatal falls occur in nursing homes. Among persons 85 years and older, 1 out of 5 fatal falls occurs in a nursing home (Baker & Harvey, 1985). In addition to physical injuries, falls also contribute to functional impairment. Fear of falling among nursing home residents has been shown to be a major reason for use of wheelchairs and other restrictions of mobility (Pawlson, Goodwin & Keith, 1986). The use of physical or chemical restraints by institutional staff to prevent a high risk person from falling clearly has negative impacts on functioning.

The real problem of falls in the elderly is not one simply of a high incidence, since young children and athletes certainly have a higher incidence of falls than all but the frailest elderly. Rather it is a combination of high incidence together with a high susceptibility to injury. The propensity for injury is due to a high prevalence of clinical diseases (e.g., osteoporosis) and age-related physiologic changes (e.g., slowed protective reflexes) that make even a relatively mild fall particularly dangerous. Moreover, once injured, the case fatality rate is much higher for elderly people than younger people (Hogue, 1982).

One of the most serious fall consequences, hip fracture, assumes epidemic proportions in old people—172,000 ocurring in 1985. The cumulative lifetime incidence of hip fracture in the United States for those reaching 90 is 32% for women and 17% for men. In 1984, the annual cost of care for hip fractures in the United States was estimated at 7 billion dollars (Melton and Riggs, 1983). Nursing home patients have a disproportionately high incidence of hip fracture, and have also been shown to have higher mortality rates following hip fracture than community-living elderly persons (Rhymes & Jaeger, 1988).

The U.S. Public Health Service has estimated that two-thirds of deaths due to falls are potentially preventable (U.S. DHHS, 1981). This might be accomplished in several ways. Identifying and eliminating environmental risks in homes or institutions could prevent many falls due primarily to environmental causes. Adequate medical evaluation and treatment for underlying medical conditions might prevent many disease-related falls. Finally, many patients who have irreversible medical problems causing their falls could still benefit from learning adaptive behavior to minimize severity of falls.

ETIOLOGIC CONSIDERATIONS

Causes of Falls

The major causes of falls and their relative frequencies based on the major published studies are presented in Table 2.1. Only 2 (Lucht, 1971; Rubenstein et al., 1989) of the 9 studies reviewed were conducted among nursing

TABLE 2.1 Causes of Falls in the Elderly Adults: Summary
of Nine Studies That Carefully Evaluated Patients Who Fell

	Percentage	Range
"Accident"/environment-related	38%	(12–53%)
Gait problems or weakness	13%	(3–39%)
Drop attack	11%	(1–25%)
Dizziness/vertigo	8%	(3–19%)
Postural hypotension	5%	(2–24%)
Syncope	1%	(0–13%)
Other specified causes*	18%	(6–37%)
Unknown	8%	(5–21%)

Source: Adapted from Rubenstein et al., 1988 and Rubenstein et al.,
1989
*This category includes: central nervous system disturbances, acute
illness, confusion, poor eyesight, drugs, alcohol, falling out of bed.

home populations. Consequently, the relative frequency of causes can be
expected to be somewhat different from frail, high risk nursing home populations, where medical factors are more important than evironmental factors. Nonetheless, the table provides some useful ranges.

In most studies 30 to 50% of falls are attributed to accidents. However,
many of these "accidental" falls really stem from the interaction between
relatively minor environmental hazards and increased individual susceptibility to hazards from accumulated effects of age. Older people have stiffer, less
coordinated, and more dangerous gaits than do younger people. Posture
control, body-orienting reflexes, muscle strength and tone, and height of
stepping all decrease with aging and impair ability to avoid a fall after an
unexpected trip. Age-associated impairments of vision, hearing, and memory, tend to increase the number of trips and stumbles. Among institutionalized populations, functional disabilities, confusion, and acute
illnesses also increase vulnerability to falling. While falls in nursing homes
are more commonly attributed to medical and less to environmental factors
than in community settings, many avoidable environmental hazards still exist
even within the best institutional settings. Environmental factors that have
been associated with falls in nursing homes are listed in Table 2.2.

Studies have shown that most falls in nursing homes occur in the bedroom
at the bedside or in the bathroom (Berry, Fisher & Lang, 1981; Dimant,
1985; Kalchthaler, Bascon, & Quintos, 1978). Certain activities that are
commonly associated with falls in these locations include arising from bed,
ambulating to and from the bathroom, and transferring to a bed, chair, or
toilet (Berry, Fisher, & Lang, 1981; Gryfe, Amies, & Ashley, 1977; Kalchthaler, Bascon, & Quintos, 1978). Environmental hazards that frequently
contribute to these falls include wet floors due to episodes of incontinence,

TABLE 2.2 Factors Associated with Falls Among
Elderly Persons in Institutions

Institutional factors
Slick hard floors
Poor lighting
Reduced number of nurses
Use of bedrails
Daytime sedation
Improper bed height

Patient factors
Recent admission or transfer
Specific activities
arising from bed
walking to and from bathroom
transferring
after meals
Improper footwear
Medical risk factors (see Table 2.3)

poor lighting, bedrails, and improper bed height. Falls have also been reported to increase when nurse staffing is low (Blake & Morfitt, 1986) and during shift changes (Dimant, 1985), presumably due to lack of staff supervision.

The broad category of gait problems and weakness is the second commonest cause for falls in community-living older persons, and it was the single most common cause of falls in the largest nursing home study that quantified fall etiology (Rubenstein et al., 1989). The etiology of gait problems and weakness is clearly multifactorial. In addition to age-related changes in gait and balance already alluded to, gait problems can stem from dysfunctions of the nervous, muscular, skeletal, circulatory, and respiratory systems as well as from simple deconditioning following a period of inactivity. Muscle weakness is an extremely common finding among the aged population and much of this stems from disease and inactivity rather than aging per se. One study found the prevalence of hip weakness to be over 80% among nursing home residents (Robbins et al., 1989), while another found that 57% of residents of an intermediate care facility had decreased lower extremity strength (Tinetti, Williams, & Mayewski, 1986). Common causes of weakness and gait problems include stroke, parkinsonism, fractures, skeletal abnormalities, arthritis, myopathies, and polyneuropathies. Several case-control studies have clearly shown gait and muscle dysfunctions to be a major risk factor for falls and fractures. (Nevitt et al., 1989; Robbins et al., 1989; Tinetti, Williams & Mayewski, 1986).

Drop attacks are defined as sudden falls without loss of consciousness or dizziness. Patients usually experience associated leg weakness, which is usually transient but can persist for hours. Sudden change in head position is often a precipitating event. This syndrome has been attributed to transient vertebrobasilar insufficiency, although it is probably due to more diverse pathophysiologic mechanisms. Tone and strength sometimes have been reported to be restored more rapidly if patients push their feet against a solid object (Sheldon, 1960). Although drop attacks are to be considered an important etiology of falls, recent more precisely documented studies indicate that they cause substantially fewer falls than the 11% average figure indicated in Table 2.1.

The sensation of dizziness is an extremely common complaint of elderly patients who fall. This requires a careful history since the description of dizziness is subjective and can arise from very different etiologies. True vertigo, a sensation of rotational movement, may indicate a disorder of the vestibular apparatus, e.g., benign positional vertigo, acute labyrinthitis, or Meniere's disease. Symptoms described as "imbalance on walking" often reflect a gait disorder. Many patients describe a vague light-headedness that may reflect cardiovascular problems, hyperventilation, orthostasis, drug side effect, anxiety, or depression.

Orthostatic hypotension, defined as a drop of over 20mm of systolic blood pressure after standing from a supine position, has a 5 to 25% prevalence among "normal" elderly people (Robbins & Rubenstein, 1984). It is more common among persons with certain predisposing risk factors, including autonomic dysfunction (frequently related to age, diabetes, or CNS damage), hypovolemia, low cardiac output, parkinsonism, metabolic and endocrine disorders, and medications (particularly sedatives, antihypertensives, and antidepressants) (Mader, Josephson, & Rubenstein, 1987). The orthostatic drop may be more pronounced on arising in the morning, since the baroceptor response is diminished after prolonged recumbency. Orthostatic hypotension may also be exacerbated by certain activities and after meals (Lipsitz & Fullerton, 1986).

Syncope is a serious and important but less common cause of falls. Syncope is defined as a sudden loss of consciousness with spontaneous recovery; it results from decreased cerebral blood flow or occasionally from metabolic causes such as hypoglycemia or hypoxia. The most frequent etiologies in elderly persons are cardiac arrhythmias, orthostatic hypotension, vasovagal reactions, and syncope of unknown cause. A history of syncope may be difficult to obtain, because many patients do not remember exactly what occurred during the fall, and drop attacks or dizziness may be confused by the patient with syncope.

Other specific causes of falls include disorders of the central nervous system, cognitive deficits, poor vision, drug side effects, alcohol intake, and acute illness. Diseases of the central nervous system (e.g., cerebrovascular disease, dementia, normal pressure hydrocephalus, parkinsonism) often result in falls by causing dizziness, orthostatic hypotension, and gait disorders. In addition, patients with cognitive deficits often are not able to recognize and avoid hazards. Drugs frequently have side effects that result in impaired mentation, stability, and gait. Especially important are agents with sedative, antidepressant, and antihypertensive effects, particularly diuretics, vasodilators, and beta blockers (Granek et al., 1987). While alcohol use is less likely to be a problem within the institutional setting than within the community, patients should be specifically questioned about this, since alcohol is an occult cause of instability, falls, and serious injury. Other less common causes of falls include anemia, hypothyroidism, unstable joints, foot problems, and severe osteoporosis with spontaneous fracture.

Risk Factors

Because most nursing home patients have more than one identifiable age-related change or medical condition that constitute risk factors predisposing to falls, the exact cause of a fall is frequently difficult to determine and requires keeping these many possibilities in mind. Rather than try to determine a specific cause for a fall, a more appropriate approach to the nursing home patient who falls may be to focus on identifying and treating relevant risk factors so that subsequent falls can be avoided. Several case-controlled studies have documented significant differences between institutionalized fallers and non-fallers, and have quantified the relative risk of various factors associated with falls in institutional settings (Table 2.3).

In the two studies that compared physical examination data between nursing home fallers and non-fallers (Robbins et al., 1989; Tinetti, Williams & Mayewski, 1986), lower extremity weakness, gait and balance impairments, postural hypotension, neurosensory deficits and impaired vision were significantly more prevalent among patients who fell. In a study examining only knee and ankle strength, weakness at both joints was found to be significantly more common among fallers than nonfallers (Whipple, Wolfson, & Amerman, 1987). In addition, lower extremity weakness has been shown to be a significant risk factor for serious injury during falls among nursing home patients (Tinetti, 1987).

Functional variables identified as risk factors in nursing home populations include: the use of assistive devices for ambulation, self-reported limitations in mobility, and difficulty in performing basic self-care activities of daily living. Although cognitive impairment has been reported to be a risk factor for falls in community-living elderly persons, it has only been found to have borderline significance in nursing home patients, possibly due to the high prevalence of dementia among these populations, or the fact that demented patients are more likely to be restrained.

TABLE 2.3 Risk Factors for Falling Identified in Case-Control Studies Among Institutionalized Populations

Reference	Wells	Tinetti	Granek	Robbins
Year published	1985	1986	1987	1989
N (subjects)	77	79	368	149
Study design	R	P	R	R
1. Physical exam data				
a. Muscle weakness	—	+	—	+
b. Gait impairment	—	+	—	+
c. Balance impairment	—	+	—	±
d. Postural hypotension	—	+	—	±
e. Neurosensory impairment	—	0	—	+
f. Visual impairment	—	+	—	±
2. Functional level				
a. Impaired ADL	—	+	—	±
b. Use assistive device	—	+	—	+
c. Mobility limitation	—	+	—	0
d. Cognitive impairment	—	±	—	±
3. Medications				
a. Total number	+	—	+	+
b. Psychoactive	0	+	+	0
c. Cardiac	+	0	+	0
4. Medical history factors				
a. Arthritis	0	0	+	0
b. Incontinence	—	+	—	+
c. Depression	—	0	+	0

Key: + = Significant risk factor ($p < .05$)   — = Not tested in study
± = Risk factor of borderline   R = Retrospective design
   significance ($.1 > p > .05$)   P = Prospective design

Polypharmacy has also been identified as an independent predictor of falls, and in 3 of the 4 studies in which medications were reviewed, it was reported that fallers received significantly more prescription medications than nonfallers. Specifically, psychotropic and cardiac drugs were found to be associated with falling.

Fallers have also been shown to have a greater number of medical diagnoses than nonfallers. Specific diagnoses assoicated with falls include arthritis, depression, and incontinence. Perhaps as important as specific diagnoses is the interaction between an increasing prevalence of multiple diagnoses.

One study (Robbins et al., 1989) found that it was possible to estimate the likelihood of a patient falling by assessing three risk factors: hip strength, balance, and number of prescribed medications taken. Using this model, the predicted 1 year risk of falling ranged from 12% for persons with none of the three risk factors to 100% for persons with all three risk factors. Another study (Tinetti et al., 1986) developed a fall risk index based on nine identified risk factors, and found that the likelihood of falling increased with the number of risk factors present. Although using slightly different approaches, both of these studies confirm that among nursing home patients falling is often the result of interacting conditions, and weakness and gait and balance disorders significantly increase the risk of falling.

DIAGNOSTIC APPROACH

The practitioner's first objective when facing a nursing home patient who has fallen is to stabilize and treat immediate problems brought on by the fall, such as head injury or fractures. Following this, a systematic search for the underlying cause of the fall should be undertaken. The basic components of this diagnostic approach are outlined in Table 2.4.

A well-directed history is the most helpful part of the diagnostic process. Obtaining a full report of the circumstances and symptoms surrounding the fall is crucial. Reports from witnesses are very important, because the patient may have poor recollection of these events. Historical factors that can point to a specific etiology, or help to narrow down the differential diagnosis, include: a sudden rise from a lying or sitting position (orthostatic hypotension), a trip or slip (gait, balance, or vision disturbance or an environmental hazard), an unexplained drop attack without loss of consciousness (vertebrobasilar insufficiency), looking up or sideways (arterial or carotid sinus compression) and loss of consciousness (syncope or seizure).

Symptoms experienced near the time of falling may also point to a potential cause—dizziness or giddiness (orthostatic hypotension, vestibular problem, hypoglycemia, arrhythmia, drug side effect), palpitations (arrhythmia),

TABLE 2.4 Approaching the Patient Who Fell

Assess and treat injury

Determine probable cause of fall
  History
  Physical examination
  Laboratory and other tests (e.g., complete blood count, serum electrolyte studies, electrocardiograms, Holter monitor)

Prevent recurrence
  Treat underlying illness
  Reduce accompanying risk factors (e.g., visual problems, orthostasis)
  Reduce environmental hazards (See Table 2.5)
  Teach adaptive behavior (e.g., slow rising, gait training, cane or walker use)

incontinence or tongue biting (seizure), asymmetric weakness (cerebrovascular disease), chest pain (myocardial infarction or coronary insufficiency), or loss of consciousness (any cause of syncope). Medications and the existence of concomitant medical problems may be important contributory factors. Other points to elicit during the history that might be helpful in directing further workup and care planning include: How long was the patient on the ground? What effect did the fall have on patient confidence, fear of further falls, and activity? Are there any effects on staff expectations and plans for future activities?

Pertinent items to be included on the post-fall physical examination include: orthostatic changes in pulse and blood pressure, presence of arrhythmias, carotid bruits, nystagmus, focal neurologic signs, musculoskeletal abnormalities, visual loss, and gait disturbances. Careful mental and functional status assessment is often crucial. Even if risk factors are discovered that did not cause the fall in question, their identification and treatment can probably reduce the likelihood of subsequent falls.

It may be useful, under carefully monitored conditions, to attempt to reproduce the circumstances that might have precipitated the fall, e.g., positional changes, head turning, urination, or carotid pressure. Gait and stability should be assessed by close observation of the patient rising from a chair, standing with eyes open and closed, walking, turning, and sitting down. One should take particular note of gait velocity and rhythm, stride length, double support time (the time spent with both feet on the floor), height of stepping, use of assistive devices, and degree of sway. Imbalance observed during head turning or flexion is an important finding associated with vestibular or vertebrobasilar pathology and a significantly increased risk of falling.

The laboratory evaluation need not be extensive, but should include several key tests when the cause is not obvious: complete blood count to search for anemia or infection; serum chemistries, especially sodium, potassium, calcium, glucose, and creatinine; electrocardiogram to document arrhythmia; and thyroid function tests, since occult thyroid disease may be difficult to diagnose clinically. Even then, the clinical evaluation and initial laboratory tests may not detect an intermittent problem that may have been the cause of the fall (orthostatic changes, arrhythmias, and electrolyte disturbances, for example).

An ambulatory cardiac (Holter) monitor is advisable in cases when a transient arrhythmia is suspected by history, in cases of otherwise unexplained syncope, or in cases when the patient with unexplained falls has a history of cardiac disease and is on cardiac medication. The likelihood of finding suggestive abnormalities on Holter monitoring in elderly patients who fall is particularly high. In one study performed among nursing home patients, 82% of both fallers and nonfaller controls had ventricular arrhythmias documented on Holter monitoring and 100% had supraventricular arrhythmias (Rosado et al., 1989). None of these patients were symptomatic during the Holter monitoring. Since transient arrhythmias are so prevalent among the elderly, it is often unclear whether a monitored abnormality was related to the fall, unless corresponding symptoms are noted during the monitoring process. The study concluded that without suggestive symptoms, the Holter monitor should not be part of the routine fall evaluation.

THERAPY AND PREVENTION
Medical Therapy

The purpose of the diagnostic approach outlined above is to uncover direct or contributing causes of falls that are amenable to medical therapy or other corrective intervention. Among the more obvious examples, cardiac dysrhythmias clearly related to a fall should be treated with antiarrhythmics or a pacemaker, or both. Hypovolemia due to hemorrhage or dehydration calls for treatment directed toward restoring hemodynamic stability. Parkinsonism usually responds to specific therapy, at least for a while; in advanced cases, however, safe ambulation can require extensive supervision and use of assistive devices. Discontinuing medication that causes postural hypotension or undue sedation is often adequate to prevent further falls in a frail elderly person.

For patients with gait and balance disturbances, specific assistive devices are often helpful. These devices include walkers, crutches, canes, and even shoe modification. Since the assistive device must be tailored to the patient, it should be prescribed in consultation with a physiatrist or physical therapist. Many such patients, those with stroke, hip fracture, arthritis, or parkinsonism for example, can also benefit from a program of gait training under supervision of a physical therapist.

Several techniques may benefit patients with persistent orthostatic hypotension due to autonomic dysfunction: sleeping in a bed with the head raised to minimize sudden drop in blood pressure on rising; wearing elastic stockings to minimize venous pooling in the legs; rising slowly or sitting on the side of the bed for several minutes before standing up, and avoiding heavy meals and activity in hot weather. If conservative mechanical measures are ineffective, circulating blood volume can be increased by liberalizing dietary salt, provided that associated medical conditions do not preclude this. If disabling postural hypotension persists, mineralocorticoid therapy can be initiated with low doses of fludrocortisone acetate (Florinef Acetate), beginning at 0.1 to 0.2 mg/d will suffice in elderly patients. Extreme caution must be used to prevent precipitating congestive heart failure, fluid overload, hypokalemia, and hypertension.

Persons subject to drop attacks from vertebrobasilar insufficiency associated with head motion may be helped by a cervical collar. The collar should be prescribed in consultation with a neurologist or physiatrist for proper fit, because an ill-fitting collar theoretically could cause carotid compression.

A more difficult task is the management and prevention of recurrent falls by patients for whom a specific cause cannot be identified or who have multiple or irreversible causes. A careful search for, and correction of, other risk factors that predispose to falling (such as visual and hearing deficits) is essential. For disabilities that do not properly resolve with treatment of the underlying medical disorder (e.g., hemiparesis, ataxia, persistent weakness, or joint deformities), a trial of short-term rehabilitation in consultation with a physiatrist or physical therapist may improve safety and diminish long-term disability. When irreversible problems exist, residual limitations should be explained and coping methods developed. Among this group of patients it is unlikely that falls can be prevented without markedly curtailing mobility. The use of restraints may be an appropriate short-term intervention for acutely ill patients, or a necessity for severely demented patients, however, for the majority of institutionalized fallers the risks of immobility (Evans & Strumpf, 1989; Lofgren et al., 1989) and the impacts on quality of life may be more detrimental than a fall. In addition, there is some evidence to suggest that physical restraints (bedrails, poseys) as well as "chemical restraints" (sedatives, tranquilizers) actually contribute to falls in some instances (Ballinger & Ramsay, 1975; Dimant 1985, Miller & Elliott, 1979). Numerous alarm systems that alert staff when patients try to get out of bed or ambulate unassisted are currently available and are one alternative to restraints.

Prevention

Fall prevention in the nursing home requires a multi-pronged approach to take into account the multifactorial causes of falls. First, as a means of identifying nursing home patients at risk for falling, a focused fall risk assessment should be incorporated into the periodic physical examination. While the efficacy of screening institutionalized populations has not been evaluated, a periodic assessment done in connection with routine medical evaluations can be helpful in identifying potentially correctable problems (e.g., decreased vision, postural hypotension, diminished strength, and impaired gait), and may prevent falls. A fall risk assessment does not need to be complex, invasive, or expensive, but should include the following: postural blood pressure measurement, visual acuity testing, manual muscle testing of the lower extremities, balance and gait evaluation, functional status and mental status evaluations, and a review of medications and dosing (Robbins et al., 1989).

Second, the environment should be designed to allow patients maximal freedom of movement without risk of injury. In order to insure a safe environment, nursing home staff must closely monitor the facility for potential hazards. Specific environmental interventions should include: adequate lighting in all hallways and stairwells, bathroom grab bars next to the toilet and in the tubs or shower, nonskid mats in tubs or shower, raised toilet seats, handrails in the hallways, secure stairway banisters, and furniture that is easy to rise from. Of special importance is bed height. Most beds are adjustable and are often in an inappropriately raised position for the convenience of the staff. Proper bed height is such that when the patient sits on the side of the bed with feet touching the floor the knees are bent at a 90° angle. Furniture can also be rearranged so as to provide support to an unstable patient for ambulation to the bathroom. Table 2.5 lists the most important items to include in an environmental assessment based upon published safety checklists and guidelines (Kellogg, 1987; Rubenstein et al., 1988). Indirect data to support the value of such modifications is contained in studies of institutions that were specially designed to meet the needs and vulnerabilities of the elderly. Such institutions have substantially lower accident rates than those without such special attention (Morfitt, 1980).

Although not usually considered as part of the environment, proper footwear are important for safety. Ill-fitting shoes, shoes with worn soles and heels, heels that are too high or too narrow, shoes that are too tight or are left untied or unbuckled are unsafe. The habit of many nursing home patients of wearing slippers without soles or backs or wearing stockings without shoes is

TABLE 2.5 Environmental Assessment:
Summary of the Most Important Items

Bedroom
    Remove throw rugs
    Reduce clutter
    Observe bed for proper height
    Remove cords and wires on floor
    Check lighting, especially pathway to bathroom
Bathroom
    Install grab bars in tub/shower and by toilet
    Use rubber mats in tub/shower
    Take up floor mats when not using tub/shower
    Install raised toilet seat if too low
Hallways and dining room
    Install handrails in hallways and stairwells
    Eliminate chairs and sofas too low to comfortably arise from
    Avoid waxing floors
    Secure carpet edges on floor and stairs
Outside
    Observe outside patient areas for uneven walking surfaces (e.g., cracked sidewalks) or unsafe stairs

particularly hazardous and should be discouraged. Footwear should fit properly, be low heeled, and have a nonslippery sole. If a callous, bunion, or hammer toe is a problem, a shoe with a soft pliable upper which can conform to the shape of the foot should be recommended (Kellogg, 1987).

Third, intervention programs, such as exercise and gait training, to treat specific risk factors should be targeted to high risk patients. Although these types of interventions have not yet been shown to be effective in preventing falls, studies in community-living elderly populations have reported that older people can achieve measurable improvement in strength and flexibility (Agre et al., 1988; Morey et al., 1989; Raab et al., 1988). The one published randomized trial to determine the impact of a fall prevention program, consisting of a careful diagnostic assessment coupled with referrals for specific treatment and preventive interventions, had some promising results (Rubenstein et al., 1989). One hundred and sixty nursing home patients who had fallen were randomized into the study. The fall assessment performed by a nurse practitioner detected large numbers of remediable problems (e.g., weakness, environmental hazards, orthostatic hypotension, drug side effects, gait dysfunction). At the end of a 2 year follow-up period, there were clear but nonsignificant trends for intervention subjects to have lower fall and mortality rates. Strikingly, the intervention group did experience significant reductions in hospitalizations (26%) and hospital days (52%) compared to controls. The results from this study confirm previous observations that falls among frail institutionalized patients are often a marker for serious, often unrecognized, underlying illnesses and disabilities—many of which are amenable to treatment (Nickens, 1985; Rodstein, 1964).

In conclusion, a large proportion of falls in nursing home patients are potentially preventable with careful medical and environmental evaluation and intervention. Just as important, falls often indicate the presence of treatable underlying conditions in need of attention. Therefore, a vigorous diagnostic, therapeutic, and preventive approach is appropriate in all nursing home patients who fall. Moreover, periodic fall risk appraisals among all nursing home patients, as well as regular environmental "rounds" to detect and correct hazards, can probably lead to reduced fall rates, although these strategies remain to be tested. Any intervention that can make inroads on reducing the incidence of falls and related morbidity in nursing homes will clearly have far-reaching impacts.

REFERENCES

Agre, J. C., Pierce, L. E., Raab, D. M., McAdams, M., & Smith, E. L. (1988). Light resistance and stretching exercise in elderly woman: Effect upon strength. *Arch Phys Med Rehabil, 69,* 273–276.

Baker, S. P. & Harvey, A. H. (1985). Falls injuries in the elderly. *Clin Geriatr Med, 1*, 501–512.

Ballinger, B. R. & Ramsay, A. C. (1975). Accidents and drug treatment in a psychiatric hospital. *Brit J Psychiat, 126*, 462–463.

Berry, G., Fisher, R. H., & Lang, S. (1981). Detrimental incidents, including falls, in an elderly institutional population. *J Am Geriatr Soc, 29*, 322–324.

Blake, C. & Morfitt, J. M. (1986). Falls and staffing in a residential home for elderly people. *Public Health, 100*, 385–391.

Campbell, A. J., Reinken, J., Allan, B. C., & Martinez, G. S. (1981). Falls in old age: A study of frequency and other related factors. *Age and Ageing, 10*, 264–270.

Dimant, J. (1985). Accidents in the skilled nursing facility. *NY State J Med, 85*, 202–205.

Evans, L. K. & Strumpf, N. E. (1989). Tying down the elderly. A review of the literature on physical restraint. *J Am Geriatr Soc, 37*, 65–74.

Granek, E., Baker, S. P., & Abbey, H. (1987). Medications and diagnoses in relation to falls in a long-term care facility. *J Am Geriatr Soc, 35*, 503–511.

Gryfe, C. I., Amies, A., & Ashley, M. J. (1977). A longitudinal study of falls in an elderly population: I. Incidence and morbidity. *Age and Ageing, 6*, 201–210.

Hogue, C. C. (1982). Injury in late life: Part I. Epidemiology. *J Am Geriatr Soc, 30*, 183–190.

Kalchthaler, T., Bascon, R. A., & Quintos, V. (1978). Falls in the institutionalized elderly. *J Am Geriatr Soc, 26*, 424–428.

Kellogg International Work Group on Prevention of Falls in the Elderly. (1987). The prevention of falls in later life. *Dan Med Bull, 34* (Suppl 4), 1–24.

Lipsitz, L. A., & Fullerton, K. J. (1986). Postprandial blood pressure reduction in healthy elderly. *J Am Geriatr Soc, 34*, 267–270.

Lofgren, R. P., MacPherson, D. S., Granieri, R., Myllenbeck, S., & Sprafka, J. M. (1989). Mechanical restraints on the medical wards: Are protective devices safe? *Am J Pub Health, 79*, 735–738.

Lucht, U. (1971). A prospective study of accidental falls and resulting injuries in the home among elderly people. *Acta Socio-med Scand, 2*, 105–120.

Mader, S. L., Josephson, K. R., & Rubenstein, L. Z. (1987). Low prevalence of postural hypotension among community-dwelling elderly. *JAMA, 258*, 1511–1514.

Melton, L. J. & Riggs, B. L. (1983). Epidemiology of age-related fractures. In Avioli, L. V. (Ed.), *The Osteoporotic Syndrome* (pp. 45–72). Orlando, FL: Grune & Stratton.

Miller M. B. & Elliott, D. F. (1979). Accidents in nursing homes: Implications for patients and administrators. In Miller, M. B. (Ed.), *Current Issues in Clinical Geriatrics* (pp. 97–137). New York: Tiresias Press.

Morey, M. C., Cowper, P. A., & Feussner, J. R. (1989). Evaluation of a supervised exercise program in a geriatric population. *J Am Geriatr Soc, 37*, 348–354.

Morfitt, J. M. (1980). Residential homes for the elderly—Which are the safest? *Pub Health, London, 94*, 223–228.

Nevitt, M. C., Cummings, S. R., Kidd, S., & Black, D. (1989). Risk factors for recurrent nonsyncopal falls. A prospective study. *JAMA, 261*, 2663–2668.

Nickens, H. (1985). Intrinsic factors in falling among the elderly. *Arch Intern Med, 145*, 1089–1093.

Pawlson, L. G., Goodwin, M., & Keith, K. (1986). Wheelchair use by ambulatory nursing home residents. *J Am Geriatr Soc, 34*, 860–864.

Raab, D. M., Agre, J. C., McAdam, M., & Smith, E. L. (1988). Light resistance and

stretching exercise in elderly women: Effect upon flexibility. *Arch Phys Med Rehabil, 69,* 268–272.

Rhymes, J. & Jaeger, R. (1988). Falls. Prevention and management in the institutional setting. *Clin Geriatr Med, 4,* 613–622.

Robbins, A. S. & Rubenstein, L. Z. (1984). Postural hypotension in the elderly. *J Am Geriatr Soc, 32,* 769–774.

Robbins, A. S., Rubenstein, L. Z., Josephson, K. R., Schulman, B. L., Osterweil, D., & Fine, G. (1989). Predictors of falls among elderly people. Results of two population-based studies. *Arch Intern Med, 149,* 1628–1633.

Rodstein, M. (1964). Accidents among the aged: Incidence, causes and prevention. *J Chron Dis, 17,* 515–526.

Rosado, J. A., Rubenstein, L. Z., Robbins, A. S., Heng, M. K., Schulman, B. L., & Josephson, K. R. (1989). The value of holter monitoring in evaluating the elderly patient who falls. *J Am Geriatr Soc, 37,* 430–434.

Rubenstein, L. Z., Robbins, A. S., Schulman, B. L., Rosado, J., Osterweil, D., & Josephson, K. R. (1988). Falls and instability in the elderly. *J Am Geriatr Soc, 36,* 266–278.

Rubenstein, L. Z., Robbins, A. S., Josephson, K. R., & Schulman, B. L. (1989). Benefits of a falls workup: A randomized clinical trial. *Clin Res, 37,* 324A.

Sheldon, J. H. (1960). On the natural history of falls in old age. *Brit Med J, 10,* 1685–1690.

Tinetti, M. E., Williams, T. F., & Mayewski, R. (1986). Fall risk index for elderly patients based on number of chronic disabilities. *Am J Med, 80,* 429–434.

Tinetti, M. E. (1987). Factors associated with serious injury druing falls by ambulatory nursing home residents. *J Am Geriatr Soc, 35,* 644–648.

U.S. Department of Health and Human Services. (1981). *Health, United States 1980 with prevention profile* (312–314). DHHS Publ. No. (PHS) 81-1232; Hyattsville, MD.

Whipple, H., Wolfson, L. I., & Amerman, P. M. (1987). The relationship of knee and ankle weakness to falls in nursing home residents: An isokinetic study. *J Am Geriatr Soc, 35,* 13–20.

3
Segregating the Cognitively Impaired: Are Dementia Units Successful?

Kathleen Coen Buckwalter

INTRODUCTION

Alzheimer's disease (AD) is a common cause of cognitive impairment and very serious health problem for the elderly. Persons with AD experience progressive mental and functional impairment. As the disorder progresses, secondary mental symptoms may develop, usually depression or delusions, and sometimes delirium. Emotional outbursts and catastrophic reactions are common. Most Alzheimer's victims show marked deterioration, and may become mute, incontinent, inattentive, and incapable of ambulation or self-care. Eventually, the problems of managing the AD patient require placement into a long-term care facility. Making up about 65% of nursing home residents (Hing, 1987), demented persons may live for years, presenting difficult problems of care and management.

In view of the many problems associated with caring for patients with cognitive impairment, such as wandering, inattention to personal hygiene, rummaging randomly in other patients' rooms and storage areas, defecating and urinating in unacceptable places, combative behavior toward other patients and staff, etc., it is imperative to devise and evaluate settings for their care (DHHS, 1984). Many nursing homes are not equipped with environmental structures or the support and service systems required to care for the person with cognitive impairment. Most nursing homes integrate the confused resident with nonconfused physically frail residents, and staff often have inadequate knowledge about how to care for persons with dementia or other forms of cognitive impairment. Because the confused and anxious resident is often involved in confrontations with family, staff, and other residents, chemical and/or physical restraints tend to be used to maintain safety and harmony. This traditional setting, with floor plans that encourage continuous pacing, may be inadequate to address the personal safety, privacy, environmental needs, and other health care needs of the cognitively impaired population (Hall, Kirschling, & Todd, 1986; Peppard, 1986).

The work of Lawton (1972; 1980), Coons (1983), and Danford (1982) suggest that the environment may have strong effects on patient behavior. However, there is much controversy about what specific characteristics of the environment are therapeutic for cognitively impaired persons. Although some nursing homes have been experimenting with environmental interventions to manage the behavior of cognitively impaired residents for more than two decades (Peppard, 1986), only recently have Special Care Units (SCU's) been proposed as a key solution for the difficult-to-manage AD patient (Ronch, 1987; OTA, 1987).

The critical elements of these units, however, appear to be quite controversial. What constitute a special unit vary among long-term care facilities as to the type and amount of changes made when a dementia unit is implemented. As Sloan and colleagues (1989) noted in a telephone survey of all nursing homes in California, New York, North Carolina, Ohio, and Texas, dementia units vary according to the philosophy of treatment, staff training, programming, number and mix of patients on a unit, and the criteria for admission.

With the increasing numbers of persons expected to develop AD and other cognitive impairments, nurses, managers of long-term care facilities (LTCs), family members and policymakers are faced with the difficult prospect of determining the most appropriate and cost effective means of caring for these patients. Often, considerable costs are involved in the construction (e.g., environmental barriers, special floor coverings, indestructable furniture, outdoor enclosures, etc.) and staffing (staff education programs, increased staff: patient ratios) of dementia units. Moreover, the potential costs and quality of care issues associated with continuing to care for AD patients on traditional integrated units, make it imperative to evaluate the effectiveness of dementia units in terms of their effect on patient cognitive and behavioral functioning; family attitudes and perceptions of care; cost; and staff stress, attrition, and job satisfaction.

WHAT'S "SPECIAL" ABOUT SPECIAL CARE UNITS?

Although many states are considering or have developed standards or regulations governing specialized dementia units, at present there is no standardized definition, set formula for constructing (Schultz, 1987), nor consistent terminology (e.g. specialized dementia unit, special needs unit, special care unit, special unit, dedicated care unit, etc.) used to characterize special units for the cognitively impaired. This chapter will use the above terms interchangeably to refer to "a distinct part of a health care facility which is clearly identifiable, containing contiguous rooms in a separate wing or building or on a separate floor of the facility, and for which a special program of care has been approved" (ADRDA Unit Rules Committee, 1988). This definition appears to capture most of the critical elements of specialized dementia units as described in the literature.

The notion of a specialized environment and program of care is one that separates special care units from merely segregated units. The American Association of Homes for the Aged (AAHA, 1989), in developing "best practices" guidelines for special units, has emphasized seven dimensions of special care, including commitment, philosophy of care, therapeutic care, physical design, specialized staff, communication, and research and education (Beltler, 1988). Similarly, there are at least five areas consistently reported in the literature in which dementia units seem to be "special": (1) staff selection and training; (2) activity programming specifically designed for cognitively impaired residents; (3) family programming; (4) physical environment and decor, including separation from other areas of the facility; and (5) admission of residents with cognitive impairment, most commonly Alzheimer's disease or a related disorder. Each of these areas is briefly summarized in the next section.

Staff Selection and Training

Most dementia units are established by an interdisciplinary team, including social services, activities, physical, occupational and rehabilitation therapists, dieticians, pastoral care, supportive services, and medical consultants. However, the nursing department generally is responsible for coordinating care, developing policies and procedures for the unit, and hiring and training unit staff (Ackerman, 1985). Some staff have special in-service training to work on a dementia unit, but the educational requirements and content of the curricula vary greatly, ranging from 2 to 40 hours of didactic and experiential training (the average appears to be around 10 hours of specialized training) (Greene, Asp, & Crane, 1985). In staff training, emphasis is usually placed on knowledge about the disease process and its behavioral and emotional manifestations, stress management techniques, communication strategies (especially nonverbal techniques), pacing of activities and communication, continuity of care, and maintaining respect for the dignity of the individual.

Staffing patterns also vary greatly from unit to unit, but in general follow patterns similar to those in Skilled Nursing Facilities (SNFs). Staff-to-patient ratios commonly reported range from 1:4 to 1:6, which reflects the heaviness of patient care (Ackerman, 1985). A few units report no increase in staff (Benson et al., 1987). Hours of patient care per patient day range anywhere from 2 to 5 (Schultz, 1987). Staff morale is an important administrative and clinical consideration, and some units report periodically rotating staff off the unit to prevent burnout and attrition, although this practice may adversely affect the consistency of care provided. Other units have implemented regular staff support meetings in an effort to diffuse problems and maintain morale. Most units recruit staff who express a willingness to work with the cognitively impaired population, their families, and other multidisciplinary staff. Peppard (1989) maintains that common sense, flexibility, and knowledge are the three key elements of a successful unit.

Activity Programming

Specialized programming for residents, usually conducted by an activities coordinator, is an important feature of many dementia units. The amount and the nature of structured programming differs according to unit philosophy, with some facilities emphasizing flexibility and creativity, whereas others stress continuity and routinization (Hall, Kirschling, & Todd, 1986; Schultz, 1987).

Most successful approaches to programming activities for persons with cognitive impairment allow for some degree of flexibility (Zgola, 1987). Like care routines, patient programming should ideally be meaningful and individualized. In general, activities should be something the resident wants to engage in and that will lead to the perception of a positive outcome on their part. That is, not everyone enjoys bingo, and there is no reason to believe that just because a person has become cognitively impaired, this disaffection will change. Further, the individual who can no longer get the letters right, nor appreciate their relationship to the bingo card may suffer from a sense of failure if forced to engage in this particular activity. The scheduling of activities also varies dramatically among specialized settings, although almost all favor a consistent routine. Some units promote a series of back-to-back, highly structured activities to prevent the resident who is unable to initiate activities from prolonged periods of idleness. Other program models implement regular mid-morning and mid-afternoon "time-out" periods, void of planned activities, in an effort to compensate for the resident's fatigue and loss of reserve energy (Hall & Buckwalter, 1987).

Much more research is needed to determine an optimal approach to activity programming. Activities found on many dementia units include, for example, sensory integration techniques, reminiscence, exercise, music, movement, and pet therapies. Other more individualized programs may focus on dressing and grooming, feeding, and socialization needs. Simple voluntary tasks (e.g., filling water glasses), light housekeeping chores, and meal preparation are also popular activities among less impaired residents. Activities that complement the resident's previous interests, such as gardening, are also encouraged (Johnson, 1989). Activities and social services programs often include the opportunity for regular interaction with nonconfused residents of the facility as well as with the community outside the facility.

The role of reality orientation, both 24-hour and classroom, remains controversial, and in general lacks empirical support in terms of long-lasting effects. Some units subscribe instead, to Feil's concept of validation or fantasy therapy (Feil, 1984). According to Hall and Buckwalter's Progressively Lowered Stress Threshold Model, which is the conceptual base for many specialized dementia units in the Midwest, "the use of active rehabilitative or educational techniques, reality testing, reality orientation, and encouraging the demented patient to engage in activities beyond their level of cognitive ability may serve as profound stressors" (Hall & Buckwalter, 1987, p. 404). Thus, although all patient questions are answered concerning reality, and environmental cues, such as clocks and calendars are provided, reality therapy and cognitive testing are modified to incorporate only that information that the resident needs to know to function safely. The philosophy of therapeutic care advanced by the AAHA (Beitler, 1988) supports the highest level of client functioning, accommodates individual differences, responds to changing abilities over time, and compensates for losses while supporting remaining abilities.

Family Programming

The role of the family of the institutionalized patient is often confusing and unclear for both family members and staff (Buckwalter & Hall, 1987). Most dementia units purport to assist the family in maintaining a relationship with their loved one and family programming is thus an element of many units. Family activities may include regular family meetings, joint family/resident activities, or education/information groups covering such topics as medical and legal issues.

Families are often encouraged to continue to attend local support groups (ADRDA) as well as those provided by the institution (Johnson, 1989). Perhaps most importantly, families need to be listened to and staff availability for this task is essential to positive family adjustment (Ackerman, 1985). On some units family members are encouraged to volunteer and to continue care-giving tasks (Hansen, Patterson, & Wilson, 1988). Others include family members in the development of resident plans of care. Visitor training programs that essentially teach the family how to visit so that catastrophic outcomes are avoided during their visit and after their departure (e.g., in small groups, for short periods of time) are increasingly being incorporated into admission procedures (Johnson, 1989; Maas, Buckwalter, & Hall, 1989). Level of family involvement and their satisfaction with the care provided appears to vary greatly from facility to facility.

Physical Environment and Decor

Not surprisingly, the architectural design of special units also varies considerably, although many units try to optimize socialization and supervision of the cognitively impaired resident (Skolaski-Pellitteri, 1983). Low or reduced stimulus units are organized somewhat differently than traditional units and are designed to minimize extraneous noise and activity (Johnson, 1989). For example, many reduced stimulus units have moved away from a congregate dining experience, as this highly stimulating activity may lead to sensory overload and withdrawal. Instead, residents are fed in small groups (3–4) in their own rooms (Hall & Buckwalter, 1987). Similarly, centralized placement of the nurses' station, with its ringing phones, blaring public address system, and general level of chaos (change of shift reports, people charting, preparing to make rounds), is believed to be disruptive for the cognitively impaired resident, and can lead to dysfunctional behaviors (Weldon, 1986). Environmental modifications aimed at reducing noxious or confusing stimuli might include removal of prints and patterns from floors, walls, furniture, or covering of floors with carpet to reduce glare. Intercom systems and mirrors are also frequently removed in an effort to keep extraneous noise and frightening reflections to a minimum. A successful feature of many specialized units is a courtyard area or other secure outdoor arena where residents may wander safely, garden, or simply relax.

Clearly, there is no set formula for constructing a dementia unit. The unit environment is one that is designed to enhance remaining functional abilities, to prevent excess disability or those reversible deficits above and beyond what might be expected from the cognitive impairment itself (Dawson, 1986), to provide comfort, security, and safety for the cognitively impaired patient while allowing freedom of movement within the unit (Beitler, 1988). Resident security thus becomes an important concern, and most units have some mechanisms (e.g., alarmed doors) to detect undesired elopement. Most specialized units are designed to increase the quality of life of the cognitively impaired resident, rather than altering the course of their disease, although a number of units purport to improve resident behaviors, life satisfaction, and social functioning.

Physical standards for dementia units may include, for example, locked or alarmed doors (with approval of the fire marshall), a secure outdoor activity area, no floor level or grade changes (steps or slopes), adequate lighting, dining and activity areas within the unit itself that are not shared by other residents, a private area for nursing staff activities, toilets that are accessible and large enough to accommodate a nonambulatory resident and two staff members, and stainless steel mirrors. Interior decor varies among facilities as well. Many encourage decor with possessions from home to personalize the resident's room and to make common areas more homelike (Beitler, 1988). Moderate color schemes, with bright colors used for accent are recommended for individual rooms, whereas interesting textures and high contrast colors are encouraged in the common areas to enable residents to differentiate one area from another. In most units, single and double occupancy rooms predominate (Greene, Asp, & Crane, 1985), although some specialized units have four-bed wards. Units are also quite diverse in size, ranging from small wings (8–10 beds) to entire buildings housing upwards of 50 residents (Hepburn et al., 1989; Schultz, 1987). Optimum size appears to be not more than 20 cognitively impaired patients per unit (Johnson, 1989), but this area needs further systematic research.

Admission Criteria

Although there appear to be no standardized admission criteria for a dementia unit, most units are designed for ambulatory residents in the middle stages of a dementing illness. However, some "bedfast" units have been developed, and residents are then moved from the ambulatory wing to the bedfast area when their deterioration from the disease process necessitates almost total dependency in activities of daily living, and when they are no longer able to participate meaningfully in the activities of the ambulatory unit.

Johnson (1989, p. 37) describes selection criteria for the low stimulus Alzheimer's disease wing he developed in a Louisiana nursing home, including that the patient be ambulatory or in a wheel chair; give evidence of having some type of irreversible dementia; must not require more than the minimum amount of medical care that can be administered by the limited number of staff; and can manage some self-care with staff assistance. Similar criteria have been set forth by Ackerman (1985, p. 91), with the addition of spelling out behavioral manifestions such as absence of or short span of attention; inability to communicate needs either verbally or nonverbally; emotionally labile or withdrawn personality; inability to provide self-care, requiring total and near total assistance with ADL's; impaired judgment requiring protection from self or others; total or near total disorientation to time, person and place; loss of recent memory; and disruptive behavior.

The state of Iowa mandates admission to a special care unit only after an evaluation team determines that the resident (1) is a serious danger to self or others; or (2) habitually wanders or would wander out of buildings and is unable to find the way back; or (3) has significant behavior problems that seriously disrupt the rights of other residents; and, in all cases (4), less restrictive alternatives have been unsuccessful in preventing harm to self or others; and (5) legal authority for such restrictive activity has been established (Special Care Unit Committee meeting, January 21, 1988). Residents are reevaluated 30 days after placement and at least every 180 days thereafter according to Iowa standards.

Higher functioning residents are not recommended for special care units; rather residents who score 5 or more on the Reisberg et al. (1982) Global Deterioration Scale are more ideally suited for segregation, and specialized programming (Peppard, 1989). The importance of preadmission home assessments is emphasized in the literature (Buckwalter & Hall, 1987; Johnson, 1989), as well as the necessity to acquaint family members with unit philosophy and practices upon admission.

In sum, dementia units reported in the literature vary greatly. At present there is no standard definition of a special unit; no one best staff mix, training, or staffing pattern; and environmental and programmatic activities are equally diverse and seem to vary from facility to facility based on treatment philosophy (e.g., high or low stimulus) and resources. However, there is some unity in the assumptions underlying the concept of special care, including the notion that special care is "good," that improvement in selected areas of client functioning can be expected through environmental enrichment and therapeutic staff support, and that aberrant behavior is a symptom of underlying resident discomfort (Beitler, 1988).

Thus, most dementia units appear to embrace similar goals, that is, to (1) assist the cognitively impaired patient to maintain or maximize his or her level of cognitive, intellectual, and physical functioning; (2) to enhance quality of life through specialized programming; (3) to allow freedom of movement, expression, and choice within the environment; and (4) to provide safety, warm and accepting care with dignity, and to promote socially acceptable behavior with judicious use of chemical and physical restraints (Ackerman, 1985; Greene, Asp, & Crane, 1985). The primary purpose of the special unit, then, is to create an environment where the cognitively impaired resident can flourish, while remaining comfortable and secure, and where the resident's autonomy is actually enhanced rather than reduced (Hegeman & Tobin, 1988).

ARGUMENTS IN FAVOR OF SEGREGATION

A number of authors have recommended that cognitively impaired patients be housed separately in units that provide a consistent daily routine to reduce the level and complexity of environmental stimuli (Grossman et al., 1986; Hall & Buckwalter, 1987; Johnson, 1989; Peppard, 1986; Wolanin & Philips, 1981). Others have noted that nondemented elderly suffer mental and emotional declines when mixed with more cognitively impaired residents (Wiltzius, Gambert, & Duthie, 1981), or, as Kane (1987) has suggested, that grouping confused residents with nonconfused transforms the latter into involuntary care givers for the rest of their lives, and while paying for their care. Hall, Kirschling, and Todd (1986) and Johnson (1989), among others, have documented the invasion of privacy, loss or damage of personal property, decreased socialization, interrupted sleep, and fear of physical harm that often befall the lucid roommate of a cognitively impaired individual. Clearly, the needs of the nondemented nursing home resident must be considered (Retsinas, 1988).

Grossman et al. (1986) surveyed clinical care staff and found that 76% of the respondents believed they could provide better and more direct care in a segregated unit, while 83% felt that the care recipients would be more comfortable if segregated according to level of care.

Descriptions of special care units are becoming more available in the literature (see, for example, Goodman, 1986). Hall, Kirschling and Todd (1986), using the principles of progressively lowered stress threshold (Hall & Buckwalter, 1987), have implemented environmental interventions (SCUs) in two settings. Although anecdotal and unsystematic, their initial results suggested that cognitively impaired residents had fewer inappropriate behaviors, and use of antipsychotic medications was reduced. In a later single group study, with two pretest and three posttest measures of the effects of a special unit (no control group), Hall (1988) found no statistically significant decrease in the use of restraints, incidence of falls, combative behaviors, and functional abilities. There was significantly less use of mood controlling medications and significant improvement in sleep through the night for cognitively impaired residents after the unit was implemented, and a nonsignificant reduction in socially unacceptable behaviors.

Cleary and colleagues (1988) developed and evaluated a reduced stimulation unit for patients with Alzheimer's disease and related disorders. They observed decreases in agitation and restraint use, as well as increases in resident weight. In contrast to the findings of Hall (1988) reported above, Cleary et al. (1988) found no change in medication usage among residents of the unit. Additionally, wandering created fewer concerns for both staff and other patients on this unit, and cognitively impaired residents were observed to interact more with staff and others. Interestingly, family satisfaction increased significantly after opening the unit, although staff satisfaction did not.

Mathew et al. (1988) undertook a detailed cross-sectional profile of dementia residents in three settings; an established special care unit, other wards of the same facility, and a nursing home without a special unit. They found that the special care units residents were better educated, younger, wealthier, and had fewer physical health problems than residents of both comparison units. The investigators concluded that otherwise the special care residents were typical of dementia residents in nursing homes, and that they did not function at a higher level than residents of a traditional nursing home setting. Their data did identify a few positive patient outcomes for residents of the special care unit, such as a trend toward being hospitalized less and developing fewer skin problems. Family satisfaction was higher on the special unit and restraint use was diminished. No differences between groups were noted on the variables of sleep disturbance or weight loss, and SCU patients actually had more frequent injuries than residents in comparison settings (Matthew et al., 1988, p. 22), a finding that is probably due to avoidance of physical restraints.

Several other special unit programs have reported that they are improving the behavior and ability of cognitively impaired residents (Cameron et al., 1987; Greene, Asp, & Crane, 1985; Linsk & Miller, 1986), as well as enhanced staff effectiveness and morale, greater family satisfaction, and a more favorable environment for lucid residents of the same facility (Benson et al., 1987). However, with the exception of Benson et al. (1987), they have failed to perform comprehensive evaluations, and offer instead more anecdotal evidence for their efficacy. Benson and his associates (1987) evaluated 32 elderly residents admitted to a specially designed dementia unit. They found increased levels of mental and emotional status as well as activities of daily living which were sustained over a 1 year follow-up period.

A study of 5 LTC's in Iowa with dementia units (Iowa Foundation for Medical Care, 1987) demonstrated positive outcomes in terms of resident weight gain, and decreased use of drugs and restraints. However, the study was cross-sectional in design and there were significant problems in substantiating diagnoses.

One of the few cost-benefit analyses of a unit (a 46-bed specialized dementia unit in an academically affiliated nursing home) revealed costs for maintaining the unit were similar to those of conventional units within the facility (Cameron et al., 1987).

ARGUMENTS AGAINST SEGREGATION

In contrast to the information presented above, some clinicians, administrators, and researchers argue against segregation of the cognitively impaired (Salisbury and Goehner, 1983), and still others stress an increased level of stimulation on units designed for their care (Loew & Silverstone, 1971; Richman, 1969). At present there is no clear-cut consensus that segregating cognitively impaired residents from other frail elderly is, in and of itself, advisable (Rabins, 1986). Moreover, preliminary data from a rigorously designed longitudinal control group evaluation of a special care unit in Texas (Chafetz & West, 1987), has demonstrated insignificant differences in resident outcomes (e.g., cognitive ability or behavior problems), staff knowledge and attitudes toward the aged, although sedative use was significantly reduced in the special unit sample.

Given the usually higher costs per day for special unit care, on average about $5.00–$10.00 (OTA, 1987), these results seem discouraging. Clearly, additional longitudinal data from the Chafetz and West study cited above, as well as other controlled studies comparing special, segregated but not special, and traditional units for the cognitively impaired, are sorely needed before further conclusions about the efficacy of dementia units can be drawn. Further, as noted in *Losing a Million Minds*, "Good studies of cost are urgently needed, but must await a determination of what components are necessary or ideal in a special unit" (DTA, 1987, p. 256).

Koff (1986) has argued for the development of standards of care before more special units are constructed, a plea that is supported by findings from a recent statewide survey of long-term care (LTC) facilities and special care units in Minnesota (Hepburn et al., 1989). Hepburn et al. (1989) found that management of disruptive patient behavior was the major problem cited by all respondents, and that the "predominant mode of available response to problemative behaviors is restrictive" (p. 21). A sub-survey was conducted on the 14% of respondents who indicated that they had or planned to have a special care unit for dementia patients. The investigators concluded that there was little concern for diagnostic precision on these units, with 96% of the facilities accepting the admitting diagnosis of the patient's own physician. Behavior, rather than diagnosis, seemed to be the major admission criterion. There was also a lack of well articulated discharge criteria, with discharge mostly due to death. Only half of the special units reported that staff were specially selected to work on the unit and only a third received specialized training to do so. Despite the well documented need for staff education and training (Rango, 1985), more than three-fourths of the SCU respondents reported no special in-service programming for unit staff. Interestingly, only 1 facility noted a support group for their staff, and another 2 reported on stress reduction programs. Few of the units surveyed incorporated special designs or structural changes (Hepburn et al., 1989). Like Koff (1986), these authors recommend the development "of standards about what makes a SCU for dementia patients" (Hepburn et al., 1989, p. 23), including identification of meaningful admission and discharge criteria, staffing issues, and elements of the physical design.

Wilson is a strong advocate for what she calls "controlled integrative environments." She maintains that there is nothing "special" about special care units—it's just good care. At the 1989 American Society on Aging Annual Conference (Washington, DC, April 1989), she and Nancy Peppard debated issues related to Special Needs Units in a stimulating "Point-Counterpoint" session. Wilson (1989) maintains that the concept of special care units may lead to more mechanized, dehumanized care environments which strive for the "lowest common denominator," making it difficult to recruit and retain quality staff. She also cites the negative effect of labeling the unit, and the lowered expectations that accompany segregation. Many of these same arguments were advanced as "cons" by Rabins (1986) in a recent article outlining the advantages and disadvantages of special care environments. Wilson reported on a study she had conducted with 96 residents that mainstreamed cognitively impaired persons with noncognitively impaired residents. Results suggested no negative impact on the mental well-being of the noncognitively impaired group, and the Alzheimer's patients improved in functional ability, bonding, and mutual helping behaviors (Wilson, 1989).

SPECIAL CARE UNITS IN OTHER SETTINGS
State Hospital

The one detailed description the author located of a special unit in a state hospital (Bullock, Reilly, & Nies, 1988) shared many of the same features as dementia units in nursing home settings. The Special Care Unit (SCU) of Eastern State Hospital is a psychosocial treatment program in a state facility, especially designed for patients with Alzheimer's disease and related disorders. The unit is part of the Hancock Geriatric Treatment Center, and has a male and female ward, each of which has a maximum capacity of 20 patients. The therapeutic milieu is designed to minimize anxiety and confusion, and uses soft music, minimum changes in routine and staffing, and visual aids to do so. Regular exercise and an enclosed outdoor area for wandering help reduce agitation and restlessness. All staff have expressed an interest in working on the unit and undergo training about the disorder and how to work with cognitively impaired residents. The goal of the unit is to maintain each patient's mental and physical abilities for as long as possible, to minimize problematic behaviors, without undue use of physical or chemical restraints, such that return to the community is possible.

Services that are available to residents of the SCU include: medical and nursing services, occupational and activities therapy, psychological and social services. Initial evaluation of the unit, using data collected from patient records ($N = 15$) and interviews with staff ($N = 14$) and patients, revealed that patients had resided at the state hospital for at least 4 months prior to transfer to the SCU. Daily and monthly frequencies of a variety of problem behaviors was assessed both before and after placement in the SCU. Results show a generally beneficial effort on patient behaviors, with anxiety, restlessness, and withdrawn and yelling behaviors decreasing most dramatically. Resistive and verbally abusive behaviors increased slightly. In the first 15 months of the SCU, 7 residents were discharged to nursing homes or homes for adults.

Data from staff members suggest the ward atmosphere is quieter, cleaner, and more relaxed, with better patient-to-staff ratios leading to more individualized care and attention to daily needs. Increasing socialization and more cooperation between staff and patients was also noted (Bullock, Reilly, & Nies, 1988).

A survey administered verbally to SCU residents revealed an overall positive attitude about the unit and its staff. All but 1 resident liked being on the unit, and the vast majority (14/18) felt happy and well treated. No dramatic change in type or quantity of medications was noted.

Adult Day Care

Dementia-specific units within day care centers are an increasing phenomenon. A recent article by Chodosh et al.(1989) details the advantages and disadvantages of establishing an Alzheimer's Disease and Related Disorders Unit integrated with an existing medical day care program. The units operated side-by-side and provided opportunities for joint activities (mainstreaming) between participants. The authors noted potential advantages in terms of financing, administration, staffing and transportation, but these outcomes weren't fully realized, as negative staff attitudes and behaviors emerged as the dementia unit enlarged. They conclude that day care units for demented clients can "provide an additional component of noninstitutional care for many moderately impaired dementia victims" (Chodosh et al., 1989, p. 13), but that the effect of a dementia unit on the clientele, their families, and the staff of a nearby medical day care center is considerable. They advise careful preparation and programming, with frequent evaluation of the program's intended goals.

PROBLEMS IN RESEARCH ON DEMENTIA UNITS

At present there is little empirical support for various environmental approaches to care of persons with cognitive impairment, and the few evaluations of dementia that are available are largely anecdotal, unsystematic, or use measures without established psychometric properties. Ohta and Ohta (1988), in a recent comprehensive overview of existing special units for Alzheimer's patients, emphasize that while there has been a proliferation of these units, and that their proponents are convinced of the success of the units, there is a paucity of systematic research to evaluate the effectiveness of interventions. They argue that studies of single special units are not adequate, particularly if the characteristics of the unit are not carefully described, including philosophy, environmental design, therapeutic approach, staffing, staff training, and patient admission and discharge criteria. They also note the serious methodological flaw of no control group that characterizes many studies. Finally, the need to provide more detailed information regarding effects for specific subcategories of patients was emphasized, e.g. level of functioning.

Ohta and Ohta (1988) assert that rigorous and informative research investigating the effectiveness of dementia units should employ an experimental design with random assignment to experimental and control groups, and should strive to test a clear taxonomy of unit characteristics on a range of cognitively impaired residents of special units. Further, investigators must use measurement instruments that are appropriate and validated on cognitively impaired residents of LTC settings (Sloan et al., 1989). The need for more rigorous research in this area was also underscored by the U.S. Congress OTA Report (1987), which noted that no appropriately designed and controlled study of special unit participant changes was found in their survey, and that such studies were needed to resolve controversies regarding the therapeutic characteristics of dementia units and their effects on patients, family, staff, and cost.

Researchers must also be aware of the many unique sources of bias when evaluating control data for Special Care Unit (SCU) studies, including facility characteristics, case mix differences, length of time the unit has been operating, and geographic and state regulatory differences (Sloan et al., 1989). Sloan et al. recommend that investigators try to "prevent, detect, and adjust for possible biases, through selection of comparison populations, matching, stratification, and/or multivariate modeling techniques" (1989, p.5). On a more positive note, several methodologically rigorous, longitudinal studies of the effectiveness of special units are currently underway, but not yet complete (Chafetz & West, 1987; Maas, Buckwalter, & Hall, 1989).

RECOMMENDATIONS FOR FUTURE RESEARCH AND TRAINING ON DEMENTIA UNITS

Although the majority of recent studies indicate that segregation of cognitively impaired patients from lucid patients is desirable and leads to better behavioral and quality of life outcomes, much more research is needed in the planning and design of special units for persons with cognitive impairment. Given the expected growth in the number of nursing home residents with AD, and the apparent lack of standardization among facilities with dementia units, it is important to fund research that evaluates various aspects of specialized care, including: (1) What is the optimum role of family members in SCUs? (2) What are the critical elements of the physical plant of these units? (3) What is the optimum level of staff training, staff mix, and staffing patterns in an SCU? (4) What specialized programming/activities lead to beneficial patient outcomes? (5) What are the costs associated with these critical elements? Is SCU care cost-effective?

There is also a need to develop a national registry of special units and to construct a taxonomy of special unit types, and to analyze unit effects according to type. In addition to reporting specific characteristics of the facility (e.g. size, operating aegis), the unit itself (e.g., staffing specifications), and patients, registry data should include information on both facility and unit philosophy, architectural design, clinical programming, admission criteria, resident characteristics, and other relevant policies. Registry data could be used to address the following questions: (1) What are the resident outcomes of dedicated units? (2) What are the morbidity and mortality rates on dedicated units? (3) What are the essential components of a successful dedicated unit? And (4) are dedicated units cost effective? Such a registry would further aid in the development and monitoring of quality assurance programs in facilities with special care units (Maas, Buckwalter, & Hall, 1989).

Finally, there is a need to develop and evaluate standardized training programs to assist the staff of special units in developing the skills necessary to effectively manage cognitively impaired residents.

ACKNOWLEDGEMENTS

The author gratefully acknowledges the contributions of Meridean Maas, Ph.D, R.N.; Geri Hall, M.A., R.N.; and Kathleen M. Bullock, M.A., in the preparation of this chapter.

REFERENCES

Ackerman, J. O. (1985). Separated, not isolated—as basic as administrative, backing, and commitment. *The Journal of Long-Term Care Administration*, 90–94.

Alzheimer's and Related Disorders Unit Rules Committee Meeting, State of Iowa, February 18, 1988.

American Association of Homes for the Aged. (1989). Best practices for special care programs for patients with Alzheimer's disease or a related disorder. Washington, DC: American Association Homes for the Aged.

Benson, D. M., Cameron, D., Humbach, E., Servino, L., & Gambert, S. (1987). Establishment and impact of a dementia unit within the nursing home. *Journal of the American Geriatrics Society*, *35*, 319–323.

Beitler, D. (1988, November) Observable criteria for judging quality of care for dementia patients in nursing homes. Symposium presented at Gerontological Society of America, San Francisco, CA.

Buckwalter, K. C. & Hall, G. R. (1987). Families of the institutionalized older adult: A neglected resource. In Brubaker, T. H. (Ed.), *Aging, Health and Family: Long-Term Care* (176–196). Beverly Hills, CA: Sage Publications.

Bullock, K. M., Reilly, L. E., & Nies, D. S. (1988). An initial evaluation of the Eastern State Hospital Special Care Unit. Unpublished manuscript.

Cameron, D. J. et al. (1987). A specialized dementia unit: Cost and benefit analysis. *The New York Medical Quarterly*, *7*, 103–107.

Chafetz, P. K. & West, H. L. (1987, November). Longitudinal control group evaluation of a special care unit for dementia patients: Initial findings. Presented at the 40th Annual Scientific Meeting of the Gerontological Society of America, Washington, DC.

Chodosh, H. L., Adelman, R., Caruso, D., Martin, F., & Muro, E. S. (1989). Combining medical and dementia day care units: problems and solutions. *The American Journal of Alzheimer's Care and Related Disorders and Research*, *4*, 7–13.

Cleary, T., Clamon, C., Price, M., & Shullaw, G. (1988). A reduced stimulus unit: Effects on patients with Alzheimer's disease and related disorders. *The Gerontologist*, *28*, 511–514.

Coons, D. H. (1983). The therapeutic milieu. In Reichel, W. (Ed.), *Clinical Aspects of Aging*. Baltimore, MD: Williams and Wilkins.

Danford, S. (1982). Therapeutic design for aging. In Norton, MacNeill (Ed.), *Mental Health Interventions for Aging*. South Hadley, MA: J. F. Bergin Publishers, Inc.

Dawson, P., Kline, K., Wiancko, D., & Wells, D. (1986). Preventing excess disability in patients with Alzheimer's disease. *Geriatric Nursing*, *7*, 298–310.

Feil, N. (1984). Communicating with the confused elderly patient. *Geriatrics*, *39*, 131.

Goodman, G. (March/April 1986). Confronting Alzheimer's at Newton-Wellesley nursing home. *Nursing Homes*, 30–34.

Greene, J., Asp, J., & Crane, N. (1985). Specialized management of the Alzheimer's patient: Does it make a difference? A preliminary progress report. *Journal of the Tennessee Medical Association*, *78*, 58–63.

Grossman, H., Weiner, A. S., Salamon, M. J., & Burros, L. (1986). The milieu standard for care of dementia in a nursing home. *Journal of Gerontological Social Work*, *9*, 73–98.

Hall, G. R., Kirschling, M. V. & Todd, S. (1986). Sheltered freedom: An Alzheimer's unit in an ICF. *Geriatric Nursing*, *7*, 132–137.

Hall, G. R. & Buckwalter, K. C. (1987). Progressively lowered stress threshold: A conceptual model for care of adults with Alzheimer's disease. *Archives of Psychiatric Nursing*, *1*, 399–406.

Hall, G. R. (1988). Evaluating a low stimulus nursing home unit for residents with chronic dementing illnesses. Unpublished Masters Thesis, Iowa City, Iowa.

Hansen, S. S., Patterson, M. A. & Wilson, R. M. (1988). Family involvement on a dementia unit: The resident enrichment and activity program. *The Gerontologist*, *28*, 508–510.

Hegeman, C. & Tobin, S. (1988). Enhancing the autonomy of mentally impaired nursing home residents. *The Gerontologist*, *28*(Supplement), 71–75.

Hepburn, K., Severance, J., Gates, B., & Christensen, M. (1989, March/April) Institutional care of dementia patients: A state-wide survey of long-term care facilities and special care units. *The American Journal of Alzheimer's Care and Related Disorders and Research*, *4*, 19–23.

Hing, E. (1987, June/July). Use of nursing homes by the elderly: Preliminary data from the 1985 National Nursing Home Survey. *National Gerontological Nursing Association Newsletter*.

Iowa Foundation for Medical Care. (1987, April). A study of Alzheimer's units in Iowa nursing homes. Des Moines, IA.

Johnson, C. J. (1989, March/April). Sociological intervention through developing low stimulus Alzheimer's wings in nursing homes. *The American Journal of Alzheimer's Care and Related Disorders and Research.* 4, 33–41.

Kane, R. (1987). Considerations before developing a special care unit for Alzheimer's patients. Beyond Folklore III: Standards of Care in Managing Alzheimer's Patients. Symposium conducted by the University of Minnesota and the Veteran's Administration. Minneapolis, MI.

Koff, T. H. (1986, Summer). Nursing home management of Alzheimer's disease: A plea for standards. *American Journal of Alzheimer's Care, 1,* 12–15.

Lawton, M. (1980). Psychosocial and environmental approaches to the care of senile dementia patients. In Cole, J. & Barrett, J. (Eds.), *Psychopathy in the Aged.* New York: Raven Press.

Lawton, M. P. (1972). Assessing the competence of older people. In Kent, D., Kastenbaum, P., & Sherwood, S. (Eds.), *Research Planning and Action for the Elderly.* New York: Behavioral Publications.

Linsk, N. L. & Miller, B. (1986). Assessment of activity, location, and interaction of an Alzheimer's disease family care unit. *The Gerontology, 26* (Special Issue), 14A.

Loew, C. A. & Silverstone, B. M. (1971). A program of intensified stimulation and response facilitation for senile aged. *The Gerontologist, 11,* 341–347.

Maas, M., Buckwalter, K. C., & Hall, G. R. (1989). National dedicated Alzheimer's unit outcome registry. Proposal submitted to National Center for Nursing Research, February 15, 1989.

Mathew, L., Sloan, P., Kilby, M., & Flood, R. (1988, March/April). What's different about a special care unit for dementia patients: A comparative study and research. *The American Journal of Alzheimer's Care and Related Disorders, 3,* 16–23.

Ohta, R. J. & Ohta, B. (1988). Special units for Alzheimer's disease patients: A critical look. *The Gerontologist, 28,* 803–808.

Peppard, N. (1986). Special nursing home units for residents with primary degenerative dementia: Alzheimer's disease. *Journal of Gerontological Social Work, 9,* 5–18.

Peppard, N. R. (1989, April) Point-counterpoint. Session on special needs units. American Society on Aging. Washington, DC.

Rabins, P. (1986). Establishing Alzheimer's disease units in nursing homes: Pros and cons. *Hospital and Community Psychiatry, 37,* 120–121.

Rango, N. (1985). The nursing home resident with dementia: Clinical care, ethics, and policy implications. *Annals of Internal Medicine, 102,* 835–841.

Reisberg, B., Ferris, M. J., Ferris, deLeon, & Crook, T. (1982). The global deterioration scale (GDS): An instrument for the assessment of primary degenerative dementia. *American Journal of Psychiatry, 139,* 1136–1139.

Retsinas, J. (1988, April). Needs of the nondemented nursing home resident. *Geriatric Medicine Today, 7,* 84–90.

Richman, L. (1969). Sensory training for geriatric patients. *American Journal of Occupational Therapy, 23,* 254–257.

Ronch, J. L. (1987). Specialized Alzheimer's units in nursing homes: Pros and cons. *American Journal of Alzheimer's Care and Research, 2,* 10–19.

Salisbury, S. & Goehner, P. (1983). Separation of the confused or integration with the lucid? *Geriatric Nurse, 6,* 157–159.

Schultz, D. J. (1987). Special design considerations for Alzheimer's facilities. *Contemporary Health Care,* 49–56.

Skolaski-Pellitteri, T. (1983). Environmental adaptations which compensate for dementia. *Physical and Occupational Therapists in Geriatrics, 3,* 31–44.

Sloan, P. D., Beitler, D. Buckwalter, K. C., et al. (1989). Methodologic issues in the study of specialized units (special care units) in nursing homes. Unpublished manuscript.

Special Care Unit Committee Meeting. (1988, January 21). Iowa Department of Inspections and Appeals, Des Moines, IA.

U.S. Congress, Office of Technology Assessment. (1987). *Losing a million minds: Confronting the tragedy of Alzheimer's disease and other dementias.* OTA-BA-323, Washington, DC: U.S. Government Printing Office.

U.S. Department of Health and Human Services, Task Force on Alzheimer's Disease. (1984). Alzheimer's Disease (DHHS Publication No. ADM 84-1323). Washington, DC: U.S. Government Printing Office.

Weldon, S. (1986, Fall). Behavioral and contexual interventions for deficit—type I and type II dementias (Alzheimer's disease). *Clinical Gerontologist, 6,* 35–43.

Wiltzius, F., Gambert, S., & Duthie, E. (1981). Importance of resident placement within a skilled nursing facility. *Journal of American Geriatrics Society, 29,* 418–421.

Wilson, K. (1989, April). Point-counterpoint session on special needs units. American Society on Aging. Washington, DC.

Wolanin, M. & Phillips, L. (1981). *Confusion: Prevention and care.* St. Louis, MO: Mosby.

Zgola, Y. (1987). *Doing things, a guide to programming activities for persons with Alzheimer's disease.* Baltimore, MD: Johns Hopkins University Press.

4

New Approaches to the Diagnosis and Treatment of Incontinence in the Nursing Home

Joseph G. Ouslander

PREVALENCE AND IMPACTS OF INCONTINENCE

Urinary incontinence (UI) is found in approximately half of residents of nursing homes (NHs) (Mohide, 1986; Ouslander, Kane, & Abrass, 1982; Ouslander & Fowler, 1985). It tends to be frequent and involve large volume urine loss, and over half of those incontinent of urine have some degree of stool incontinence (Ouslander, Kane, & Abrass, 1982; Ouslander & Fowler, 1985). Male NH residents appear to be as equally predisposed to incontinence as females (Ouslander, Kane, & Abrass, 1982; Ouslander & Fowler, 1985). Impairments of cognitive and physical functioning are strongly associated with incontinence among NH residents (Ouslander, Kane, & Abrass, 1982; Warren et al., 1987). As will be discussed later, these associations have important implications for diagnosis and treatment, because dementia and immobility make extensive diagnostic evaluations difficult and some forms of treatment impractical or too risky. Incontinence is associated with skin problems and urinary tract infections (UTIs) in NHs (Ouslander, Kane, & Abrass, 1982), but with the exception of catheter-related UTIs (Warren et al., 1987; Ouslander et al., 1987b), a cause-and-effect relationship has not been shown. The adverse psychosocial effects of incontinence among NH residents are difficult to document using existing scales (Ouslander et al., 1987a), but incontinent residents who do not have significant cognitive deficits are frequently embarrassed and uncomfortable, and may tend to isolate themselves. UI has been shown to be stressful for many NH nursing staff (Yu & Kaltreider, 1987). The economic costs of managing UI and its complications in the NH, including labor, laundry, and supplies, are enormous and amount to close to $2 billion per year (Ouslander & Kane, 1984; Hu, 1986). Thus, strategies that reduce the frequency of UI among NH residents could lead to substantial physical, psychosocial, and economic benefits.

PATHOPHYSIOLOGY OF INCONTINENCE IN THE NURSING HOME

Detailed discussions of the pathophysiology of UI in the geriatric population are available in the literature (Resnick & Yalla, 1985; Ouslander, 1986). Several aspects that are most relevant to UI in the NH will be briefly discussed herein. When a previously continent NH resident becomes incontinent, a search for acute and reversible causes of the UI should be undertaken. These causes include delirium (which can be associated with a variety of underlying conditions), restricted mobility, urinary retention, UTI, urethritis, fecal impaction, conditions that cause polyuria (e.g., poorly controlled diabetes, volume expanded states) and a variety of drugs (e.g., diuretics, psychotropics, autonomic agents) (Kane, Ouslander, & Abrass, 1989). NH residents with persistent forms of UI may also have one or more of these reversible factors contributing to their incontinence that need to be diagnosed and treated before further evaluations are undertaken.

There are four basic types of persistent UI: stress, urge, overflow, and functional (Kane, Ouslander, & Abrass, 1989). Because of the association between UI and impairments of cognitive and physical functioning (Ouslander, Kane, & Abrass, 1982; Ouslander et al., 1987a), there is a tendency to ascribe UI among NH residents to dementia and/or immobility. While functional disabilities may play an important role in the pathogenesis of UI among many NH residents, most incontinent NH residents also have abnormalities of lower urinary tract function that are amenable to specific treatments (Resnick, Yalla, & Laurino, 1989). In addition to these abnormalities, bacteriuria is also common among incontinent NH residents (Ouslander et al., 1987b; Boscia et al., 1986a; Nicolle et al., 1983). Studies to date suggest that eradicating bacteriuria among NH residents is not beneficial in terms of morbidity and mortality (Boscia et al., 1986; Nicolle et al., 1983; Abrutyn, Boscia, & Kaye, 1988). Two studies have also suggested that eradicating bacteriuria does not significantly effect UI; one was done in ambulatory bacteriuric elderly with infrequent UI (Boscia et al., 1986), and the other was done in a small number of NH residents (Ouslander, Blaustein, & Connor et al., 1988b). Until better data are available, this author still recommends eradicating the bacteriuria among incontinent NH residents once before further evaluations are done, and observing for any effects on the

UI (Ouslander, 1989a). While it is very unlikely that sterilizing the urine will cure the UI, it is possible that the frequency of UI will decrease and thus make the resident more responsive to other behavioral and/or pharmacologic interventions (see below). Further research is needed in order to clarify the role, if any, of chronic or intermittent bacteriuria in the pathogenesis of UI in the NH.

The most common urodynamic abnormality found among incontinent NH residents is detrusor hyperactivity (detrusor instability, detrusor hyperreflexia). Detrusor hyperactivity has been found in over half of NH residents with UI in several studies (Resnick, Yalla, & Laurino, 1989; Brocklehurst & Dillane, 1966; Pannill, Williams, & Davis, 1988; Ouslander et al., 1989). In a substantial proportion, however, this urodynamic finding occurs in concert with others that may have important implications for treatments, such as sphincter weakness with stress incontinence, and outflow obstruction (Resnick, Yalla, & Laurino, 1989; Pannill, Williams, & Davis, 1988; Ouslander et al., 1989a). Further, elegant complex urodynamic studies by Resnick and colleagues have indicated that about half of those with detrusor hyperactivity empty less than one-third of their bladder contents when an involuntary bladder contraction occurs (detrusor hyperactivity with impaired contractility or DHIC) (Resnick, Yalla, & Laurino, 1989; Resnick and Yalla, 1987). The nosologic, pathophysiologic, and clinical implications of this urodynamic finding are not yet clear. It may be that incontinent individuals with DHIC are more responsive to certain interventions such as bladder relaxant drug therapy; on the other hand they may be more likely to have problems with urinary retention with these drugs, or respond less well to simple behavioral intervention. More research on the clinical implications of DHIC is clearly needed.

Because many incontinent NH residents with urodynamically documented detrusor hyperactivity also have functional limitations that could play an important role in their UI, the precise relationship of detrusor hyperactivity to the pathogenesis of UI in this population remains unclear. Further research is necessary to determine the relative roles of detrusor hyperactivity vs. functional factors. Studies that determine if continent NH residents also have detrusor hyperactivity, and whether this urodynamic finding is important in predicting responsiveness to treatment interventions would be of great value in this area.

DIAGNOSTIC EVALUATION

The diagnostic evaluation of persistent types of urinary incontinence generally includes a history, physical examination, urinalysis and culture, and a basic assessment of lower urinary tract function. In the NH, some type of monitoring record that assists in determining the frequency and pattern of UI can be helpful in the assessment, as well as in implementing and following the results of treatment (Ouslander, Uman, & Urman, 1986). Further evaluation with cystourethroscopy, radiology, and complex urodynamic tests is of value in some instances. Urodynamic tests including simultaneous video urodynamic studies, have been shown to be feasible, safe, and informative even among very frail and elderly institutionalized patients (Resnick, Yalla, & Laurino, 1989). The role of complex urodynamic testing in the evaluation of geriatric urinary incontinence is, however, controversial. The controversy arises because these tests, where available, generally require a special trip to the site of the equipment and personnel trained in its use and the interpretation of test results; can be uncomfortable and cause bacteriuria in some patients (Sabanathan, Duffin, & Castleden, 1985); may be difficult to perform and interpret in functionally disabled and cognitively impaired patients (Eastwood & Smart, 1985); are relatively expensive (Ouslander & Kane, 1984); have not, until recently, been well standardized, especially in relation to aging (Abrams et al., 1988; Staskin, 1986); and most importantly, may not be necessary to determine an effective treatment plan for many incontinent NH residents.

We have designed and prospectively tested an assessment strategy that includes a detailed history (including the use of some type of bladder record in the NH), a targeted physical examination, a urinalysis and culture, a series of simplified tests of lower urinary tract function, and several criteria for referral for further evaluation. Details of this assessment strategy can be found in other publications (Kane, Ouslander, & Abrass, 1989; Ouslander et al., 1989a). A nurse practitioner, physician's assistant, or clinical nurse specialist can be trained to carry out the assessment. They must, however, have a basic understanding of lower urinary tract function and the types and causes of UI in the geriatric population. The assessment (including history, physical exam and simplified tests) takes 60–90 minutes and generally requires a nurse assistant in NH residents. In our experience, even frail, functionally impaired NH residents tolerate the assessment well, and the incidence of symptomatic UTI has been less than 5% (Ouslander, Leach, & Abelson, et al. 1988c).

The objectives of the assessment are threefold: first, to identify and treat the reversible factors discussed above (including bacteriuria); second, to identify residents who might benefit from further urologic, gynecologic, and urodynamic evaluation; and third, to identify residents who are candidates for a treatment trial with behavioral and/or pharmacologic therapy.

The equipment and supplies necessary for the simplified tests are listed in Table 4.1; the procedures are detailed in Table 4.2; and the criteria for referral are listed in Table 4.3 (Kane, Ouslander, & Abrass, 1989; Ouslander et al., 1989a; Ouslander, Leach, & Staskins, 1989b). In carefully selected residents the simple cystometry procedure may be unnecessary. They in-

**TABLE 4.1 Equipment and Supplies for Simple
Tests of Lower Urinary Tract Function**

12 or 14 French straight catheter
Sterile catheter insertion tray
50 ml catheter-tip syringe (without piston)
Liter bottle of sterile water
Fracture pan (females)
Urinal (males)
Commode (either portable or adjacent to exam room)
Small absorbent pads (for stress test)

clude women who (1) give a precise history of either pure stress (leaking small amounts of urine coincident with increases in intra-abdominal pressure) or pure urge incontinence without symptoms of voiding difficulty (leakage after precipitant urge to void unassociated with change in body position or increase in intraabdominal pressure); (2) are examined at a time when their bladder is full to ensure an accurate stress test; and (3) void a reasonable volume (e.g., > 200 ml) with no signs of voiding difficulty, and empty their bladder adequately (i.e., residual volume <100 ml). In the majority of our patients, however, we find the simple cystometry procedure helpful because patients either have mixed or unclear symptoms, and because it is often impractical to examine a patient at a time when his or her bladder is full and the patient is able to void in a normal fashion. In these types of patients the simple cystometry is helpful in (1) performing a stress test with the bladder full (the sensitivity of the stress test has been shown to be dependent on bladder volume [Lose, Gammelgaard, & Jorgensen, 1986]); (2) attempting to reproduce the patient's symptoms; and (3) determining an accurate residual volume after the bladder has been filled to capacity and the patient voids with a full bladder.

Preliminary results from one study suggest that a clinical algorithm, that does not include simple cystometry, may have a high diagnostic and therapeutic accuracy (Resnick, Yalla, & Laurino, 1986). Further research is needed to determine the optimal approach to the diagnostic evaluation of UI in the NH. Until this research is completed, NH residents with persistent UI who are not so severely impaired or terminally ill that specific treatment would be unlikely to benefit them, should have some type of assessment along the lines described above (NIH Consensus Conference, 1989; Ouslander, 1989b).

TREATMENT

Several different treatment modalities can be used to manage UI in the NH. Detailed discussions of these interventions can be found elsewhere (Ouslander, 1986; Kane, Ouslander, & Abrass, 1989). This review will focus on

TABLE 4.2 Procedures for Simple Tests of Lower Urinary Tract Function

Procedure	Observations	Interpretation
Stress maneuvers If possible, start the tests when the patient feels his/her bladder is full. He/she is asked to cough forcefully 3 times in the standing position with a small pad over the urethral area.	Timing (coincident or after stress) and amount (drops or larger volumes) of any leakage	Leakage of urine coincident with stress manuever confirms presence of stress incontinence.
Normal voiding The patient is asked to void privately in his/her normal fashion into a commode containing a measuring "hat" after a standard prep for clean urine specimen collection.	Signs of voiding difficulty (hesitancy, straining, intermittent stream) Voided volume	Signs of voiding difficulty may indicate obstruction or bladder contractility problem.
Post-void residual determination A 14 French straight catheter is inserted into the bladder using sterile technique within 5–10 minutes of the patient's voiding.	Ease of catheter passage Post-void residual volume	If there is great difficulty passing the catheter, obstruction may be present. If the residual volume is elevated (e.g., over 100 ml) after a normal void, obstruction or a bladder contractility problem may be present.

Procedure	Observation	Comments
Bladder filling* For females, position a fracture pan under their buttocks, and for males, have a urinal available to measure any leakage during filling. A 50ml catheter tip syringe without the piston is attached to the catheter and used as a funnel to fill the bladder. The bladder is filled with room temperature sterile water, 50 ml at a time, by holding the syringe so that it is approximately 15cm above the pubic symphysis (bladder pressure should not normally exceed 15cm of water during filling) until the patient feels the urge to void, and 25ml increments until bladder capacity is reached (an involuntary contraction, or "I would rush to the toilet now, I can't hold anymore"). The catheter is then removed.	First urge to void ("I'm starting to feel a little full"). Presence or absence of involuntary bladder contractions—detected by continuous upward movement of the column of fluid (sometimes accompanied by leaking around or expulsion of the catheter) in the absence of abdominal straining, which the patient cannot inhibit. Amount lost with involuntary contraction and subsequent bladder emptying. Bladder capacity—amount instilled before either an involuntary contraction or the strong urge to void is perceived).	Involuntary contractions or severe urgency at relatively low bladder volume (e.g., <250–300 ml) suggest urge incontinence, especially if consistent with the patient's presenting symptoms.
Repeat stress maneuvers The patient is asked to cough forcefully 3 times in the supine and standing positions.	Timing (coincident or after stress) and amount (drops or larger volumes) of any leakage.	See above. Stress maneuvers with a full bladder are more sensitive for detecting stress incontinence.
Bladder emptying The patient is asked to empty his/her bladder again privately into the commode with the measuring "hat."	Signs of voiding difficulty (see above). Voided volume. Calculated post-void residual (amount instilled minus amount voided).	See above. Calculated post-void residual may be more valid if patient did not feel full at beginning of tests.

*If an involuntary contraction does occur, it may be useful in selected patients to refill the bladder slowly (to at least 200 ml if possible) after the contraction subsides in order to have an adequate volume for a stress test, or for assessing bladder emptying.

**TABLE 4.3 Criteria Used for Referral for Further Urologic
and Urodynamic Evaluation**

History
   History of lower urinary tract or pelvic surgery or irradiation in the last 6 months.
   Relapse or rapid recurrence of symptomatic urinary tract infections.

Physical examination
   Marked pelvic prolapse.
   Marked prostatic enlargement and/or suspicion of carcinoma.

Simplified diagnostic tests
   Severe hesitancy and/or interrupted urinary stream.
   Severe stress incontinence in a woman who is a candidate for surgery, and in
      whom behavioral and/or pharmacologic treatment has failed, or stress in-
      continence in a man.
   Difficulty passing a 14 French straight catheter.
   Post-void residual >100 ml.

Urinalysis
   Microhematuria in the absence of bacteriuria and pyuria.

Diagnostic uncertainty; i.e., inability to make presumptive diagnosis after history,
physical examination and simplified diagnostic tests.

Failure to respond to an adequate therapeutic trial for urge and/or stress incontinence.

aspects of treatment that are most relevant to the NH setting. Even among
NH residents, the optimal treatment approach generally depends on the type
of UI, as depicted in Table 4.4. With the exception of overflow UI, behaviorally oriented therapies play a key role in treatment. Table 4.5 lists
examples of behavioral therapies. This classification is similar, but not identical, to the nosology presented in recent reviews of this topic (Hadley, 1986;
Burgio & Burgio, 1986). The use of these techniques in the NH is discussed
in the sections that follow.

STRESS INCONTINENCE

Pelvic floor (Kegel) exercises are generally the initial approach to treating
stress incontinence in young and middle-aged women. These exercises must
be done repetitively several times per day in order to be successful. Many
incontinent NH females may be unable to cooperate with such training.
Biofeedback has been used successfully for elderly female outpatients (Burgio, Whitehead, & Engel, 1985); the effectiveness of this type of therapy
(which requires special equipment and trained therapists) in NH settings has
not been well studied. Medical therapy for stress incontinence includes

**TABLE 4.4 Primary Treatments for Different Types
of Geriatric Urinary Incontinence**

Type of incontinence	Primary treatments
Stress	Pelvic floor (Kegel) exercises Alpha adrenergic agonists Estrogen Biofeedback, behavioral training Surgical bladder-neck suspension
Urge	Bladder relaxants Estrogen (if vaginal atrophy present) Training procedures (e.g., biofeedback, behavioral therapy) Surgical removal of obstructing or other irritating pathologic lesions
Overflow	Surgical removal of obstruction Intermittent catheterization (if practical) Indwelling catheterization
Functional	Behavioral therapies (e.g., habit training, scheduled toileting) Environmental manipulations Incontinence undergarments and pads External collection devices Bladder relaxants (selected patients)[a] Indwelling catheters (selected patients)[b]

[a]Many patients with functional incontinence also have detrusor hyperreflexia and some may benefit from bladder relaxant drug therapy (see text). From Castleden et al. (1983). *Age and Aging, 12,* 249–255.
[b]See Table 4.7.

alpha-adrenergic agonists and estrogen. The optimal dosage, route of administration, and duration of therapy for estrogen in this situation have not been clearly defined, but prolonged treatment is necessary to strengthen periurethral tissues. Women with bothersome stress incontinence who fail behavioral and medical therapies should be considered for a bladder-neck suspension procedure if no contraindications to surgery are present and an experienced surgeon is available (Schmidbauer, Chiang, & Raz, 1986).

OVERFLOW INCONTINENCE

Patients with urinary retention and incontinence require either surgical removal of an obstructing lesion or bladder emptying by intermittent or continuous catheterization. Although clean intermittent catheterization has been used successfully in young paraplegics, elderly female outpatients, and

TABLE 4.5 Examples of Behaviorally Oriented Training Procedures for Urinary Incontinence

Procedure	Definition	Types of incontinence	Comments
Patient dependent			
Pelvic floor (Kegel) exercises	Repetitive contraction of pelvic floor muscles	Stress	Requires adequate function and motivation May be done in conjunction with biofeedback
Biofeedback	Use of bladder, rectal, or vaginal pressure recordings to train patients to contract pelvic floor muscles and relax bladder	Stress and urge	Requires equipment and trained personnel Relatively invasive Requires adequate cognitive and physical function and motivation
Behavioral training	Use of educational components of biofeedback, bladder records, pelvic floor, and other behavioral exercises	Stress and urge	Requires trained therapist, adequate cognitive and physical functioning, and motivation
Bladder retraining[a]	Progressive lengthening or shortening of intervoiding interval, with adjunctive techniques[b] intermittent catheterization used in patients recovering from overdistension injuries with persistent retention	Acute (e.g., post-catheterization with urge or overflow, post-stroke)	Goal is to restore normal pattern of voiding and continence Requires adequate cognitive and physical function and motivation

Care giver dependent			
Scheduled toileting/ prompted voiding	Fixed toileting schedule with prompted voiding; adjunctive techniques may also be used	Urge and functional	Goal is to prevent wetting episodes Can be used in patients with impaired cognitive or physical functioning Requires staff/caregiver availability and motivation
Habit training	Variable toileting schedule with positive reinforcement and adjunctive techniques[b]	Urge and functional	Goal is to prevent wetting episodes Can be used in patients with impaired cognitive or physical functioning Requires staff/caregiver availability and motivation

[a]Techniques to trigger voiding (running water, stroking thigh, suprapubic tapping), completely empty bladder (bending forward, suprapubic pressure), and alterations of fluid or diuretic intake patterns.

Source: After Castleden et al. (1983), *Age and aging, 12,* 249–255.

among hospitalized patients after total joint replacement surgery (Bennett & Diokno, 1984; Michelson, Latke, & Steinberg, 1988), its practicality and safety compared with continuous catheterization in the NH setting are uncertain. One study has suggested that, at least over the short term, this technique may be a reasonable approach among elderly males (Terpenning, Allada, & Kauffman, 1989). Its acceptability to NH residents and staff, its long-term efficacy, and its cost (sterile rather than clean catheters should probably be used in the NH) need to be further delineated. Pharmacologic attempts to promote bladder emptying with the cholinergic agonist bethanechol on a chronic basis are usually not successful. Other drugs, including alpha-adrenergic antagonists and muscle relaxants, have also been used in patients with urinary retention (Ouslander & Sier, 1986), but their efficacy in NH patients has not been documented.

URGE INCONTINENCE

NH residents with urge-type incontinence associated with detrusor instability or hyperreflexia can be treated with a variety of training and behavioral procedures, with or without the concomitant use of bladder-relaxant drug therapy. The training/behavioral procedures and techniques outlined in Table 4.5 are only basic examples of various protocols that have been described. In developing and implementing such procedures in the NH setting, it is important to distinguish between protocols that depend on the functional capabilities of the patient and attempt to restore a normal pattern of voiding and continence (e.g., biofeedback, bladder retraining) and protocols that are less dependent on the functional abilities of the patient and more dependent on the availability and motivation of the staff (e.g., habit training, prompted voiding, scheduled toileting). The objective of the latter types of procedure is to attempt to keep the patient dry rather than to restore a normal pattern of voiding; these interventions are appropriate for incontinent NH residents with substantial impairments of cognitive and physical functioning (see below).

Bladder-relaxant drugs have systemic anticholinergic effects and must be used carefully in elderly NH residents. The relative efficacy of bladder-relaxant drug therapy and training/behavioral procedures for incontinent NH residents, either alone or in combination, has not been studied (Hadley, 1986; Burgio & Burgio, 1986; Ouslander & Sier, 1986). Oxybutynin, in doses of 2.5–5mg three times per day, does appear to be safe but its efficacy has not been documented among NH residents (Ouslander et al., 1988a). Using both modalities for residents who have no contraindications for, and can tolerate, bladder-relaxant drugs is a reasonable approach. Because functional disability appears to be associated with a poorer response to bladder relaxant medication (Ouslander et al., 1988a; Castleden, Duffin, & Clarkson, 1983; Zorzitto et al., 1986), and behavioral interventions appear to be effective in selected residents (see below), a reasonable strategy would be to use behavioral treatment first, and then add drug treatment in appropriate residents if the response is not adequate. Because many NH residents probably have detrusor hyperactivity in conjunction with impaired bladder contractility and incomplete bladder emptying (a condition that can only be diagnosed at present by formal urodynamic studies [Resnick, Yalla, & Laurino, 1989]), all elderly NH residents treated for urge incontinence with bladder relaxant drugs should be followed closely for the development of urinary retention, as well as other side effects. This is especially true with symptoms such as excessive dry mouth, constipation, and fecal impaction.

FUNCTIONAL INCONTINENCE

Incontinent NH residents frequently have severe impairments of cognitive and/or physical functioning that render them unable to toilet themselves independently. Many of these residents will also have detrusor hyperactivity and can potentially benefit from bladder-relaxant drug therapy; however, drug therapy alone will not be successful without some type of protocol implemented by NH staff. Maintaining dryness in these residents will largely depend on the motivation of the NH staff (Igou, 1986; Colling, 1988). Whether staff-dependent protocols for the management of incontinence in NHs are feasible and cost-effective has been the subject of several recent studies. These studies have generally shown that prompted voiding or habit training can reduce the frequency of UI by about 20–25% overall (Ouslander et al., 1988a; Schnelle et al., 1988; Hu et al., 1989; Burgio et al., 1988; Colling et al., 1988). From a cost-effectiveness standpoint, implementing these interventions may be more costly than simply changing residents when they are wet (Schnelle et al., 1988; Hu et al., 1989). Targeting these interventions to subgroups of residents who are most likely to benefit will make them more cost-effective (Schnelle et al., 1988; Hu et al., 1989). Targeting criteria are not as yet well developed, but it appears from the work of Schnelle and Hu that residents with larger bladder capacities and those with better cognitive function respond better (Hu et al., 1989; Schnelle, 1989). Further studies are needed to better define criteria that will help NH staff target these interventions in a cost-effective manner. A variety of supportive and environmental approaches, discussed below, can also be helpful in managing residents with functional UI as well (Brink & Wells, 1986).

MIXED TYPES OF INCONTINENCE

Many elderly NH residents have mixed types of incontinence (Resnick, Yalla, Laurino, 1989; Ouslander et al., 1989a). In general, formal urodynamic testing is necessary in order to diagnose accurately these mixed conditions, although they may be suspected from the history, physical exam, and simple bedside diagnostic maneuvers.

A subgroup of elderly women have both detrusor instability or hyperreflexia with urge incontinence, and sphincter weakness with stress incontinence. Surgical bladder-neck suspension has been shown to cure both conditions in younger women (McGuire & Savastano, 1985), but surgery may be neither desired nor feasible in an elderly NH resident. Imipramine (in doses of 10–25 mg three times per day) may have some theoretical advantages over pure bladder relaxants in these patients because of its anticholinergic and alpha-adrenergic effects, but it can have cardiovascular toxicity and must therefore be used very carefully.

In elderly men, obstruction is frequently accompanied by detrusor instability (Abrams, 1985; Frimont-Moller et al., 1984). Similar to the situation in women, surgery (prostate resection) will often cure both conditions (Abrams, 1985), but may not be appropriate for many NH residents. Patients who have urge incontinence and do not have significant degrees of urinary retention can be given a judicious trial of a bladder relaxant, observing post-void residual volumes carefully to detect the development of anticholinergic-induced urinary retention. Depending on the response and the patient's clinical condition and preferences, a prostate resection would be the alternative therapeutic approach.

NONSPECIFIC TREATMENTS FOR INCONTINENCE IN THE NH SETTING

Several nonspecific and supportive measures can be helpful in managing incontinent NH residents. Environmental manipulations, a variety of toilet substitutes, external collection devices, and specially designed undergarments and padding, when used appropriately, can be effective adjuncts to more specific forms of therapy. These techniques and devices have been reviewed in detail elsewhere (Brink & Wells, 1986; Ouslander et al., 1985). They should not substitute, however, for a diagnostic evaluation that seeks underlying causes for the incontinence for which there are more specific treatments, and should not be utilized in a manner that fosters further dependency among the incontinent patients.

TABLE 4.6 Example of a Bladder Retraining Protocol

Objective: To restore a normal pattern of voiding and continence after the removal of an indwelling catheter.[a]

1. Remove the indwelling catheter (clamping the catheter before removal is not necessary).

2. Treat urinary tract infection if present.[b]

3. Initiate a toileting schedule.
   a. Begin by toileting the patient:
      1) upon awakening
      2) every 2 hours during the day and evening
      3) before getting into bed
      4) every 4 hours at night

4. Monitor the patient's voiding and continence pattern with a record that allows for the recording of:
   a. Frequency, timing, and amount of continent voids
   b. Frequency, timing, and amount of incontinence episodes
   c. Fluid intake pattern
   d. Post-void or intermittent catheter volume

5. If the patient is having difficulty voiding (complete urinary retention or very low urine outputs, e.g., <240 cc in an 8-hour period while fluid intake is adequate):
   a. Perform in and out catheterization, recording volume obtained, every 6 to 8 hours until residual values are <100 cc[c]
   b. Instruct the patient on techniques to trigger voiding (e.g., running water, stroking inner thigh, suprapubic tapping) and to help completely empty bladder (e.g., bending forward, suprapubic pressure, double voiding)

6. If the patient is voiding frequently (i.e., more often than every 2 hours):
   a. Perform post-void residual determination to ensure the patient is completely emptying the bladder
   b. Encourage the patient to delay voiding as long as possible and instruct him/her to use techniques to help completely empty bladder (above)

7. If the patient continues to have frequency and nocturia, with or without urgency and incontinence, in the absence of infection:
   a. Rule out other reversible causes (e.g., medication effects, hyperglycemia, congestive heart failure)
   b. Consider urologic referral to rule out bladder instability (unstable bladder, detrusor hyperreflexia)

---

[a]Indwelling catheters should be removed from all patients who do not have an indication for their acute or chronic use. Clamping routines have never been shown to be helpful, and are not appropriate for patients who have had overdistended bladders.
[b]Significant bacteriuria with pyuria (>10 white blood cells per high-power field on a spun specimen).
[c]In patients who have been in urinary retention, it may take days or weeks for the bladder to regain normal function. If residuals remain high, urologic consultation should be considered before committing the patient to a chronic indwelling catheter.

Chronic indwelling urinary catheters are probably used too often for the management of incontinent NH residents (Marron et al., 1983; Kunin, 1987). Frequently, patients are admitted to a NH with a catheter already in place. Unless an appropriate indication exists, the catheter should be removed because of the potential morbidity from these devices (Warren et al., 1987; Ouslander et al., 1987b; Warren et al., 1981). A bladder-retraining protocol, such as the one outlined in Table 4.6, should be implemented after the catheter is removed (Greengold & Ouslander, 1986). Table 4.7 outlines the basic indications for chronic indwelling catheter use and key principles of

TABLE 4.7 Chronic Indwelling Catheter Use and Care

Indications
  Urinary retention that:
    is causing persistent overflow incontinence, symptomatic infections, or renal dysfunction
    cannot be corrected surgically or medically
    cannot be managed practically with intermittent catheterization
  Skin wounds, pressure sores, or irritations that are being contaminated by incontinent urine
  Care of terminally ill or severely impaired for whom bed and clothing changes are uncomfortable or disruptive
  Preference of patient or caregiver when patient has failed to respond to more specific treatments
Key principles of management
  Maintain sterile, closed, gravity drainage system
  Avoid breaking the closed system
  Use clean techniques in emptying and changing the drainage system; wash hands between patients in institutionalized setting
  Secure the catheter to the upper thigh or lower abdomen to avoid perineal contamination and urethral irritation due to movement of the catheter
  Avoid frequent and vigorous cleaning of the catheter entry site; washing with soapy water once per day is sufficient
  Do not routinely irrigate
  If bypassing occurs in the absence of obstruction, consider the possibility of a bladder spasm—which can be treated with a bladder relaxant
  If catheter obstruction occurs frequently, increase the patient's fluid intake and acidify the urine if possible
  Do not routinely use prophylactic or suppressive urinary antiseptics or antimicrobials
  Do not do routine surveillance cultures to guide management of individual patients because all chronically catheterized patients have bacteriuria (which is often polymicrobial) and the organisms change frequently
  Do not treat infection unless the patient develops symptoms; symptoms may be nonspecific and other possible sources of infection should be carefully excluded before attributing symptoms to the urinary tract
  If a patient develops frequent symptomatic urinary tract infections, a genitourinary evaluation should be considered to rule out pathology such as stones, periurethral or prostatic abscesses, and chronic pyelonephritis

caring for patients who are managed with these devices. NHs should establish policies and procedures for the management of indwelling catheters (Ouslander & Fowler, 1985). The use and care of indwelling catheters are reviewed in more detail elsewhere (Warren, 1986).

CONCLUSIONS

Urinary incontinence is a major health problem among NH residents, is stressful for NH staff, and contributes substantially to morbidity and health care costs in this setting. Recent studies have led to improvements in our understanding of the pathophysiology of UI in the NH, but much more remains to be learned. The role of bacteriuria, the relative importance of detrusor hyperactivity vs functional factors, and the clinical significance of detrusor hyperactivity with impaired contractility are especially important to understand. While severely impaired and terminally ill incontinent NH residents can be managed supportively, most incontinent residents should have some type of basic diagnostic evaluation. The appropriate extent of this evaluation remains to be determined; the simplified tests of lower urinary tract function and criteria for referral outlined in this review should be helpful to primary care health professionals in NHs. It is essential that UI not simply be attributed to dementia and/or immobility, and that a search for reversible and specifically treatable conditions be undertaken. Care giver-dependent behavioral interventions such as habit training and prompted voiding are the mainstays of managing UI in the NH. Although proven to be effective, further research is necessary to validate targeting criteria that will make them more cost-effective. The role of drug treatment, especially for detrusor hyperactivity, remains to be better defined. Chronic indwelling catheterization has been overused and specific indications should be present for these devices to be used on a long-term basis. Appropriate catheter care protocols should be developed and implemented for those situations in which the catheter is necessary.

REFERENCES

Abrams, P. (1985). Detrusor instability and bladder outlet obstruction. *Neurourology and Urodynamics 4*, 317–238.
Abrams, P., Blaivas, J. G., Staton, S. L., et al. (1988). Standardisation of terminology of lower urinary tract function. *Neurourology and Urodynamics, 7*, 403–427.
Abrutyn, E., Boscia, J. A., & Kaye, D. (1988). The treatment of asymptomatic bacteriuria in the elderly. *Journal of the American Geriatric Society, 36*, 473–475.
Bennett, C. J., & Diokno, A. C. (1984). Clean intermittent self-catheterization in the elderly. *Urology, 24*, 43–45.

Boscia, J. A., Kobasa, W. D., Knight, R. A., Abrutyn, E., Levinson, M. E., & Kaye, D. (1986a). Epidemiology of bacteriuria in an elderly ambulatory population. *Am J Med 80*, 208–214.

Boscia, J. A., Kobasa, W. D., Levison, M. E., et al. (1986b). Lack of association between bacteriuria and symptoms in the elderly. *American Journal of Medicine 81*, 979–982.

Brink, C. A., & Wells, T. J. (1986). Environmental support for geriatric incontinence: Toilets, toilet supplements and external equipment. In *Geriatric Clinics* (Vol. 2, No. 4, pp. 829–840). Philadelphia: Saunders.

Brocklehurst, J. C. & Dillane, J. B. (1966). Studies of the female bladder in old age. II. Cystometrograms in 100 incontinent women. *Gerontology Clinics, 8*, 306–319.

Burgio, K. L. & Burgio, L. D. (1986). Behavior therapies for urinary incontinence in the elderly. In *Geriatric Clinics* (Vol. 2, No. 4, pp. 809–827). Philadelphia: Saunders.

Burgio, L., Engel, B., McCormick, K., & Scheeve, A. (1988). Behavioral treatments for urinary incontinence in geriatric long term care facilities: An update. *Gerontologist, 28* (Special Issue), 200A.

Burgio, K. L., Whitehead, W. E., & Engel, B. T. (1985). Urinary incontinence in elderly—bladder-sphincter biofeedback and toilet skills training. *Annals of Internal Medicine, 104*, 507–515.

Castleden, C. M., Duffin, H. M., & Clarkson, E. J. (1983). In vivo and in vitro studies on the effect of sodium antagonists on the bladder in man and rat. *Age and Ageing, 12*, 249–255.

Colling, J. (1988). Educating nurses to care for the incontinent patient. *Nursing Clinics of North America, 23*(1), 279–289.

Colling, J., Ouslander, J., Hadley, B., et al. (1988). Determining incontinence episodes among nursing home residents by electronic monitoring. *Gerontologist, 28* (Special Issue), 5A.

Eastwood, H. D. H., & Smart, C. J. (1985). Urinary incontinence in the disabled elderly male. *Age and Ageing, 14*, 235–239.

Frimont-Moller, P. C., Jensen, K. M., Iversen, P., et al. (1984). Analyses of Presenting Symptoms in Prostatism. *Journal of Urology, 132*, 272–276.

Greengold, B. A. & Ouslander, J. G. (1986). A bladder retraining program for elderly patients post-indwelling catheterization. *Journal of Gerontological Nursing, 12*, 31–35.

Hadley, E. (1986). Bladder training and related therapies for urinary incontinence in older people. *JAMA, 256*, 372–379.

Hu, T-W. (1986). The economic impact of urinary incontinence. *Clinics in Geriatric Med, 2*, 673–687.

Hu, T. W., Igou, J. F., Kaltreider, D. L., et al. (1989). A clinical trial of a behavioral therapy to reduce urinary incontinence in nursing homes. *JAMA, 261*, 2656–2662.

Igou, J. (1986). Incontinence in nursing homes: Research and treatment issues from the nursing perspective. *Clinics in Geriatric Medicine, 2*, 873–885.

Kane, R. L., Ouslander, J. G., & Abrass, I. B. (1989). *Essentials of Clinical Geriatrics* (pp. 139–189). New York: McGraw-Hill.

Kunin, C. M. (1987). *Detection, Prevention and Management of Urinary Tract Infections*. Philadelphia: Lea & Febiger.

Lose, G., Gammelgaard, J., & Jorgensen, T. J. (1986). The one-hour pad weighing test: Reproducibility and the correlation between the test result, the start volume in the bladder, and the diuresis. *Neurourology and Urodynamics, 5*, 17–21.

Marron, K. R., Fillit, H., Peskowitz, M., et al. (1983). The Nonuse of Urethral Catheterization in the Management of Urinary Incontinence in the Teaching Nursing Home. *Journal of the American Geriatric Society, 31,* 278–281.

McGuire, E. J. & Savastano, J. A. (1985). Stress incontinence and detrusor instability/urge incontinence. *Neurourology and Urodynamics, 4,* 313–316.

Michelson, J. D., Lotke, P. A., & Steinberg, M. E. (1988). Urinary-bladder management after total joint-replacement surgery. *New England Journal of Medicine, 319,* 321–326.

Mohide, E. A. (1986). The prevalence and scope of urinary incontinence. *Clinics in Geriatric Medicine, 2,* 639–655.

Nicolle, L. E., Bjornson, J., Harding, G. M. K., et al. (1983). Bacteriuria in elderly institutionalized men. *New England Journal of Medicine, 309,* 1420–1425.

NIH Consensus Conference. (1989). Urinary incontinence in adults. *JAMA, 261,* 2685–2690.

Ouslander, J. G. (1986). Diagnostic evaluation of geriatric urinary incontinence. In *Geriatric Clinics* (Vol. 2, No.4, pp. 715–730). Philadelphia: Saunders.

Ouslander, J. G. (1989a). Asymptomatic bacteriuria and incontinence. *J Am Geriatr Soc, 37,* 197–198.

Ouslander, J. G. (1989b). Urinary incontinence: Out of the closet. *JAMA, 261,* 2695–2696.

Ouslander, J. G., Blaustein, J., Connor, A., et al. (1988a). Pharmacokinetics and Clinical Effects of Oxybutynin in Geriatric Patients. *Journal of Urology, 140,* 47–50.

Ouslander, J. G., Blaustein, J., Connor, A., & Pitt, A. (1988b). Habit training and oxybutynin for incontinence in nursing home patients: A placebo-controlled trial. *Journal of the American Geriatric Society, 36,* 40–46.

Ouslander, J. G. & Fowler, E. (1985). Incontinence in VA nursing home care units. *Journal of the American Geriatric Society, 33,* 33–40.

Ouslander, J. G., Greengold, B. A., & Chen S. (1987b). Complications of chronic indwelling urinary catheters among male nursing home patients: A prospective study. *Journal of Urology, 138,* 1191–1195.

Ouslander, J. G. & Kane, R. L. (1984). The costs of urinary incontinence in nursing homes. *Medical Care, 22,* 69–79.

Ouslander, J. G., Kane, R. L., & Abrass I. B. (1982). Urinary incontinence in elderly nursing home patients. *JAMA, 248,* 1194–1198.

Ouslander, J. G., Kane, R. L., Vollmer, S., & Menzes, M. (July, 1985). Technologies for managing incontinence. (Health Technology Case Study 33), OTA-HCS-33 Washington, DC: US Congress, Office of Technology Assessment.

Ouslander, J. G., Leach, G., Abelson, S., et al. (1988c). Simple vs multichannel cystometry in the evaluation of bladder function in an incontinent geriatric population. *Journal of Urology 140,* 1482–1486.

Ouslander, J. G., Leach, G., Staskin, D., et al. (1989a). Prospective evaluation of an assessment strategy for geriatric urinary incontinence. *Journal of the American Geriatric Society, 37,* 715–724.

Ouslander, J. G., Leach, G. E., & Staskin, D. R. (1989b). Simplified tests of lower urinary tract function in the evaluation of geriatric urinary incontinence. *Journal of the American Geriatric Society, 37,* 706–714.

Ouslander, J. G., Morishita, L., Blaustein, J., et al. (1987a). Clinical, functional, and psychosocial characteristics of an incontinent nursing home population. *Journal of Gerontology, 42,* 631–637.

Ouslander, J. G. & Sier, H. C. (1986). Drug therapy for geriatric urinary incontinence. In *Geriatric Clinics* (Vol. 2, No. 4, pp. 789–808). Philadelphia: Saunders.

Ouslander, J. G., Uman, G. C., & Urman, H. N. (1986). Development and testing of an incontinence monitoring record. *Journal of the American Geriatric Society, 34*, 83–90.

Pannill, F. C., Williams, T. F., & Davis, R. (1988). Evaluation and treatment of urinary incontinence in long term care. *Journal of the American Geriatric Society, 36*, 902–910.

Resnick, N. M., & Yalla, S. V. (1985). Management of urinary incontinence in the elderly. *New England Journal of Medicine, 313*, 800–805.

Resnick, N. & Yalla, S. V. (1987). Detrusor hyperactivity with impaired contractile function: An unrecognized but common cause of incontinence in elderly patients. *JAMA, 257*, 3076–3081.

Resnick, N. M., Yalla, S. V., & Laurino, E. (1986). An algorithmic approach to urinary incontinence in the elderly. *Clinical Research, 34*, 832A.

Resnick, N. M., Yalla, S. V., & Laurino, E. (1989). The pathophysiology of urinary incontinence among institutionalized elderly persons. *New England Journal of Medicine, 320*, 1–7.

Sabanathan, K., Duffin, H. M., & Castleden, C. M. (1985). Urinary tract infection after cystometry. *Age and Ageing, 14*, 291–295.

Schmidbauer, C. P., Chiang, H., & Raz, S. (1986). Surgical treatment for female geriatric incontinence. In *Geriatric Clinics* (Vol. 2, No. 4, pp. 759–776). Philadelphia: Saunders.

Schnelle, J. F. (1989). Treatment of urinary incontinence in nursing home patients by prompted voiding. *Journal of the American Geriatric Society, 37*, 1051–1057.

Schnelle, J. F., Sowell, V. A., Hu, T. W., & Traughber, B. (1988). Reduction of urinary incontinence in nursing homes: Does it reduce or increase costs? *Journal of the American Geriatric Society, 36*, 34–39.

Staskin, D. R. (1986). Age-related physiologic and pathologic changes affecting lower urinary tract function. In: *Geriatric Clinics* (Vol. 2, No. 4, pp 701–710). Philadelphia: Saunders

Terpenning, M. S., Allada, R., & Kauffman, C. A. (1989). Intermittent urethral catheterization in the elderly. *Journal of the American Geriatric Society, 37*, 411–416.

Warren, J. W. (1986). Catheters and catheter care, In: *Geriatric Clinics* (Vol 2, No. 4, pp. 857–871). Philadelphia: Saunders.

Warren, J. W., Damron, D., Tenney, J. H., et al. (1987). Fever, bacteremia and death as complications of bacteriuria in women with long-term urethral catheters. *Journal of Infectious Diseases, 155*, 1151–1158.

Warren, J. W., Muncie, H. L., Berquist, E. J., et al. (1981). Sequelae and management of urinary infection in the patient requiring chronic catheterization. *Journal of Urology, 125*, 1–7.

Yu, L. C. & Kaltreider, D. L. (1987). Stressed nurses dealing with incontinent patients. *J Gerontological Nursing, 13*, 27–30.

Zorzitto, M. L., Jewett, M. A. S., Fernie, G. R., Holliday, P. J., & Bartlett, S. (1986). Effectiveness of propantheline bromide in the treatment of geriatric patients with detrusor instability. *Neurourology and Urodynamics, 5*, 133–140.

5

Redefining A Standard of Care for Frail Older People: Alternatives to Routine Physical Restraint

Lois K. Evans
Neville E. Strumpf
Carter Williams

INTRODUCTION

In nearly every nursing home in the United States, residents are secured to beds and chairs with vest, waist, or crotch restraints; locked into geriatric chairs with fixed tray tables; and/or wear mitts or wrist ties to discourage pulling at feeding tubes and catheters. While motivation for restraint use is perhaps understandable—prevention of injury from falls, facilitation of medical treatment, or modification of disturbing behavior—both means and efficacy are increasingly questioned. Concerns regarding iatrogenic effects, ethical considerations, and legal rights are fundamental issues. Equally compelling are perceptions regarding liability, staffing patterns, and availability of alternatives, making this a complex problem without easy solution.

In this chapter, the context of routine use of restraints with older people is examined as background for a revised standard of care. A mechanism for meeting this new standard, especially by nursing homes, is also recommended. It is our position that restraint use is *rarely* appropriate in the care of older people, that it is inappropriate as a routine treatment of choice, and that any use must be temporary. Selection of restraint as a short-term intervention should be based on continuing assessment of individual needs and awareness of current knowledge regarding effects, consequences, and alternatives.

Definition

Physical and mechanical restraints are defined as any device applied to the body or immediate personal environment to limit freedom of voluntary movement. These include chest/vest, wrist or ankle ties; mitt, belt, crotch, harness, sheet, full body suit; or geriatric chair with fixed tray table, bed nets, and full-length bedrails. Not included are orthopedic casts or intravenous arm boards, bed or door alarm devices, velcro "gates," special door latches, or half- or three-quarter bedrails.

Current Practice in North America

Prevalence

Restraint use varies by type of setting. In the acute care hospital, incidence rates up to 22% for older patients are reported (Mion, Frengley, & Adams, 1986), while in nursing homes, the prevalence is considerably higher (DHEW, 1979; Dube & Mitchell, 1986; Editorial, 1980; Evans & Strumpf, 1987; Zimmer, Watson, & Treat, 1984). Throughout the United States in skilled nursing facilities certified by Medicare and Medicaid, an average of 41% of the residents are restrained daily; a few states report an even greater prevalence, 55–58% (HCFA, 1988). At least 96% of American nursing homes report using physical restraints (Farnsworth, 1973); only a very few do not permit it.

Restraints differ by setting, with more chest, belt, and chair restraints found in nursing homes (Evans & Strumpf, 1989). Once initiated, restraint is often continued on a daily basis for months or years (Evans & Strumpf, 1987; Strumpf & Evans, 1988); in one study of 15 nursing home residents with senile dementia, 5–14 waking hours were spent in restraint, an average of 9.5 hours per day (Buckwalter, 1988). Restraint use in nursing homes may also vary by unit and by time of day (Cohen-Mansfield, 1988; Evans & Strumpf, 1987).

Patient Characteristics

Patient characteristics that reliably predict restraint use have been summarized (Evans & Strumpf, 1989) and include physical frailty, presence of monitoring or treatment devices, and poor body alignment. In addition, cognitive impairment is an important risk factor (Evans & Strumpf, 1989; Gillick, Serrel, & Gillick, 1982). In one exploratory study (Strumpf & Evans, 1987) no significant difference was found in Mini-Mental State scores between restrained and nonrestrained nursing home residents; staff ratings of disorientation, however, were greater for restrained residents. The possible role of staff perceptions in labeling and treatment cannot be ignored.

Facility Characteristics

No formal study comparing nursing homes with high and low restraint use has been reported. Most nursing homes in North America, however, share common concerns and characteristics that may bear on restraint use. One of these is patient mix. In addition to medical disorders and functional limitations, as many as 94% of today's nursing home residents have cognitive impairments and/or serious behavioral problems (Burgio et al., 1988; German, Shapiro, & Kramer, 1986; Rovner et al., 1986). While it is generally accepted that personnel in nursing homes are able to manage physical care, few have training or skills in handling behavioral problems (Westlake & Rubano, 1983). Inappropriate attitudes include hostility and infantilization (Podransky & Sexton, 1988; Rovner & Rabins, 1985). Further, personnel in "total institutions" like nursing homes are less sensitive to individual differences among residents, engage in more efforts to control impulses and behavior, and desire orderliness and conformity to rules and regulations (Friedman & Ryan, 1986). Staff must manage difficult care on a daily basis with few resources and scarce consultation. Thus, for "social-psychologic problems," medical solutions, as demonstrated by the high use of psychotropic drugs (over 60% in 2 recent studies [Beers et al., 1988; Buck, 1988]) and physical restraints (Burnside, 1984; Covert, Rodrigues, & Solomon, 1977; English & Morse, 1988) are frequently sought. By accident, today's nursing homes in many ways are forced to act as "long-term care psychiatric facilities," without the resources of the psychiatric hospital (Rovner et al., 1986). Although restraints are still used to ensure patient safety in many psychiatric settings, older patients are seldom restrained (Soloff, 1978; Soloff, 1984; Soloff, Gutheil, & Wexler, 1985). Psychiatric staff are generally better trained than nursing home personnel in verbal and social alternatives to restraint use, including a therapeutic milieu, interpersonal techniques, and environmental manipulation (Guirguis, 1978; Gutheil & Tardiff, 1984; Strome, 1988; Whitehead, 1987).

Negative attitudes by nursing home staff (Cubbin, 1970), normative values (Maxwell, Bader, & Watson, 1972), and ready availability of devices (Mitchell-Pedersen et al., 1985) contribute considerably to use of physical restraints. In a randomized survey of staff in 31 nursing homes, excessive restraint was the most frequent type of physical abuse reported by observers (21%) and by perpetrators (6%) (Pillemer & Moore, 1989). Nursing staff believe that restraints are efficacious in the care of older people and lack a repertoire of alternative management strategies for behaviors that commonly result in restraint (Strumpf & Evans, 1987; Strumpf & Evans, 1988; Yarmesch & Sheafor, 1984). Lower staff levels are sometimes named as contributors to increased restraint in nursing homes (Rose, 1987), although the practice is known to require increased staff time (Kendal Corporation, 1989;

Rosen & DiGiacomo, 1978; Young, Muir-Nash, & Ninos, 1988), and the prevalence is actually lower in intermediate care as compared with skilled nursing facilities (31.7% vs. 41.3%; HCFA, 1988). Nevertheless, a recent cross-cultural study demonstrated a significant difference in restraint use between American and Scottish facilities with similar staffing levels (Evans & Strumpf, 1987). Lack of discussion by the health care team regarding decisions to restrain has been noted by several (Code, 1984; Frengley & Mion, 1986; Strumpf & Evans, 1988). Finally, in some nursing homes, residents are restrained because of institutional concern about the consequences of falls, thus contributing to "defensive practice" (Editorial, 1980; Editorial, 1984; Granek et al., 1987; Rubenstein et al., 1983; Schwab, 1975; Wiener & Kayser-Jones, 1989).

Comparison with Other Models

In sharp contrast, care is provided for frail older people in other countries without the use of restraining devices. Although health care systems and legal environments are very different from the United States, the following two models are compelling reminders of the possible.

Scotland

In a comparison of restraint practice between 1 exemplary American nursing home ($n = 62$) and 9 Scottish geriatric facilities with similar types of patients ($n = 826$), prevalence in the American home was 25% and in Scottish facilities 3.8% (chairs only) (Evans & Strumpf, 1987). Scottish nurses had a broad repertoire of alternative interventions (5.1 average) and did not view restraints as efficacious, or even appropriate, in the care of older people. Several differences in philosophy and practice seemed relevant: a strong emphasis on rehabilitation, interdisciplinary team practice, and knowing and responding to individual needs (Kayser-Jones, 1989). Low (16") beds, multiple walking aids, and a variety of chairs were observed (Millard, 1978). Nurses (erroneously) believed that restraint of older people is illegal. An observation that falls and other incidents on a ward were infrequent suggested to supervisors that the staff were being "too protective." A greater proportion of trained staff (but similar staff-resident ratios), tolerance for a range of "deviant" behaviors, less reliance on technology, unavailability of restraining devices, and architectural features that facilitated visibility and monitoring and stimulated residents' socialization and orientation further distinguished Scottish facilities from their North American counterparts.

Scandinavia

Like Scotland, the use of restraints in long-term care settings in Sweden and Denmark is virtually unknown. At Grobergets Sjukhem, Goteborg, Sweden, a home for 210 residents with functional levels similar to those in

American skilled nursing facilities, a conceptual framework termed "individualized care" by Ulla Turemark (1987) Administrator and Director of Nursing, provided many alternatives to restraints. The model at Grobergets requires elements often missing in nursing homes in the United States (Williams, in press): increased opportunities for choice; homelike atmosphere; careful selection of a comfortable chair and positioning pillows for each resident; beds that can be lowered to within 18 inches of the floor; regard for mobility, even to the point of some risk-taking; and value for the needs and feelings of residents, especially those suffering from dementia. Knowledge of each resident as a person is purposefully enhanced by continuity in staff assignment. Continuous education for all staff, particularly in regard to attitudes and close work with families are also emphasized.

In Denmark, at the Health Center for the municipality of Skaevinge, the importance of response to individual needs of the person with dementia was reiterated. As at Grobergets, emphasis was placed on gaining knowledge of the individual, especially during the first weeks following admission, so that appropriate responses could be made in times of stress (Wagner, 1987). As a result, evidence of agitation in residents of these Swedish and Danish homes appeared far less often than in American homes.

In summary, the concept of individualized care places the resident at the center of care, with the accomplishment of routines and tasks in a secondary position, just the reverse of the approaches to practice in nursing homes in the United States.

Impetus for Change

Change in restraint practices with frail older people has been given renewed impetus by increasing awareness both of its prevalence and serious consequences, and of the rights of people living in nursing homes. Clearly, recent examinations of restraint practices have raised the consciousness of legislators, regulators, and providers, further supported and promoted by the longstanding efforts of several advocacy groups (Holder & Frank, 1984). Emphasis on resident autonomy in long-term care (Collopy, 1988) has accelerated discussion regarding decision making about quality of life issues in nursing homes among care givers, consumers, and their advocates (Hastings Center, 1987; NCCNHR, 1985; Wiener & Kayser-Jones, 1989), including ethical dilemmas inherent in nonconsensual treatment by physical restraints (Evans & Strumpf, 1989; Robbins, 1986; Strumpf & Evans, 1988; Veatch & Fry, 1987). Building on a 25-year history, consumer advocacy groups, now joined by a strengthened ombudsman program, have intensified efforts to ensure the rights of nursing home residents, including the right to be free from unnecessary restraints and the right to respectful, individualized treatment. (While these rights had been a part of federal nursing home legislation since 1974, various obstacles to their full implementation [including industry response, administrative delay, and regulatory weaknesses (Holder & Frank 1984)] permitted a rise in the prevalence of restraint use from 25% in 1977 (DHEW, 1979) to 41% by 1987 [HCFA 1988]).

Growing congressional concern about quality of care in nursing homes, and possible weakening of regulations, resulted in a commissioned study by the Institute of Medicine (IOM, 1986) which called for many reforms, including effective enforcement of residents' rights, quality of care, and quality of life. Many of these recommendations were eventually enacted in the Omnibus Budget Reconciliation Act (OBRA) of 1987 (PL 100-203). Court-ordered improvements in regulatory survey procedures (NCCNHR, 1987, 1988) in the 1980s also resulted in greater attention to *outcomes* of care for residents as opposed to the former practice of examining only the *ability* of homes *to provide* care. Thus, a readiness, opportunity, and mandate for change in the practice of physical restraint exist, as never before, in long-term care. An examination of the effects and consequences of restraints serves to reinforce that need for change.

EFFECTS AND CONSEQUENCES OF PHYSICAL RESTRAINT OF OLDER PEOPLE
Morbidity and Mortality

Euphemisms for physical restraints—safety or protective devices, postural supports or patient aids—all convey the idea of protection or assistance. What is relatively unknown and rarely considered is that, regardless of the label, these mechanisms are restraints, with little or no safety value. Yet, evidence that restraints are not benign, especially for older people, is considerable.

Safety Hazards

While the primary purpose of physical restraint is prevention of falls and subsequent injury in older people, studies conclude that restraints seldom eliminate falls or the risk of injury (Coyle, 1979; Feist, 1978; Hernandez & Miller, 1986; Innes & Turman, 1983; Kustaborder & Rigney, 1983; Lund & Sheafor, 1985; Maciorowski et al., 1989; Rubenstein et al., 1983; Tinker, 1979; Walshe & Rosen, 1979). As an example, Hart and Sliefert's (1986) study in a 185-bed skilled nursing facility showed that 42% of falls occurred among restrained residents. Little difference in incidence rates between facilities that do or do not restrain has been shown; serious injury rates, however, are higher in the facilities using restraints (Thankachan, 1987). When restraint use was reduced by 97% in one 180-bed geriatric unit, there were more falls, but no significant difference in serious injuries (Mitchell-Pedersen et al., 1985).

Injuries resulting directly from physical restraints include severe hyperthermia (Greenland & Southwick, 1978); brachial plexus injury (Scott & Gross, 1989); acute renal failure (Lahmeyer & Stock, 1983); rhabdomyolysis (Lahmeyer, 1983), and severe ischemic contracture of the intrinsic muscles of the hands (McLardy-Smith, Burge, & Watson, 1986).

Higher mortality rates have been associated with restrained elders in at least 4 hospital-based studies (Frengley & Mion, 1986; Lofgren et al., 1989; Robbins et al., 1987; Strumpf & Evans, 1987). Among elderly hospitalized patients, 20% who were restrained did not survive the hospital stay, regardless of the length of restraint period (Lofgren et al., 1989). Further, accidental strangulation from physical restraint has been reported (Cape, 1983; DiMaio, Dana, & Bux, 1987; Dube & Mitchell, 1986; Katz, Weber, & Dodge, 1981; MacLean et al., 1982), and the Long Beach Press–Telegram in California (Editorial, 1987) identified 35 restraint-related strangulation deaths and two deaths by burning since 1980.

Physical and Physiologic Consequences

Immobilization is known to have many serious consequences, especially in frail older people (Harper & Lyles, 1988; Selikson, Damus, & Hamerman, 1988; Steinberg, 1980). Lofgren and associates (1989) provide strong support for the association between prolonged physical restraint and adverse outcomes. Following all restrained patients prospectively through their acute medical hospitalization, a significant relationship between restraint use greater than 4 days and development of nosocomial infection and new pressure sores was found (Lofgren et al., 1989). In addition to these iatrogenic consequences, many other physiologic problems may occur. Functional capacity is quickly reduced since older people lose steadiness and balance, and develop muscle weakness, when restrained to bed or chair (Buchner & Larson, 1987; Warshaw et al., 1982). Furthermore, problems with constipation and incontinence (Editorial, 1980; Harper & Lyles, 1988); atelectasis and pneumonia (Harper & Lyles, 1988; Patrick, 1967); circulatory obstruction (Gutheil & Tardiff, 1984); cardiac stress (Robbins et al., 1987); poor appetite and dehydration (Gerdes, 1968) have been reported in association with restraint use. Immobilization by prolonged restraint use may also lead to serious changes in biochemical and physiologic processes including abnormalities in body chemistry, basal metabolic rate, and blood volume; orthostatic hypotension; lower extremity edema; bone demineralization; decreased muscle mass and tone; and brain wave changes (Miller, 1975; Oster, 1976; Zubek & MacNeill, 1966).

Psychologic and Behavioral Consequences

In studies of mechanically restrained animals, the resultant stress response was observed to trigger an increase in corticosterones (Morey-Holton et al., 1982) and decreased function of the blood brain barrier in the autonomic region (Belova & Jonsson, 1982). Some of the perceptual and psychologic responses noted with immobilization in humans (Bolin, 1974; Downs, 1974; Miller, 1975; Oster, 1976; Roslaniec & Fitzpatrick, 1979) are consistent with this finding. Such physiologic changes may help account for the disorganized or confused behavior so often found in restrained patients. It has been observed that restraint, especially of frightened delirious patients, actually increases panic and fear and produces increasingly angry, belligerent, agitated, or combative behavior (Dietsche & Pollman, 1982; Fawdry & Berry, 1989; LaPorte, 1982; MacLean et al., 1982; Misik, 1981; Patrick, 1967; Zimmer, Watson, & Treat, 1984), just the reverse of the desired effect. Loss of self-image, increased psychologic dependency, increased confusion, regressive behavior, resistance, agitation, and withdrawal are also observed (Castelberry & Seither, 1982; Cohen-Mansfield, 1986; Fawdry & Berry, 1989; Gerdes, 1968; Rose, 1987; Schilder, 1987; Tadsen & Brandt, 1973). These behaviors may actually be healthy coping strategies in response to restriction of freedom and represent an attempt to regain a sense of competence, dignity, and autonomy (English & Morse, 1988; Friedman & Ryan, 1986). Initially patients may be angry and hostile, but with repeated failure at achieving their goals, many eventually become passive and regressed (McHutchion & Morse, 1989). Engel (1968) has suggested that this response may induce a predisposition to illness and premature death.

Psychologic complications of immobilization also derive from sensory deprivation (Harper & Lyles, 1988; Steinberg, 1980). Cognitive, affective, and perceptual changes have been reported in immobilized patients. In the restrained elder, sensory deprivation may result from decreased stimulation in several areas: kinesthetic, visual, auditory, tactile, or social (Harper & Lyles, 1989). In one study, restrained nursing home residents clearly socialized less than nonrestrained residents, and these same residents differed in their social behavior between periods of restraint and nonrestraint (Folmar & Wilson, 1989). Others have noted that the restrained patient is often viewed as disturbed, dangerous, or mentally incompetent (Mitchell-Pedersen et al., 1985) and is thus avoided.

Responses and Beliefs

Patients

To our knowledge, only a few studies (most of these in hospitals) have documented explicitly the personal responses of patients to physical restraint. In Schilder's (1987) interviews with 42 hospitalized patients concerning physical restraints, half expressed feelings of anger and fear, characterizing the experience as a "nightmare," "punishment," "loss of control," "being a prisoner," and feeling "nailed down" or "like a child." Many thought staff explanations concerning the reasons for restraint were "ridiculous" or "illogical." For those over age 80, Schilder noted in the informants a keen "threat to personal integrity" and a "loss of confidence in the ability to maintain independent functioning" (pp. 164–168).

Lichtenstein and Stone (1987) interviewed 38 restrained patients in one veterans' hospital; of these, 40% made negative comments, 42% gave neutral comments, and 18% simply agreed with the treatment, perhaps because they saw no choice but acquiescence. The researchers were especially struck by the eloquence of their informants, despite impaired cognition. Mion, Marino, and Frengley (1989) confirmed reactions of anger, resistance, denial, compliance, demoralization, and resignation from restrained patients on an acute general medical ward and a rehabilitation unit. McHutchion and Morse (1989) reported their observation of 2 elderly patients, 1 of whom had been restrained for 17 months and the other for $2\frac{1}{2}$ years. The first reported anger at being restrained, and when the devices were finally removed, she remained practically immobile as if she were still "psychologicaly restrained" (p. 20). The second patient also displayed considerable distress at being tied; once restraints were removed, the patient appeared aware of her limitations and took no unnecessary risks.

Strumpf and Evans have also interviewed patients concerning perceptions of their restraint experiences during hospitalization. Several months after the restraint episode, three noninstitutionalized women over age 80 provided vivid evidence for the profound personal impact of physical restraint on sense of self (Strumpf, Evans, & Schwartz, in press). A second set of interviews with 20 restrained elders took place in a hospital as part of an exploratory study of perceptions of patients and nurses about the experience of physical restraint. Using a semistructured interview guide, 9 categories of responses by the patients emerged, most of them negative: anger, fear, resistance, humiliation, demoralization, discomfort, resignation, denial, and agreement. Selected brief examples of each of these categories have been reported (Strumpf & Evans, 1988). Comments by several patients suggest lingering memories and significant emotional effects, indicating a need for ongoing explanation, reassurance, and debriefing after discontinuation of restraint.

As part of a study of restraint patterns and resident responses in the nursing facility of a life care community (Strumpf & Evans, 1987), 1 resident who had suffered a broken pelvis spoke in considerable detail about the 11 months since her injury:

> They're afraid I would fall again and break something, [but] I hate it [the restraints]. I've hated it from the beginning. I felt they were taking away my privileges. I don't think it [the restraint] is very satisfactory. It's very uncomfortable and it tightens around my chest sometimes. No, I don't think I should have to wear it. I feel like a criminal. I started to fight them; it takes

three nurses to put it on. I asked them if they're going to take it off, and they said "in about 10 months." Sometimes they forget to put it on. Just who is it [the restraint] supposed to help? (material from investigator's files)

In Farnsworth's (1973) survey of restraint use in nursing homes, ¼ of the homes cited resident complaints about restraint. Lack of sanction for restraint use is supported by 2 studies (Bourland & Lundervold, in press; Lundervold, Lewin, & Bourland, 1989) in which older adults in the community consistently rated restraint as the least acceptable of 8 possible interventions employed for behavioral problems in nursing homes.

Families

While no systematic collection of data about family attitudes toward use of physical restraints has been reported, meetings with families, reports from care settings which are reducing or eliminating restraint use, and accounts in the press provide a broad outline of family responses.[1] These range from the occasional family member who insists on physical restraint for her/his relative to those who are adamant and vocal in their rejection of restraints. The large group in between is characteristically confused as to the best course of action: The usual initial reaction upon finding a relative restrained is one of distress and dislike of the procedure (Hiatt, 1986), but when informed by staff that no alternatives exist, families often acquiesce, albeit with uneasiness.

A son may feel so apprehensive after his mother has suffered 1 hip fracture and repair, and so fearful that the experience may be repeated with the other hip, that he will insist that his mother be tied down. At the other end of the spectrum is the family who so abhors the sight of a hospitalized beloved grandfather struggling against restraints that the entire family organizes to provide 24-hour companionship instead. In another instance, a frail woman in her 80s persistently requests removal of her husband's restraints so that he can maintain mobility and a sense of self-respect and dignity. Another woman, herself a post-stroke patient, longs to have her husband's restraint removed so that he can walk outside with her and "see one more spring." Yet another was unsuccessful in having the vest restraint removed from her mother who suffered increasing dementia, and who on one occasion soon after admission walked out of the nursing home. The daughter is certain that several months of continuous restraint, during which her mother expressed increasing despair, contributed to her fatal heart attack.

Family members are uncertain about physical restraint use, and at the same time feel impotent to make changes. A recent experience reported by the Jewish Home in Rochester, NY, illustrates this point: Families were informed about a special project to eliminate physical restraints from one unit at the home. According to the Director of Social Service, their response, with 2 exceptions out of 22 families, was one of general approval and support, and none chose to move a relative to another floor where restraints were still being used (Silver, 1989). Thus, there are many indications that families are ready for information, discussion with and support from staff in reduction of restraint use, and implementation of alternative care practices.

Staff

In regard to nurses' responses to physical restraints, the literature suggests general adherence to beliefs concerning patient safety, control of behavior, and maintenance of treatment plans. Few investigators, however, have questioned nurses directly about their responses to application of physical restraints to patients. Stilwell (1988) noted nurses' concerns regarding use of restraints. In one study, hospital nurses were asked how they felt about restraining their elderly patients (Strumpf & Evans, 1988). Their responses illustrated the complexity of the legal-ethical dilemma. Some based decisions entirely on a strict interpretation of the moral duty to "do no harm," which for them meant safety before other considerations (p. 135). Others struggled to reconcile their decisions to protect the patient against competing values for respecting patient autonomy and dignity. Interviews of these primary nurses also suggested that the nurses were not fully aware of the impact of physical restraint on their patients. Although physicians were not interviewed, a careful review of the progress notes pointed out their ignorance of or disinterest in the outcomes of physical restraint.

IMPACT OF LEGAL BELIEFS AND THE REGULATORY SYSTEM

While awareness is increasing regarding the negative effects of routine restraint use on older adults and the dilemmas experienced by their families and caregivers, nursing home administrators often feel caught, on the one hand, between a need for what they perceive as responsible risk management and, on the other, by rapidly changing ethical perspectives and legal regulations. With regard to physical restraint, quality care and risk management are closely intertwined.

Risk Management: The Legal Situation

An expanding technology and a litigious society have profoundly affected the rules and regulations governing health care (Fagerhaugh, 1987). Concerns are increasingly voiced regarding the impact of potential liability on practice

(Francis, 1989; Kapp, 1989a; Kayser-Jones & Kapp, 1989; Rubenstein et al., 1983). The widespread prevalence of physical restraints is a case in point, for these devices are clearly assumed to be protective, with scant attention paid to the actual evidence of their value in promoting safety. Evidence against these devices is impressive, although frequently denied in anticipation of malpractice suits. Indeed, beliefs about risk of litigation for failure to apply a physical restraint are apparently entrenched and powerful. Colleagues in the United Kingdom have pointed to fear of litigation following patient injury due to falls as the single most compelling rationale for the increasing use of restraints for elderly patients in the United States (Editorial, 1984; Evans & Strumpf, 1987).

Fear of litigation in American health care does, unfortunately, have its basis in recent interpretations of the law. According to the Regan Reports on Nursing Law (1982, 1983), "the nurse or other attendant can always apply as much restraint as is needed to protect the patient from hurting himself or others" (1982, p. 4). The institution and the nurses may be held liable when patients are injured because of failure to use restraints or improper use of restraints (Yob, 1988). As the first line of defense in the event of a lawsuit, case law reinforces the documentation of restraint use for any patient for whom safety is a concern (Yorker, 1988). In regard to the cognitively impaired, administrators believe suit is more likely for failure to restrain a nonconsenting, confused, or combative patient than for violating patients' rights by applying restraints (Creighton, 1982; Kapp, 1987).

The pressures felt by care providers in institutions are obvious when the American Nurses' Association develops a "colorful and informative poster" that can be hung in every nursing station giving tips on malpractice issues. "Failure to ensure patient safety" leads the list of "most frequent allegations against nurses" who are urged to "use restraints appropriately" (American Nurses' Association, 1989, p. 28). Nevertheless, a recent review of physical restraint policies in 37 skilled nursing facilities in Western New York demonstrated many gaps in the typical restraint policy, especially the need for documentation describing alternatives attempted before the restraint was applied (Janelli, 1989).

In court cases personal behavior is judged against current standards of practice. Rubenstein et al. emphasize the need to "distinguish between *valid* medical standards based upon *scientific evidence*, and *alleged* medical 'standards' based upon *assumptions* about what is in the best interest of patient care" (1983, p. 276). In the *New England Journal of Medicine*, Francis laments that the "specter of malpractice . . . threatens to stymie any attempt to modify . . . standard(s) on the basis of a better appreciation of the needs of the elderly" (1989, p. 870). The writer states emphatically that the agenda for care must be set by physicians and nurses with the interests of patients in mind, instead of leaving it to be guided by concerns about liability. One lawyer at the

Brookdale Center on Aging in New York City asks, "What do you mean that restraint is in the patient's best interest?" (Lindeman, 1987).

The decision to restrain in no way lessens the standard of care. Restraints are an intervention; harm caused by an intervention places direct liability on the agency or nurse (Yorker, 1988). The institution is especially exposed to potential liability when involuntary interventions are imposed, since the facility may be held liable when an employee invades a resident's bodily integrity without first obtaining valid consent (Kapp, 1987, p. 97). As Kapp notes, nonconsensual or involuntary treatment including imposition of physical restraints by nursing staff is "legally perilous" (1987, p. 103). Several established rights of patients and nursing home residents are important here: right to refuse treatment, right to give informed consent, and right to treatment in the least restrictive environment (Yorker, 1988).

When a competent resident knowledgeably and voluntarily accepts risks, the institution is not held liable (Kapp, 1987, p. 14). In the same way, a responsible surrogate can make a decision for no restraint. As an added measure when families refuse restraint, some facilities ask that a release-from-liability form be signed (Farnsworth, 1973; Hart & Sliefert, 1986), although the weight of this practice is yet to be fully tested (Kapp, 1989b).

Despite fears of litigation, several lawsuits and legal opinions are enlightening. In *People* v. *Coe* (1986) the court held that the civil rights of nursing home patients are similar to those of normal, healthy, noninstitutionalized adult citizens. Similarly, a Missouri circuit court (*Owens* v. *Missouri*, 1988) held that restraining a patient in order to feed was unjustified since the nurse could not lawfully force-feed a "normal citizen" who refused to eat, irrespective of the objective risks of such refusal. In a discussion of the legal rights of a no-restraint policy, Hunt points out that law concerning *negligence* does not make liability depend *automatically* on whether one *does* or *does not* restrain. "The question in every case is whether 'due care' was exercised under the circumstances . . . And courts certainly have not said . . . that refusal to tie someone in a chair is automatically evidence of anything . . . The fact that someone falls does not establish that anyone was negligent" (1986, p. 1). Hunt concludes that the legal risks of restraint-free care are low and that the widespread practice of physical restraint for reasons of safety and protection is unwarranted. Furthermore, as described in the next section, federal and state regulations, and voluntary accreditation standards, all contain statements ensuring the right to freedom from chemical and physical restraints.

In the end, a nursing home's best legal protection lies in providing residents with quality care and humane, respectful treatment. "Conduct that is ethically, socially and clinically appropriate and represents the nursing home's good faith and considered judgment almost always represents the surest form of legal risk management" (Kapp, 1987, p. xiii). Being responsive to patient concerns and problems—creating a humanistic environment—reduces the likelihood that patients/families will sue if incidents do occur (Bowling, Vroom, & Sommers, 1983).

The Current Regulatory Climate

Since 1984 the nursing home regulatory system has been in a transitional state, moving from a survey focused on the examination of nursing home capability to give care to a survey focused on outcomes for the resident. This change requires refinement of survey instruments and retraining of surveyors over a period of time. The new provisions of the nursing home reform legislation (PL 100-203, 1987) have now to be incorporated as well. A preliminary draft of restraint regulations for implementation of OBRA (effective October 1990) indicates that use of restraint will be strictly monitored, and development of alternatives will be expected (Hoyer, 1989). Should the regulations and interpretive guidelines, in their final form, fulfill expectations, they will combine with other important and relevant provisions of OBRA promoting individualized care and a rehabilitative approach which will help reduce restraint use (PL 100-203). There are requirements for assessment, comprehensive plans of care, and quality of life; provision of services and activities; and maintenance of "the highest practicable" levels of functioning.

The outcomes of OBRA, and the achievement of restraint-free care, will surely be influenced by the stance of the industry, variations in state regulations, and the urgent need for retraining and sensitization of surveyors. The stated objective of the Health Care Financing Administration (HCFA) is to give greater enforceability to the new regulations than was previously the case (Rules and Regulations, 1989). It remains to be seen whether the provisions honoring residents' rights, including restraint-free care, will be recognized both in word and deed.

RESTRAINT-FREE CARE

A Philosophy of Individualized Care

Individualized care is person-centered. The elements identified in care settings where restraints are rarely, if ever, used evolve from an awareness of the needs of the individual resident, continuous monitoring of health status, and appropriate adjustments in the care plan. The practice of examining those aspects and circumstances of daily life, through which individuality is expressed and a sense of control is gained, grows from the recognition of each person's physical, social, emotional, psychologic, and spiritual uniquenesses.

In order for individual needs to be understood and met, certain elements must be recognized and valued: (1) opportunities for choice in care decisions; (2) independence, and the strengthening of independence, in every aspect of daily living; (3) the right of residents to take risks; (4) the importance of relationships and their continuity for residents and staff; (5) the practice of an interdisciplinary team approach with an integral role for the nurse assistant; (6) homelike qualities and relative quiet in the physical environment; (7) creativity by staff and residents in problem solving; and (8) education of, and partnership with, families.

Individualized care calls for profound changes in staff attitudes away from paternalism. The importance for the resident of respect for adulthood through an individualized approach to care is supported by recent research by Rosalie Kane on the small details of everyday life in which residents most want control (Kolata, 1989), and on the importance of opportunities for choice and a sense of responsibility demonstrated by Rodin and Langer (Rodin, 1986; Rodin & Langer, 1976). The concepts of validation (Feil, 1982) and agenda behavior (Rader, Doan, & Schwab, 1985) provide tools to understand feelings and needs of the cognitively impaired. In three recent papers, care which addresses first the person and second the task has been described (Wagner, 1989; Wilson, 1988; Nicholson & Nicholson, 1988). All emphasize elements essential to individualized care and which are clearly necessary for any reductions in restraint use. At the core is meaningful survival of the whole person, physically and psychologically, as discussed by Atchley (1989) and Tobin and Lieberman (1983).

Alternate Management Methods

Common standards for restraint use with frail older people have been delineated from the literature (Evans & Strumpf, 1989). In general, restraints:

1. should be used only on a short-term basis and as a last resort by staff properly trained in their use;
2. should trigger further investigation and treatment aimed at elimination of the problem causing the need for restraint;
3. should be applied only as a result of collaborative decision-making between nurse, physician, and other health team members;
4. should incorporate informed decision-making by patients and families;
5. are never used as a substitute for monitoring and surveillance; and
6. require attention to patient comfort and safety during periods of their use.

Given myriad serious iatrogenic effects of physical restraints, are they ever warranted? We have argued elsewhere (Evans & Strumpf, 1989; Strumpf &

Evans, 1988) that, from an ethical point of view, restraint to protect patients during short-term treatment for acute illness may have different burdens and benefits than for long-term use. The goal of treatment during acute illness is often cure or improvement in health through use of sophisticated technologies. In long-term care, however, the chief goals are rehabilitation, maintenance of function, quality of life, and a dignified and comfortable death. Restraint use is incompatible with these latter goals (Millard, 1978). Thus, anticipated length of time in restraint, acceptability to the patient, and likely outcome are important considerations in evaluating burden vs. benefit. No studies have been done of older people for whom restraints appear beneficial, although Tinetti's (1989) work may shed light on the topic. Until then, Rubenstein et al. have argued that certain circumstances unrelated to age do warrant mechanical restraints (at least in the form of bedrails): hyperactivity associated with delirium, transport by stretcher, pre- or post-op sedation, unconsciousness, intoxication, and patient request for reasons of personal security (1983, p. 274). Additionally, mitts or wrist restraint may be temporarily appropriate while undergoing short-term treatment, e.g. intravenous therapy; bedrails or tilting geriatric chair may be used at the resident's request for assistance in turning in bed or ease in eating (Evans & Strumpf, 1987); and restraints may be appropriate in an emergency when the patient's behavior is of immediate danger to self or others (Covert, Rodrigues, & Solomon, 1977).

Professional standard-based practice of restraint use rests on the systematic process of comprehensive physical, pharmacologic, and social assessment, including observation and trials of less restrictive alternatives; planning; implementation; monitoring, evaluation, and removal; and debriefing following discontinuation of restraint (Strumpf, Evans, & Schwartz, in press). Perhaps most important is the need for comprehensive assessment. When a resident falls, pulls out a catheter, becomes restless and agitated, or begins to wander off, staff must ask the question, "What is the meaning of this behavior?" Effects of a medication, dehydration, onset of acute illness, discomfort of full bladder, boredom, homesickness, frustration, or desire to feel secure or in control may each produce what may appear to be "unsafe," "noncompliant," or "troublesome" behaviors. Proper attention to diagnosing the cause of the behavior and developing an appropriate response will seldom necessitate the use of physical restraints or, if so, only on a temporary basis.

If physical restraint is to become the exception rather than the rule in long-term care, then staff must be aware of available alternatives. For the three major problematic behaviors for which restraints are used there are four general categories of alternatives—physical, psychosocial, activities, and environment.

Proper data collection and assessment will usually require observation of the behavior over a number of days to determine precipitants; circumstances and location of occurrence; who was involved; duration, interventions, and outcomes, in order to determine meaning. Depending on the identified precipitant of the behavioral change, any of a number of alternative strategies or interventions can be used. With the exception of wandering behavior, research is lacking on satisfactory alternatives to restraint (Schwartz, 1985). Many alternatives, however, have been suggested in the literature and by nurses from their practice (Evans & Strumpf, 1989; Friedman, 1983).

Fall Risk

For the resident who is judged to be at risk of injury from falling, many strategies are available other than restraints (Blakeslee, 1988; Evans & Strumpf, 1989; Sunnybrook Medical Centre, 1988; Tedeiksaar, 1989; Whedon & Shedd, 1989). Following evaluation of drugs and other treatable causes of falls, safe mobility may be enhanced by ambulation, physical therapy, gait and fall training; walking aids, safe footwear, and nonskid strips on the floor near bed or chair; padded clothing, elbow and knee pads, helmet, and carpeted floors; and development of a buddy system. Injury from falls out of bed can be reduced by using a low bed, accessible call light, bedside commode, mattress on floor (or protective floor pads around the bed to cushion a fall), or bed alarm system together with adequate monitoring. Bedrails are used only to help a patient avoid *falling*, not *getting* out of bed; thus ½ or ¾ siderails, if any, are most appropriate (Johnson, 1980).

Falls from a chair can be reduced by fitting size and type of chair to the patient; using a wedge cushion to produce a slanting contour (Tedeiksaar, 1989), having available a variety of chair types; using pillows and "mould and hold" props for trunk and limb alignment (Harris, 1987); and employing reminders or delayers such as placement of the overbed table in front of the chair. Help in getting to the toilet at frequent, regular intervals often lessens unsafe attempts at independent ambulation. Although a resident is judged at risk of falling, with no effective alternatives, families and residents may still value risks associated with freedom of movement over those associated with nonconsensual immobilization.

Treatment Interference

Commonly occurring oppositional behavior among nursing home residents includes refusal to eat, to take medications, to cooperate with activities of daily living (Friedman & Ryan, 1986), and self-extubation of feeding tubes (Ciocon et al., 1987). Residents can often be assisted to cooperate with short-term treatment when adequate explanations are given and needs for elimination, comfort, and pain relief are met. Companionship, close supervision, placement near the nurse's station for increased psychosocial stimulation and monitoring; distraction with television, radio, music, objects to hold or fold; and camouflage or padding of the site may be effective. When possible, a change in the form of treatment should be made; for example, resume oral feeding or remove urinary catheter. Finally, when a resident consistently rejects intrusive treatment, ethical decision making regarding its continuation should be initiated with resident/surrogate, with the possibility of a decision for termination of treatment (Hastings Center, 1987; Lo & Dornbrand, 1984).

Disruptive Behaviors

Disruptive and disturbing behaviors are a third common reason for restraint use. *Agitation or restlessness* frequently signals underlying problems which can be corrected, such as dehydration, infection, pain, discomfort, full bladder, or sensory misperception. Positioning, providing sensory aids, companionship, touch and massage, listening, distraction, recreation or social activity, exercise, quiet environment (free from "intercom"), lighting, soothing music in a personal headset, beverage or snack, and personal items and mementos have all been recommended as effective aids. For *wandering*, the only disruptive behavior with a beginning research base, several recommendations can be made, depending on whether the wandering behavior is goal-directed, busy wandering, or aimless wandering (ANA, 1988; Blakeslee, 1988; Dawson & Reid, 1987; Gaffney, 1986; Hegeman, 1986; Heim, 1986; Hiatt, 1980; Huey, 1985; Rader, 1987; Snyder et al., 1978). Residents identify others entering the wrong room as the behavior most disruptive to their living environment (Bernier & Small, 1988). Some wanderers are searching for a toilet. Others may be bored, restless, seeking exercise, or attempting to recreate activities of their work lives. Reducing precipitating stimuli, increasing physical and social activity, developing buddy systems and a safe environment for exploring and walking are required. Many facilities have developed wandering gardens or areas to satisfy the need for walking, or have used tape on the floor (Hussien & Brown, 1987), velcro tape "gates" across doorways (Rader, 1988), or camouflage of exits to indicate boundaries for wanderers. "Baffle latches" and alarm systems are also commonplace. Wanderers are made known to all staff and given special identification. Staff can be trained in use of validation techniques in order to identify and honor the residents' agendas while walking with them and returning to the unit (Rader, Doan, & Schwab, 1985). White noise (Young, Muir-Nash, & Ninos, 1988) is effective in facilitating sleep; for residents who awaken and wander at night, special nighttime activities such as an open kitchen facilitate a return to bed. Broad-based or stationary rockers may satisfy movement needs of some wandering or agitated residents (McConnell, 1987). *Other behaviors* such as noisemaking, public exposure or masturbation, catastrophic reaction, and physical aggression may be precipitated by sensory overload or deprivation, need for stimulation; or by pain, fearfulness, and/or short-term memory loss. Meeting these needs in other ways that protect the dignity of the resident requires creativity on the part of staff and a thorough knowledge of the person; sensory stimulation, verbal reassurance, calm voice, redesign of units to maximize social interaction and monitoring of residents, and special units for residents with dementia have been demonstrated effective in decreasing restraint use (Benson et al., 1987; Cleary et al., 1988; Hegeman, 1986).

System Change

A cursory examination of the history of physical restraint use, initially for the insane housed in asylums and later with older people in hospitals and nursing homes, suggests the necessity for fundamental changes in the entire system if adoption of alternatives is to occur. Nineteenth century reformers like Pinel (1806), the Tuke family (1813, 1885), and Connolly (1856) led a movement in Europe to abolish restraints in mental institutions by convincing a wide public constituency that such treatment was inhumane, ineffective, and unwarranted. Through their efforts and convictions, an entire system of care was essentially transformed. Although restraints are occasionally used to this day for psychiatric patients, the modern therapeutic milieu remains philosophically opposed to these devices (Soloff, 1978). That institutional systems can be changed through administrative support and staff education is demonstrated by reports describing psychiatric facilities which have reduced or eliminated restraints (Cohen, 1977; Hay & Cromwell, 1980; Jacoby et al., 1958).

Interestingly, the use of restraining devices with elders in nonpsychiatric settings appears to have become routine only recently. A review of early nursing journals and general texts (1885–1950) suggests that physical restraints were to be avoided, and the first textbook of geriatric nursing (Newton, 1950) *never* mentions their use. Articles discussing restraint, first appearing in nursing journals in the late 1960s, have increased dramatically since 1980. Many converging factors in a complex system have no doubt contributed to changing patterns of restraint use during the past 20 years: an expanding older population; societal values; a rising number of nursing home beds; a change in locus of care for the mentally ill; staff beliefs, knowledge, and skills; a medical vs. psychosocial model of care; failure to enforce regulations concerning residents' rights; and fear of litigation. Any efforts to change restraint practices in the United States will require an understanding of these potent external forces.

Philosophical stance is important, as is evident from observations and other reports of restraint-free care in the United Kingdom (Cape, 1983), Denmark (Innes & Turman, 1983), and Sweden (Williams, in press). In these countries, basic respect for the rights of the older person, awareness of the physical and psychologic effects and consequences of physical restraints, and institutional commitment to a range of alternative measures form the basis for treatment decisions.

Systems change toward reduction in restraints, accomplished mainly through staff education, is supported by a modest literature and anecdotal accounts, many received in personal letters to the authors. In general, these reports not only suggest few negative consequences from a change in restraint policies, but significantly seem linked to improvements in patient and staff outcomes (Mitchell-Pedersen et al., 1985). Educational interventions aimed at improving practice and given for staff in nursing homes (Almquist & Bates, 1980; Almquist et al., 1981; Crawford, Waxman, & Carner, 1983; Hyerstay, 1978; Lehman & Vargo, 1979) have demonstrated a positive effect on quality of care of residents; improved staff attitudes, increased job satisfaction, and better work habits, along with a decrease in turnover and frustration were noted as well. Finally, strong administrative support and policy change are essential if restraint practices are to be altered (Blakeslee, 1988; Editorial, 1980; Huey, 1985; McHutchion & Morse, 1989; Robbins, 1986; Rovner et al., 1986).

When one considers the range of very difficult behavioral problems encountered in nursing homes (Burgio et al., 1988) as well as the degree of emotional exhaustion experienced by nurses in long-term care (Hare & Pratt, 1988), the frequency of restraint is not entirely surprising. Conditions in many nursing homes, 75% of which are proprietary and known for higher stress and turnover, less organizational commitment, and decreased job satisfaction (Bell & Curry, 1989), may also contribute to the use of restraints as the "first choice of treatment" rather than "last resort." That these almost overwhelming problems in the system *can* be overcome is given testament by correspondents from the growing number of restraint-free (or nearly so) facilities around the United States, and listed in a published bulletin *Untie the Elderly*, available from Kendal-Crosslands in Kennett Square, PA, 19348.

CONCLUSION

Physical restraint of the frail older adult is a commonplace intervention with known, although generally unacknowledged, serious consequences. The prevalence of the practice can be reduced to extreme, short-term circumstances through the implementation of an individualized, person-centered approach to care, a rehabilitative philosophy, administrative support, staff training regarding assessment and alternative management strategies, close work with families, and adherence to a standard of care that is based on science rather than fear of litigation. Recent legislative and regulatory changes at the federal level point to a movement toward restraint-free care. Alteration in the practice must be managed through responsible, interdisciplinary approaches to assessment and decision making involving residents and families, and which consider, from an ethical perspective, the best interest of the resident in terms of quality of life.

As poet Celia Gilber (1988, p. 84) has written in *One Sounding for a Final Note,* " . . . Last courtesies remove restraints . . . "

NOTE

1. Except where otherwise indicated, content for this section is based on the clinical and consulting work of C. W., including discussions with members of Friends and Relatives of the Institutionalized Aged, New York City, April 30, 1989.

REFERENCES

Almquist, E., & Bates, D. (1980). Training program for nursing assistants and LPNs in nursing homes. *Journal of Gerontological Nursing, 6,* 622–627.

Almquist, E., Stein, S., Weiner, A., & Linn, M. (1981). Evaluation of continuing education for long-term care personnel: Impact upon attitudes and knowledge. *Journal of American Geriatrics Society, 29,* 117–122.

American Nurses' Association. (1988). Nurse studies wanderers. *American Nurse, 20,* 6.

American Nurses' Association. (1989). Poster gives tips on malpractice issues. *American Nurse, 21,* 28.

Atchley, R. (1989). A continuity theory of normal aging. *Gerontologist, 29,* 183–190.

Beers, M., Avorn, J., Soumerai, S. B., Everitt, D. E., Sherman, D. S., & Salem, S. (1988). Psychoactive medication use in intermediate-care facility residents. *JAMA, 260,* 3016–3020.

Bell, S. E., & Curry, J. P. (1989). The healing mission versus the profit mission: The impact on nursing morale. Paper read at the Society for Applied Anthropology, Santa Fe, NM.

Belova, T. I., & Jonsson, G. (1982). Blood-brain barrier permeability and immobility stress. *Acta Physiol Scand 116,* 21–29.

Benson, D. M., Cameron, D., Humbach, E., Servino, L., & Gambert, S. 1987. Establishment and impact of a dementia unit within the nursing home. *Journal of American Geriatrics Society, 35,* 319–323.

Bernier, S. L., & Small, N. R. (1988). Disruptive behaviors. *Journal of Gerontological Nursing, 14,* 8–13.

Blakeslee, J. (1988). Untie the elderly. *American Journal of Nursing, 88,* 833–834.

Bolin, R. H. (1974). Sensory deprivation: An overview. *Nursing Forum, 13,* 240–258.

Bourland, G. & Lundervold, D. A. (In press). Acceptability ratings for interventions for problematic behavior of older adults. *Journal of Clinical & Experimental Gerontology.*

Bowling, T. E., Vroom, D. M., & Sommers, K. M. (1983). *Nursing home management.* Springfield, MA: Charles C Thomas.

Buchner, D. M. & Larson, E. B. (1987). Falls and fractures in patients with Alzheimer-type dementia. *JAMA, 257,* 1492–1495.

Buck, J. A. (1988). Psychotropic drug practice in nursing homes. *Journal of American Geriatrics Society, 36,* 409–418.

Buckwalter, K. (1988, 20 May). Interview with L. Evans, Minneapolis, MN.

Burgio, L. D., Jones, L. T., Butler, F., & Engel, B. T. (1988). Behavior problems in an urban nursing home. *Journal of Gerontological Nursing, 14,* 31–34.

Burnside, I. M. (1984). Are nurses taught to tie people down? *Journal of Gerontological Nursing, 10,* 6.

Cape, R. D. T. (1983). Freedom from restraint (abstract). *Gerontologist 23,* 217.

Castelberry, K. & Seither, F. (1982). Disorientation. In Norris, C. M. (Ed.)., *Concept Clarification in Nursing.* Rockville, MD: Aspen.

Cleary, T. A., Clamon, C., Price, M., & Shullaw, G. (1988). A reduced stimulation unit: Effects on patients with Alzheimer's disease and related disorders. *Gerontologist, 28,* 511–514.

Ciocon, J. D., Silverstone, F. A., Graver, L. M., & Foley, C. (1987). Indications, benefits and complications of tube feedings in elderly patients (abstract). *Gerontologist, 27,* 13A.

Code, J. (1984). Letter to editor. *Journal of Gerontological Nursing, 10,* 345.

Cohen, S. I. (1977). The first year at the New Esrath Nashim Hospital, Jerusalem 1968–69: Abolition of physical restraints. *British Journal of Psychiatry, 130,* 544–547.

Cohen-Mansfield, J. (1986). Agitated behavior in the elderly II: Preliminary results in the cognitively deteriorated. *Journal of American Geriatrics Society, 34,* 722–727.

Cohen-Mansfield, J. (1988, March 10). Telephone conversation with L. Evans.

Collopy, B. (1988). Autonomy in long-term care: Some crucial distinctions. *Gerontologist, 28,* (Supplement), 10–17.

Connolly, J. (1856). Treatment of the insane without mechanical restraints. London: John Taylor (Reprinted London: Dawson of Pall Mall, 1973).

Covert, A. B., Rodrigues, T., Soloman, K. (1977). The use of mechanical and chemical restraints in nursing homes. *Journal of American Geriatrics Society, 25,* 85–89.

Coyle, N. (1979). A problem-focused approach to nursing audit: Patient falls. *Cancer Nursing, 2,* 389–391.

Crawford, S., Waxman, H., & Carner, E. (1983). Using research to plan nurse aide training. *Journal of American Health Care Association, 9,* 59–61.

Creighton, H. (1982). Are siderails necessary? *Nursing Management, 13,* 45–48.

Cubbin, J. K. (1970). Mechanical restraints: To use or not to use? *Nursing Times, 66,* 752.

Dawson, P., & Reid, D. W. (1987). Behavioral dimensions of patients at risk of wandering. *Gerontologist, 27,* 104–107.

Department of Health Education and Welfare. (1979). *National nursing home survey: 1977.* PHS 79–1794. Hyattsville MD, NCHS.

Dietsche, L. M. & Pollman, J. N. (1982). Alzheimer's disease: Advances in clinical nursing. *Journal of Gerontological Nursing, 8,* 97–100.

DiMaio, V. J. M., Dana, S. E., Bux, R. C. (1987). Deaths caused by restraint vests. *JAMA, 255,* 905.

Downs, F. S. (1974). Bedrest sensory disturbances. *American Journal of Nursing, 74,* 434–438.

Dube, A. & Mitchell, E. (1986). Accidental strangulation from vest restraints. *Journal of American Medical Association, 256*, 2725-2726.

Editorial. (1987, June 21). Care that kills. *Long Beach [CA] Press-Telegram.*

Editorial. (1984). Cotsides—Protecting whom against what? *Lancet, 35*, 383-384.

Editorial. (1980). Restrained in Canada—Free in Britain. *Health Care, 22*, 22.

Engel, G. (1968). A life setting conducive to illness: The giving up—given up complex. *Annals of Internal Medicine, 69*, 293-300.

English, J., & Morse, J. M. (1988). The 'difficult' elderly patient: Adjustment or maladjustment? *International Journal of Nursing Studies, 25*, 23-39.

Evans, L. K., & Strumpf, N. E. (1987). Patterns of restraint: A cross-cultural view (abstract). *Gerontologist, 27*, 272A-273A.

Evans, L. K., & Strumpf, N. E. (1989). Tying down the elderly: A review of the literature on physical restraint. *Journal of American Geriatrics Society, 37*, 65-74.

Fagerhaugh, S. et al. (1987). *Hazards in hospital care.* San Francisco: Jossey-Bass.

Farnsworth, E. L. (1973). Nursing homes use caution when they use restraints. *Modern Nursing Home, 30*, 4, 9-10.

Fawdry, K. & Berry, M. L. (1989). Fear of senility: The nurse's role in managing reversible confusion. *Journal of Gerontological Nursing, 15*, 17-21.

Feil, N. (1982). *Validation: The Feil method.* Cleveland: Edward Feil Productions.

Feist, R. (1978). A survey of accidental falls in a small home for the aged. *Journal of Gerontological Nursing, 4*, 15-17.

Folmar, S. & Wilson, H. (1987). The effect of physical restraints on the social behavior of nursing home residents (abstract). *Gerontologist, 27*, 55A-56A.

Francis, J. (1989). Using restraints in the elderly because of fear of litigation. *New England Journal of Medicine, 320*, 870-871.

Frengley, J. D. & Mion, L. (1986). Incidence of physical restraints on acute general medical wards. *Journal of American Geriatrics Society, 34*, 565-568.

Friedman, F. B. (1983). Restraints: When all else fails, there still are alternatives. *RN, 76*, 79-80, 82, 84, 86, 88.

Friedman, S. & Ryan, L. S. (1986). A systems perspective on problematic behaviors in the nursing home. *Family Therapy, 13*, 265-273.

Gaffney, J. (1986). Toward a less restrictive environment. *Geriatric Nursing, 7* 94-97.

Gerdes, L. (1968). The confused or delirious patient. *American Journal of Nursing, 68*, 1228-1233.

German, P. S., Shapiro, S., & Kramer, M. (1986). Nursing home study of the Eastern Baltimore Epidemiologic Catchment Area Study. In Harper, M. & Lebowitz (Eds.), *Mental illness in nursing homes* (pp. 27-40). Rockville, MD: NIMH.

Gilbert, C. (1988, September 19). One sounding for a final note (poem). *New Yorker*, 84.

Gillick, M. R., Serrell, N. A., & Gillick, L. S. (1982). Adverse consequences of hospitalization in the elderly. *Social Science and Medicine, 16*, 1033-1038.

Granek E., Baker, S. P., Abbey, H., Robinson, E., Myers, A. H., Samkoff, J. S., et al. (1987). Medications and diagnoses in relation to falls in a long-term care facility. *Journal of American Geriatrics Society, 35*, 503-511.

Greenland, P., & Southwick, W. H. (1978). Hyperthermia associated with chlorpromazine and full-sheet restraint. *American Journal of Psychiatry, 135*, 1234-1235.

Guirguis, E. F. (1978). Management of disturbed patients: An alternative to the use of mechanical restraints. *Journal of Clinical Psychiatry, 39*, 295-303.

Gutheil, T. G., & Tardiff, K. (1984). Indications and contraindications for seclusion and restraint. In Tardiff, K. (Ed.), *The psychiatric uses of restraint and seclusion* (pp. 11-17). Washington: APA Press.

Hare, J., & Pratt, C. C. (1988). Burnout: Differences between professional and paraprofessional nursing staff in acute care and long-term care health facilities. *Journal of Applied Gerontology, 7*, 60–72.

Harper, C. M., & Lyles, Y. M. (1988). Physiology and complications of bedrest. *Journal of American Geriatrics Society, 36*, 1047–1054.

Harris, B. (1987, January). Interview with L. Evans. Littlemore Hospital, Oxford, England.

Hart, M. A., & Sliefert, M. K. (1986). Monitoring patient incidents in a long-term care facility. In Chapman-Cliburn, C. (Ed.), *Risk management and quality assurance* (pp. 96–104). Chicago: JCAH.

Hastings Center. (1987). *Guidelines on the termination of life-sustaining treatment and the care of the dying.* Briarcliff Manor, NY: Author.

Hay, D., & Cromwell, R. (1980). Reducing the use of full-leather restraints in an acute adult inpatient ward. *Hospital and Community Psychiatry, 31*, 198–200.

Health Care Finance Administration. (1988). *Medicare/Medicaid nursing home information: 1987–1988.* Washington: U.S. Government Printing Office.

Hegeman, C. (1986). *Maintaining the autonomy of the mentally impaired elder in long-term care.* Report to Research Retirement Foundation. Albany, NY: Foundation for Long Term Care.

Heim, K. M. (1986). Wandering behavior. *Journal of Gerontological Nursing, 12*, 4–7.

Hernandez, M., & Miller, J. (1986). How to reduce falls. *Geriatric Nursing, 7*, 97–102.

Hiatt, L. G. (1986). Effective trends in interior design. *Provider, 12*, 28–30.

Hiatt, L. G. (1980). The happy wanderer. *Nursing Home, 29*, 27–31.

Holder, E., & Frank, B. (1984). Resident participation in nursing homes. Unpublished paper. Washington, DC: National Citizens Coalition for nursing Home Reform.

Hoyer, T. (1989). Proposed revisions to the long term care nursing facility conditions of participation: 483.13(a) restraints. Baltimore, MD: HCFA.

Huey, F. L. (1985). What teaching nursing homes are teaching us. *American Journal of Nursing, 85*, 678–683.

Hunt, A. (1986). Legal risks of a no-restraint policy. In *Physical restraints: A dilemma in long-term care.* Symposium Proceedings, Tirlawyn: An Academic Geriatric Center, Kendal-Crosslands, Kennet Square, PA.

Hussien, R. A., & Brown, D. L. (1987). Use of two-dimensional grid pattern to limit hazardous ambulation in demented patients. *Journal of Gerontology, 42*, 558–560.

Hyerstay, B. (1978). The political and economic implications of training nursing home aides. *Journal of Nursing Administration, 8*, 22–24.

Innes, E. M. & Turman, W. G. (1983). Evolution of patient falls. *Quality Review Bulletin, 9*, 30–35.

Institute of Medicine. (1986). *Improving the quality of care in nursing homes.* Washington, DC: National Academy Press.

Jacoby, M. G., Babikian, H., McLamb, E., & Hohlbein, B. (1958). A study in non-restraint. *American Journal of Psychiatry, 115*, 114–120.

Janelli, L. M. (1989). What restraint policies don't say. *Geriatric Nursing, 10*, 7.

Johnson, J. (1980). Thoughts on 'cotsides.' *Nursing Focus 2*, 120–121.

Kapp, M. B. (1989a). Enforcing patient preferences. *Journal of American Medical Association 261*, 1935–1938.

Kapp, M. B. (1989, May 8). Telephone conversation with N. Strumpf.

Kapp, M. B. (1987). *Preventing malpractice in long-term care.* New York: Springer Publishing Co.

Katz, L., Weber, F., & Dodge, P. (1981). Patient restraint and safety vests: Minimizing the hazards. *Dimensions in Health Services, 58*, 10–11.

Kayser-Jones, J. (1989). The environment and quality of life in long-term care institutions. *Nursing and Health Care, 19*, 125–130.

Kayser-Jones, J. & Kapp, M. B. (1989). Advocacy for the mentally impaired elderly: A case study analysis. *American Journal of Law & Medicine, 14*, 353–376.

Kendal Corporation. (1989). What is the law? *Untie the elderly, 1*, 3.

Kolata, G. (1989, January 19). Life's basic problems are still top concern in the nursing homes. *New York Times*, B14.

Kustaborder, M., & Rigney, M. (1983). Intervention for safety. *Journal of Gerontological Nursing*, 159–173.

Lahmeyer, H. H. (1983). PCP, physical restraints, and rhabdomyolysis. *Journal of Clinical psychiatry, 44*, 234.

Lahmeyer, H. H., & Stock, P. G. (1983). Phencyclidine intoxication, physical restraint and acute renal failure: Case report. *Journal of Clinical Psychiatry, 44*, 184–185.

LaPorte, H. J. (1982). Reversible causes of dementia: A nursing challenge. *Journal of Gerontological Nursing, 8*, 74–80.

Lehman, J., & Vargo, J. (1979). The effects of an in-service program upon the attitudes of nursing aides. *Canadian Journal of Occupational Therapy, 46*, 105–108.

Lichtenstein, H., & Stone, J. T. (1987, March). Restraints in the elderly. Paper read at American Geriatrics Society meeting, Salt Lake City.

Lindeman, B. (1987, December). Whose best interest? *50 Plus*, 4.

Lo, B., & Dornbrand, L. (1984). Guiding the hand that feeds. *New England Journal of Medicine, 311*, 401–403.

Lofgren, R. P., MacPherson, D. S., Granieri, R., Myllenbeck, S., & Sprafka, J. M. (1989). Mechanical restraints on the medical wards: Are protective devices safe? *American Journal of Public Health, 79*, 735–738.

Lund, C., & Sheafor, M. (1985). Is your patient about to fall? *Journal of Gerontological Nursing, 11*, 37–41.

Lundervold, D., Lewin, L. M., & Bourland, G. (1989). Older adults' acceptability of treatments for behavior problems. Unpublished paper, Oregon Research Institute, Eugene.

MacLean, J., Shamian, J., Butcher, P., Parsons, R., Selcer, B., & Barrett, M. (1982). Restraining the elderly agitated patient. *Canadian Nurse 78*, 44–46.

Maciorowski, L. F., Munro, B. H., Dietrick-Gallagher M., McNew, C. D., Sheppard-Hinkel E., Wanich C., et al. (1989). A review of the patient fall literature. *Journal of Nursing Quality Assurance 3*, 18–27.

Maxwell, R. J., Bader, J. E., & Watson, W. H. (1972). Territory and self in a geriatric setting. *Gerontologist 12*, 413–417.

McConnell, J. (1987, October 8). Interview with L. Evans, Stoddard Baptist Home, Washington, DC.

McHutchion, E., & Morse, J. M. (1989). Releasing restraints: A nursing dilemma. *Journal of Gerontological Nursing, 15*, 16–21.

McLardy-Smith, P., Burge, P. D., & Watson, N. A. (1986). Ischaemic contracture of the intrinsic muscles of the hands: A hazard of physical restraint. *The Journal of Hand Surgery, 1-B*, 65–67.

Millard, P. H. (1978). To rehabilitate or to vegetate? *Nursing Mirror, 146*, 14–16.

Miller, M. (1975). Iatrogenic and nursigenic effects of prolonged immobilization of the ill aged. *Journal of American Geriatrics Society, 23*, 360–369.

Mion, L. C., Marino, J. A., & Frengley, J. D. (1989, April 7). Use of physical retraints in the hospital setting: Patient characteristics and outcomes. Paper read at Elder Care: Today's Research, Tomorrow's Practice conference at Beth Israel Hospital, Boston.

Mion, L., Frengley, J. D. & Adams, M. (1986). Nursing patients 75 years and older. *Nursing Management, 17,* 24–28.

Misik, I. (1981). About using restraints with restraint. *Nursing '81 11,* 50–55.

Mitchell-Pederson, L., Edmund, L., Fingerole, E., & Powell, C. (1985). Let's untie the elderly. *OAHA Quarterly, 21,* 10–14.

Morey-Holton, E. R., Bomalski, M. D., Enayati-Gordon, E., Gonsalves, M. R., & Wronski, T. J. (1982). Is suppression of bone formation during simulated weightlessness related to glucocorticoid levels? *Physiologist, 25,* S145–S146.

National Citizens Coalition for Nursing Home Reform. (1985). *A consumer perspective on quality care: The residents' point of view.* Washington: NCCNHR.

National Citizens Coalition for Nursing Home Reform. (1987). Editorials. *Quality Care Advocate, 2*(1), 2; *2*(2), 1; *2*(4), 3; *2*(5–6), 2.

National Citizens Coalition for Nursing Home Reform. (1988). Editorials. *Quality Care Advocate, 3*(2), 3.

Newton, K. (1950). *Geriatric Nursing.* St. Louis, MO: C. V. Mosby.

Nicholson, C. & Nicholson, J. (1988). Personalized care model: An overview. Unpublished paper, Jewish Home and Hospital for Aged, New York, NY.

Oster, C. (1976). Sensory deprivation in geriatric patients. *Journal of American Geriatrics Society, 24,* 461–463.

Owens v. Missouri Department of Social Services, Division of Aging, No. cv386–46100 (Filed 26 Aug. 1988).

Patrick, M. L. (1967). Care of the confused elderly patient. *American Journal of Nursing, 67,* 2536–2539.

People v. Coe, NY Sup., 501 NYS2d 997, 131 Misc 2d 807, aff. and remitted 510 NYS2d 470, 126 AD2d 436, appeal gr 515 NYS2d 1026, 69 NY2d 878, 507 NE2d 1096 (1986).

Pillemer, K. & Moore, D. W. (1989). Abuse of patients in nursing homes: Findings from a survey of staff. *Gerontologist, 29,* 314–320.

Pinel, P. (1806). *A treatise on insanity* (trans. D. D. Davis). London: Cadell & Davies (Reproduced New York; Hofner, 1962).

PL 100–203. (1987). Omnibus Budget Reconciliation Act, Subtitle C, Nursing Home Reform. Washington: U.S. Government Printing Office.

Podransky, D. L. & Sexton, D. L. (1988). Nurses' reactions to difficult patients. *Image, 20,* 16–21.

Rader, J. (1987). A comprehensive staff approach to problem wandering. *Gerontologist, 27,* 756–760.

Rader, J. (1988, May 19). Interview with L. Evans, Minneapolis, MN.

Rader, J., Doan, J., & Schwab, M. (1985). How to decrease wandering, A form of agenda behavior. *Geriatric Nursing, 6,* 196–199.

Regan, W. (1982). Restrain as needed: Nursing judgment required. *Regan Report on Nursing Law, 23,* 4.

Regan, W. (1983). Restraints and bedfalls: Most frequent accidents. *Regan Report on Nursing Law, 23,* 4.

Robbins, L. J. (1986). Restraining the elderly patient. *Clinics in Geriatric Medicine, 2,* 591–599.

Robbins, L. J., Boyko, E., Lane, J., Cooper, D., & Jahnisen, D. W. (1987). Binding the elderly: A prospective study of the use of mechanical restraints in an acute care hospital. *Journal of American Geriatrics Society, 35,* 290–296.

Rodin, J. (1986). Aging and health: Effects of the sense of control. *Science, 233,* 1271–1276.

Rodin, J. & Langer, E. (1976). The effects of choice and enhanced personal responsibility for the aged: A field experiment in an institutional setting. *Journal of Personality and Social Psychology, 34*, 191–198.

Rose, J. (1987). When the care plan says restrain. *Geriatric Nursing, 8*, 20–21.

Rosen, H. & DiGiacomo, J. N. (1978). The role of physical restraints in the treatment of psychiatric illness. *Journal of Clinical Psychiatry, 39*, 228–232.

Roslaniec, A. & Fitzpatrick, J. J. (1979). Changes in mental status in older adults with 4 days of hospitalization. *Research in Nursing and Health, 2*, 177–187.

Rovner, B. W. & Rabins, P. V. (1985). Mental illness among nursing home patients. *Hospital and Community Psychiatry, 36*, 119–120, 128.

Rovner, B. W., Kafonek, S., Filipp, L., Lucas, M. J., & Folstein, M. F. (1986). Prevalence of mental illness in a community nursing home. *American Journal of Psychiatry, 143*, 1446–1449.

Rubenstein, H., Miller, F. H., Postel, S., & Evans, H. B. (1983). Standards of medical care based on consensus rather than evidence: The case of routine bedrail use for the elderly. *Law, Medicine & Health Care, 11*, 271–276.

Rules and Regulations. (1989). *Federal Register, 54*, 5317–5318.

Scott, T. F. & Gross, J. A. (1989). Brachial plexus injury due to vest restraints. *New England Journal of Medicine, 320*, 598.

Schilder, E. J. (1987). The use of physical restraints in an acute care medical ward. Doctoral dissertation, School of Nursing, University of California, San Francisco.

Schwab, M. (1975). Nursing care in nursing homes. *American Journal of Nursing, 75*, 1812–1815.

Schwartz, D. (1985). Call for help. *Geriatric Nursing, 4*, 9.

Selikson, S., Damus, K., & Hamerman, D. (1988). Risk factors associated with immobility. *Journal of American Geriatrics Society, 36*, 707–712.

Silver, R. (1989, June 6) Telephone conversation with C. Williams.

Snyder, L. H., Rupprecht, P., Pyrek, J., Brekhus, S., & Moss, T. (1978). Wandering. *Gerontologist, 18*, 272–280.

Soloff, P. H. (1978). Behavioral precipitants of restraint in the modern milieu. *Comprehensive Psychiatry, 19*, 179–184.

Soloff, P. H. (1984). Historical notes on seclusion and restraint. In Tardiff, K. (Ed.), *The psychiatric uses of seclusion and restraint*. Washington: APA Press.

Soloff, P. H., Gutheil, T. G., & Wexler, D. B. (1985). Seclusion and restraint in 1985: A review and update. *Hospital and Community Psychiatry, 36*, 652–657.

Steinberg, F. U. (1980). *The immobilized patient*. New York: Plenum Medical Book Co.

Stilwell, E. (1988). Use of physical restraints in older adults. *Journal of Gerontological Nursing, 14*, 42–43.

Strome, T. M. (1988). Restraining the elderly. *Journal of Psychosocial Nursing and Mental Health Services, 26*, 18–21.

Strumpf, N. E., & Evans, L. K. (1988). Physical restraint of the hospitalized elderly: Perceptions of patients and nurses. *Nursing Research, 37*, 132–137.

Strumpf, N. E., & Evans, L. K. (1987). Patterns of restraint use in a nursing home (abstract). *Nursing advances in health*. Proceedings of the American Nurses' Association Council of Nurse Researchers Meeting, 410. Kansas City: ANA.

Strumpf, N. E., Evans, L. K., & Schwartz, D. (In press). Physical restraint of the elderly: 'I would write a story if I could.' In Chenitz, W. C., Stone, J. T., & Salisbury, S. (Eds.), *The clinical practice of gerontological nursing*. Phildelphia: Saunders.

Strumpf, N. E., & Evans, L. K. (1988). Prolonged physical restraint: Promoting good vs doing harm (abstract). *Gerontologist 28*, 299A.

Sunnybrook Medical Centre. (1988). *Policy and protocols relating to adult restraint use.* Toronto, Canada: Sunnybrook Medical Centre.

Tadsen, J., & Brandt, R. W. (1973). Rules for restraint: Hygiene and Humanity. *Modern Nursing Home 30,* 57–58.

Thankachan, G. (1987). Physical restraint: A dilemma in long-term care. Report of unpublished study. TirLawyn: Kendal-Crosslands, Kennett Square, PA.

Tideiksaar, R. (1989). *Falling in old age: Its prevention and treatment.* New York: Springer Publishing Co.

Tinker, G. M. (1979). Accidents in a geriatric department. *Age and Ageing 8,* 196–198.

Tinetti, M. (1989, March 21) Telephone conversation with L. Evans.

Tobin, S., & Lieberman, M. (1983). *The experience of old age.* New York: Basic Books.

Tuke, D. H. (1885). *The insane in the United States and Canada.* London: H. K. Lewis.

Tuke, S. (1813). Description of the Retreat, an institution near York, for insane persons of the Society of Friends. Philadelphia: Issac Pierce (Reprinted London: Dawson of Pall Mall, 1964).

Turemark, U. (1987, May 25 & 27). Consultation with C. Williams, Grobergets Sjukhem, Stortoppsgatan, 41457 Göteborg, Sweden.

Veatch, R. M., & Fry, S. T. (1987). *Case studies in nursing ethics.* Philadelphia: Lippincott.

Wagner, L. (1989). A proposed model for care of the elderly. *International Nursing Review, 36,* 50–53, 60.

Wagner, L. (1987, June 1–2). Consultation with C. Williams, Skaevinge Health Center, Skaevinge, Denmark.

Walshe, A., & Rosen, H. 1979. A study of patient falls from bed. *Journal of Nursing Administration, 9,* 31–35.

Warshaw, G. A., Moore, J. T., Friedman, S. W., Currie, C. T., Kennie, D. C., & Kane, W. J. et al. (1982). Functional disability in the hospitalized elderly. *JAMA, 248,* 847–850.

Westlake, R. J., & Rubano, G. L. (1983). Psychogeriatric seminars for nursing home nurses. *Hospital and Community Psychiatry, 34,* 1056–1058.

Whedon, M. B., & Shedd, P. (1989). Prediction and prevention of patient falls. *Image 21,* 108–114.

Wiener, C., & Kayser-Jones, J. (1989). Defensive work in nursing homes: Accountability gone amok. *Social Science and Medicine 28,* 37–44.

Whitehead, T. (1987). Difficult people. *Geriatric Nursing and Home Care 7,* 23–25.

Williams, C. (In press). The experience of long-term care in the future. *Journal of Gerontological Social Work.*

Wilson, K. (1988). *Beyond loving care: Developing a social model of care.* Portland: Oregon Gerontological Association.

Yarmesch, M., & Sheafor, M. (1984). The decision to restrain. *Geriatric Nursing, 5,* 242–244.

Yob, M. O. (1988). Use of restraints: Too much or not enough? *Focus on Critical Care, 15,* 32–33.

Yorker, B. C. (1988). The nurse's use of restraint with a neurologically impaired patient. *Journal of Neuroscience Nursing, 20,* 390–392.

Young, S. H., Muir-Nash, J., & Ninos, M. (1988). Managing nocturnal wandering behavior. *Journal of Gerontological Nursing, 14,* 6–12.

Zimmer, J. G., Watson, N., & Treat, A. (1984). Behavioral problems among patients in skilled nursing facilities. *American Journal of Public Health, 74,* 1118–1121.

Zubek, J. P., & MacNeill, M. (1966). The effects of immobilization: Behavioral and EEG changes. *Canadian Journal of Psychology, 20,* 316–336.

6

Limiting Medical Interventions for Nursing Home Residents: The Role of Administrative Law

Marshall B. Kapp

INTRODUCTION

To put it only semi-facetiously, the topic of legal and ethical implications of withholding or withdrawing life-sustaining medical interventions from critically ill patients is one that has virtually been "beaten to death" in the last several years in the legal, ethical, and medical literature (Kapp, 1988). A substantial amount of the discussion in the literature focuses directly upon, or at least is indirectly pertinent to, medical decision making by and for nursing home residents.

Discussions in the literature concerning legal aspects of the limitation of life-sustaining medical treatment invariably concentrate on two forms of relevant law: (a) legislative law, or statutes, especially state Living Will or Natural Death Acts and Durable Power of Attorney Acts and (b) court decisions interpreting state statutes, common law principles of informed consent, or federal constitutional protections of personal privacy and the free exercise of religion. This chapter makes no attempt to repackage the already ample guidance available to physicians and others serving nursing home residents regarding legislative and judicial parameters of limiting life-sustaining medical interventions—parameters which the medical and other health professions are slowly learning to understand and operate within to some degree comfortably.

Instead, the chapter examines relevant law emanating from the third part of government, the executive or administrative branch. The nursing home industry is heavily regulated by state government, much more so than acute care hospitals where the primary quality control enforcement mechanism is voluntary accreditation by private organizations like the Joint Commission on Accreditation of Healthcare Organizations. State regulation of nursing homes is accomplished through survey and certification by an executive or administrative agency of government, usually the state health or social service department. The survey and certification process ordinarily is based on standards set forth both in statutes and in administrative regulations, and detected violations of these standards may result in serious penalties such as delicensure, loss of certification to participate in the Medicaid or Medicare financing programs, or intermediate sanctions such as civil fines, restrictions on admissions, or receivership.

There is a tremendous amount of free-floating anxiety among health care professionals involved in nursing home care concerning the effect of administrative regulations generally, and particularly regarding restrictions imposed by state administrative agencies (e.g., health or social service departments) on permissible options for decision making about the limitation of life-sustaining medical interventions for critically ill nursing home residents. Many times, this author has heard comments from physicians, nurses, and administrators to the effect, "We would really like to honor the expressed or inferred preferences of the resident and family and withhold or withdraw futile or disproportionately burdensome medical interventions, and we believe that our state's statutes and court decisions would permit this course of conduct, but we live in fear that state surveyors will adversely cite us for violation of administrative regulations if we do so. Consequently, as a matter of legal defensive medicine, we inflict medical interventions on residents that neither they, their families, nor we in our clinical judgment would choose in the absence of regulatory oppression."

This chapter aims to illuminate the basis for this anxiety and to dispel it, or at least render the psychological intimidation manageable. The section entitled "Nature of Administrative Law" delineates the nature of administrative law generally. The following section then looks specifically at the impact of administrative law on medical decision making by and for residents of nursing homes. In "Dealing with State Surveyors" advice is advanced to health care professionals for productive, protective interaction with state surveyors over issues connected to limiting life-sustaining interventions. The next section emphasizes the importance of staff education about these issues and their effective management.

NATURE OF ADMINISTRATIVE LAW

One cannot speak of "the law" as a monolithic entity in the sense of it being easily discernible by looking to one particular source. Rather, ascertaining the legal ramifications of any particular question—especially one as complex and sensitive as limitation of life-sustaining medical treatment for nursing home residents—may require an examination of legal authorities stemming from a variety of sources.

The federal government and each state government are based on a written constitution, which is the fundamental building block of a society and defines the relationship between the government and the people. Basic citizen rights against government intrusion, such as the right to privacy which has been interpreted by the courts to include the right to make personal medical decisions, are spelled out in the federal and state constitutions. When a court interprets a constitutional provision, that court decision becomes part of the body of constitutional law.

A constitution grants power to a legislature to enact laws that are consistent with the constitution. Laws that are enacted by legislatures composed of elected representatives are called statutes. Examples of state statutes would include Living Will or Natural Death Acts and Durable Power of Attorney Acts. Judicial interpretations of statutes are considered part of the statutory law.

When a legislature passes a statute in a particular subject area, frequently it will leave absent many of the specific operational details necessary to proper effectuation of the legislature's intent. Instead of filling in all the details itself, a legislature routinely will delegate to an executive or administrative agency (e.g., the state health department) the authority and responsibility to create administrative law to carry out the legislative purpose. Administrative law promulgated under the authority of a statute in this way is called a rule or regulation. When a court interprets a rule or regulation, the decision is part of administrative law.

At the federal level (Title 5, United States Code, Chapter 5) and within each state there exists a statute called the Administrative Procedure Act, which spells out in detail the process that an administrative agency must follow in the course of creating a rule or regulation. Among other things, the agency must publish a proposed version of the rule and allow for public comment prior to its effective date. In some states (e.g., Ohio), the state legislature retains authority to hold hearings on proposed administrative rules and to veto or amend them. Once a rule has been put into final form and becomes legally effective, the agency must publish it and make it available to the public.

Assuming that a regulation is consistent with the statute upon which it is based, that it violates no constitutional principle, and that it was created in conformity with proper procedural requirements, that regulation carries the full force of law, and is just as mandatory and enforceable as a statute. A regulation is part of "the law."

Administrative agencies sometimes create documents variously termed "Guidelines," "Directives," or "Opinions" that purport to help in interpreting and operationalizing particular regulations. Guidelines or Opinions may be issued for the benefit of those who are required to comply with the regulations, but often are written to assist the agency bureaucrats (such as state health department nursing home surveyors) to interpret and apply those regulations in their enforcement activities. Administrative Guidelines or Opinions do not carry the force of law; unlike regulations, they are not developed under statutory authority and developed according to an Administrative Procedure Act. The significance of Guidelines or Opinions is discussed further below.

An addition to the sources of law already mentioned is the common law. Common law is the law announced by a court in the context of an individual litigation, when the decision is not based on the interpretation of a specific constitutional clause, statute, or regulation. Common law results from a judge's application of general moral and social principles, history, tradition, and legal precedent drawn from analogous situations. Most of our current principles of medical malpractice, informed consent, and confidentiality have been forged incrementally, on a case-by-case basis, as a matter of common law.

Health care professionals who work in nursing homes are correct that the body of law that influences their options and actions may include administrative rules or regulations as well as statutes, constitutional provisions, and court decisions based on common law. Thus, understanding the legal boundaries surrounding decision making about limitation of life-sustaining medical interventions in the nursing home necessarily entails delineating the existence and intent of any relevant regulations and their interaction with law emanating from the other branches of government.

IMPACT OF ADMINISTRATIVE LAW ON MEDICAL DECISION MAKING

As noted earlier, apprehension teetering on paranoia of state surveyors and the administrative law arsenal that they wield runs furiously throughout the nursing home industry. This anxiety infects the realm of medical decision making for critically ill residents. Health care providers err conservatively (that is, refuse to withhold or withdraw burdensome, futile, and/or unwanted medical interventions) in an effort to guard against anticipated sanctions based on violations of regulations, guidelines, and opinions that are perceived to prohibit the limitation of life-sustaining medical interventions within nursing homes.

In order to test the validity of this apprehension of administrative law running throughout the nursing home industry and adversely coloring medical decision making for the critically ill, this author conducted a research project in the winter of 1988–1989. A letter was mailed to the director of each state health department ($n = 53$, including District of Columbia, Puerto

Rico, and Virgin Islands, which each have Medicaid programs), that requested "a copy of any state regulations or administrative policies or guidelines relating to the subject of withholding or withdrawing of medical treatment from residents of long-term care facilities in your state." After a period of 2 months, 39 responses (73.5%) had been received (many of them from the health department's office of General Counsel). An important working hypothesis of this study is that jurisdictions with a positive response to the inquiry would be the most likely to reply.

The results of this survey are quite interesting. First, 29 of the 39 responding jurisdictions replied that they did not have any administrative rules or guidelines directly relevant to the issue of decision making about life-sustaining medical interventions for nursing home residents. These states are: Alabama, Alaska, Arkansas, Connecticut, Delaware, District of Columbia, Hawaii, Idaho, Illinois, Indiana, Iowa, Kansas, Kentucky, Louisiana, Missouri, Montana, Nevada, New Hampshire, North Carolina, Oregon, Pennsylvania, Rhode Island, South Dakota, Texas, Utah, Vermont, Virginia, Washington, and Wyoming.

Almost all of these states, though, did quite correctly indicate that the survey agencies are charged with the responsibility of surveying for compliance with existing statutory and case law. Relevant state statutes in this regard include most prominently Living Will or Natural Death Acts and Durable Power of Attorney Acts (a complete survey of these statutes, plus court decisions, is found in Society for the Right to Die, 1985 and 1988). Other state statutes that guide surveyors at least tangentially in this area, and with which long-term care professionals need to be conversant, include those covering general nursing home licensure standards, resident Bills of Rights, informed consent, and guardianship of incapacitated persons. General state regulations published by administrative agencies under statutory authority on facility licensure and resident rights were also cited by many state responders (e.g., Indiana, Iowa, Kansas) and should be well-known to long-term care professionals.

Other than those in the Living Will or Durable Power of Attorney category, these state statutes fail to deal expressly with the subject of life-sustaining medical interventions for nursing home residents, beyond generally assuring mentally competent individuals the right to make personal medical decisions. One notable statute at the time of this survey that did purport to set out specific legal parameters was the provision in the District of Columbia guardianship law that disallowed the guardian of an incompetent person from refusing life-sustaining medical interventions without a specific authorizing court order (District of Columbia, 1987). This provision has since been superceded, however, by enactment of a family consent statute in the District of Columbia that contains no such limitation (District of Columbia, 1989).

The central point of this discussion is that, in these 29 jurisdictions, it is the published and readily available statutory and case law that governs the enforcement conduct of survey agencies. In some states, this body of law may be confusing and less than rational in the clinical and ethical judgment of health care professionals. However, apprehension and speculation about some mystical collection of administrative rules or guidelines that are un-known and unknowable to any but the select group of state surveyors who privately keep them under lock and key and rely on them to impose sanctions on facilities for improper decisions about life-sustaining medical in-terventions, and that run counter to generally understood statutory and common law requirements, is not well-founded.

Moreover, even those relatively few states that presently do have some form of formal or informal administrative law in this specific subject area emphasize that their administrative principles and practices are intended purely to clarify and implement—and not in any way to alter—prevailing statutes and court decisions in that state. The following examples emphasize this essential concept.

The California Department of Health Services issued on December 14, 1988, revised "Guidelines Regarding Withdrawal or Withholding of Life-Sustaining Procedure (s) in Long-Term Care Facilities" (OHLP 88–79). The cover letter for this document, sent from the director of the department to all long-term care facilities and general acute care hospitals in California, ex-pressly noted that, "It is important to keep in mind that the guidelines reiterate applicable California case law and as such are not enforceable as a separate document. It would be more accurate to describe the guidelines as a reference source. They do not establish public policy specific to the decision whether to withdraw or withhold life-sustaining procedures."

The Maryland Office of Attorney General in 1988 issued an opinion to the director of the state Office on Aging restricted to the issue of foregoing artificially administered sustenance when a person in a health facility is terminally ill or permanently unconscious (State of Maryland, 1988). In this document, the Attorney General is unambiguous in his intent *not* to create new requirements apart from existing statutes and judicial decisions. At page 9 of the opinion he asserts, "In this opinion, we will try to clarify *what current law* allows and what it does not" (emphasis added).

A similar caveat is contained in the Massachusetts Department of Public Health's 1987 "Policy Guidelines for Evaluation of LTC Facility Practices and Procedures Regarding Decisions About Resuscitation of Terminal Patients." At page 4 of that administrative agency document, the reader is admonished: "*the standards and criteria set forth here are advisory guidelines not regulations or new legal requirements.* the Department believes that facility policies and practices with respect to making and/or implementing decisions about resuscitation of irreversibly terminally ill patients should be consistent with the generic patient care and patients' rights requirements expressed in existing state and federal regulations . . . The Guidelines themselves do *not* have the force or effect of law, nor do they impose any legal requirements above and beyond those actually expressed in the cited regulations" (emphasis in original).

The New Jersey Office of the Ombudsman for the Institutionalized Elderly issued a letter to all nursing homes on August 30, 1988, captioned "Decisions to Withdraw or Withhold Life-Sustaining Medical Diagnosis or Treatment from Patients Age 60 and Over." The instruction was conveyed by that document that every proposal to forego life-sustaining medical diagnosis or treatment for any psychiatric hospital or nursing home resident age 60 or over who had not been currently and legally determined able to make such decisions on his/her own must be reported to the Ombudsman as a possible case of illegal abuse. The Ombudsman explicitly predicated this instruction on his interpretation of current New Jersey case law (*In the Matter of Kathleen Farrell*, 1987) and the state Mandatory Reporting of Adult Abuse Law (*N.J.S.A.* 52:27G-7.1), rather than any intention to create new law.

Interestingly, this Ombudsman opinion, which is not administrative law promulgated in accordance with the state Administrative Procedure Act (indeed, the ombudsman has no authority to create law) and whose validity has not yet been tested in the context of litigation, was not supplied to the author as part of this study. Instead, the response of the New Jersey Department of Health to this study inquiry was that "We do not have regulations governing the withholding or withdrawing of medical treatment from residents of long term care facilities" (Goldberg, 1988).

Also of interest is the fact that this Ombudsman opinion generated a strong backlash, leading to serious proposals for both legislative and regulatory action to undo the anxiety and virtual paralysis that the opinion had brought about, by restricting explicitly the role of the ombudsman in the area of treatment decision oversight (Price & Armstrong, 1989). Further, the New Jersey Hospital Association and the Princeton Medical Center filed a lawsuit charging the ombudsman with violation of the state Administrative Procedure Act. By the summer of 1989, the ombudsman, Hector Rodriguez, had resigned from his post.

The New York State Hospital Review and Planning Council in 1988 issued regulations on Orders Not to Resuscitate (New York, February 4, 1988). These regulations were issued under the statutory authority, and are intended to clarify and implement—not to change—New York State Public Health Law Article 29-B, effective April 1, 1988. A Department of Health Memorandum (New York, March 18, 1988) accompanied distribution of these implementing regulations and summarized their contents.

The Georgia Department of Human Resources has issued regulations (Chapter 290-5-39, 1982) on "Long-Term Care Facilities: Residents' Bill of Rights," which contains the following at Section 290-5-39-.08:

Each resident or guardian shall have the right to refuse any aspect of medical treatment, dietary restriction or any medication, subject to the following:

(a) When a resident or guardian makes such refusal such person shall be notified by the appropriate facility staff person or physician of the immediate and possible long-term consequences of the refusal. The refusal shall be documented in the resident's record as shall the possible consequences of the refusal, and the resident's physician shall be notified as soon as practical.

(b) If such refusal would result in serious injury, illness or death, the facility shall:

1. Promptly notify the resident's physician and if serious injury, illness or death is imminent, transport the resident to a hospital; and

2. Notify the resident's guardian, representative or responsible family member in that order of priority . . .

This Georgia regulation is based upon legislative authority found at Georgia Code Annotated Section 88-1914B, 1924B (1981). Assuming that no person other than the resident (e.g., the fetus of a pregnant resident) would be physically jeopardized by the limitation of life-sustaining medical intervention, this regulation does not preclude a competent resident or one acting on behalf of an incompetent resident from authorizing such treatment limitation.

Several states responded to the author's inquiry that, although they did not have in place formal regulations pertaining to life-sustaining medical interventions for nursing home residents, their surveyors regularly use informal guidelines that are based upon interpretations of relevant statutes and cases. For instance, the Arizona Department of Health Services noted that "We strongly recommend that the physician provides medical record documentation of a discussion held with the resident's family or guardian. Many facilities require the responsible family member/guardian to sign indicating agreement" (Caldwell, 1989). The Maine Department of Human Services likewise indicated that, while lacking regulations or guidelines specifically addressing withholding or withdrawing treatment, "We do require, however, that there be documentation in the resident's record of family/ client/physican involvement in the decision not to resuscitate" (Fuller, 1988). The New Mexico Health and Environment Department offered the information that, "As a matter of practice, we encourage long-term care facilities to enlist the social worker and physician to discuss treatment options. This discussion should be documented in the medical record" (Gervase, 1988).

In examining the small body of state administrative rules, guidelines, and opinions that this study found to be directly relevant to the issue of limitation of life-sustaining medical intervention in nursing homes, several constant threads emerge. First, as already mentioned, there is not a separate body of administrative law that guides state surveyors in a manner that is inconsistent with or contradictory to existing, widely published statutes and judicial decisions. Instead, the administrative documents upon which surveyors rely are expressly intended to clarify, restate, and interpret legal parameters in a way that conforms to and emphasizes the statutory and common law.

Second, all of the administrative documents explicitly or implicitly permit the limitation of certain life-sustaining medical interventions (cardiopulmonary resuscitation is the type of intervention specifically mentioned most often) in specified (some states being more or less restrictive than others, with the case of a person in a persistent vegetative state being cited most frequently) situations in the nursing home. Of course, individual state law in one's own jurisdiction must be consulted for particulars, especially regarding the status of artificial nutrition and hydration.

Third, most of the administrative documents focus on the process of medical decision making rather than the correctness of the decision reached. Specifically, both the formal documents and the informal philosophies that guide state survey agencies stress the importance of such process factors as: the indispensable involvement of the physician in ordering the imposition or the limitation of life-sustaining interventions; careful documentation of decisions made and actions taken, underlying reasons, and the process of making and implementing decisions; and open, ample communication of options, values, and preferences among members of the health care team, guardian, family, and (where capable) the resident.

DEALING WITH STATE SURVEYORS

In light of the foregoing, how may health care professionals who care for nursing home residents successfully relate to state surveyors regarding decision making about life-sustaining medical interventions in a manner that protects both the dignity and autonomy of residents and the legal and financial integrity of the provider? There is often a complex set of interpersonal dynamics at play in these circumstances, but a few suggestions from a legal perspective might be ventured.

First, just like any other citizens, health care professionals have a fundamental right to know the law against which they will be held accountable. Many potential conflicts may be preempted by timely notification and clarification of legal provisions involved. Every nursing home administrator, director of nursing, medical director, and staff physician ought to request from the state health department copies of any pertinent regulations, guidelines, or opinions; these are public documents and should be available for the asking. These are the primary materials of the law. A great deal of time and effort may be saved by obtaining, studying, and keeping on file readily available these primary sources rather than becoming exorcised over second-hand gossip about imagined legal requirements that no one ever has actually seen.

Where a surveyor threatens to or does issue a citation based upon violation of an administrative requirement and nursing home staff is not familiar with, and does not possess a copy of, the *specific* source of that legal requirement, nursing home staff should demand of the surveyor the *specific* regulatory citation upon which he or she is relying and a copy of that legal authority. As a matter of basic procedural due process as guaranteed by the federal and state constitutions, a surveyor as an agent of state government is required to reply with specificity to such an inquiry before taking any action that would jeopardize the rights of the nursing home or its staff.

Perhaps even more importantly, where nursing home staff are apprehensive about being cited for a regulatory violation by a surveyor, even though the surveying agency itself has made no particular enforcement threat, staff should request from the agency copies of any of its relevant regulations. Desirable approaches to resident care frequently are "chilled" or inhibited unnecessarily by apprehensions that could be dissolved by getting the legal facts out on the table before crises materialize.

When a demand for regulatory information is exerted, one of several results will ensue. In rare instances, the agency may refuse or drag its feet in reply. In such situations, the nursing home should consider seriously invoking the advice of legal counsel to help clarify the pertinent regulatory atmosphere, to conduct further discussions with the agency on this matter, and to invoke the state's Freedom of Information Act if necessary.

It should also be remembered that formally published state regulations (and sometimes but not always administrative guidelines or opinions) ordinarily are obtainable by any member of the public from local law or decent-sized public libraries. In addition, the office of a state legislator representing one's local district usually will be glad to furnish or facilitate the furnishing of requested administrative agency documents as a constituent service.

In the more usual situation, the agency will respond to the nursing home's inquiry. In the majority of states, as indicated above, the response will be that no administrative rules specifically addressing the issue of limitation of life-sustaining medical interventions for nursing home residents presently are in effect. Instead, the agency should inform the nursing home that its survey activities in this sphere, to the extent that the agency becomes involved at all with the treatment limitation issue, are controlled by state statutes (e.g., Living Will, Durable Power of Attorney, general Resident Rights statute) or judicial decisions. Where such statutes or judicial precedent are cited by the survey agency as the basis for its inspection and enforcement, the nursing home should utilize legal counsel to interpret that law and its implications in advance, before an actual crisis mandating quick decisions arises.

In some jurisdictions, as explained above, the survey agency's response to a demand for information about its regulatory foundation will consist either in providing the nursing home with administrative rules that specifically affect the limitation of life-sustaining medical interventions, if such rules exist, or informing the facility that no specific rules on this topic have been promulgated in that jurisdiction. In most of these situations, once the nursing home staff is operating on the basis of legal knowledge rather than speculation, a productive process of clarification, mutual education, negotiation, and compromise between the individual facility staff and the survey agency may be started. In many cases, the staff will quickly discover that the legal context and its permissible treatment or limitation of treatment choices is not as constrained as previously imagined and that surveyor-imposed sanctions in this area are much less likely than thought.

Aided by qualified legal counsel and timely initiated (i.e., begun before a concrete, crisis-oriented situation engulfed in controversy and demanding immediate action develops), such a process can help avoid potential misunderstandings and conflicts later on. Most state agencies will issue informal opinion letters to members of the industry being regulated in response to inquiries about the application of relevant law to specific real or hypothetical cases. For example, in response to this study the New York Department of Health provided a copy of a 1986 opinion letter sent to a nursing home administrator in response to requested advice concerning a life-sustaining intervention for a particular dying patient. Although these opinion letters do not carry the force of law in the sense of binding the agency or the courts, they do provide a valuable indication of the agency's intentions and expectations in the area of enforcement and therefore facilitate orderly decision making within the nursing home.

Achieving a meeting of the minds may not be as formidable a task as feared. Every nursing home should have in place written policies and procedures dealing with such matters as limitation of life-sustaining medical interventions, and these documents should be developed and implemented in the context of negotiation and discussion with the survey agency to forestall subsequent charges that actions based on institutional policies and procedures violate state legal prohibitions. North Carolina's response in this study indicated an expectation by the survey agency that individual facilities would each develop their own policies and procedures (Hamilton, 1988). Survey agency attitudes toward the value and status of Institutional Ethics Committees may also be explored in these discussions.

In many situations, the process of clarification, mutual education, negotiation, and compromise with the survey agency concerning the legal parameters of limiting life-sustaining medical interventions for residents may best be undertaken by a state or local trade (e.g., state affiliate of American Health Care Association or American Association of Homes for the Aging or local nursing home association) or professional (e.g., county medical society) organization, rather than or in addition to being undertaken by individual providers. Where interests and issues are common among many different facilities, this sort of representative process is capable of yielding more efficient results and results which, because of the political and legal clout of the organization as compared to individuals, may be more palatable and flexible to the effected providers.

In a small number of situations, an understanding of the legal requirements concerning treatment limitation cannot satisfactorily be reconciled between the survey agency and nursing home staff, that is, staff concludes that it cannot readily function—clinically, ethically, and financially—within the survey agency's interpretation of the law. One manifestation of such legal conflict could be a violation citation of the facility issued by surveyors, accompanied by regulatory sanctions. The nursing home could then attempt to defend itself by litigating either the accuracy of the surveyor's interpretation of the applicable law or the constitutional or statutory validity of the administrative regulation upon which the surveyor is relying.

This type of litigation is expensive, time-consuming, and places the nursing home at serious legal and economic jeopardy. Where conflicting views of what the law is and what the law ought to be are inescapable and some form of resort to judicial clarification cannot be avoided, the preferred strategy would be for the nursing home to initiate a lawsuit prior to the imposition of any regulatory sanction for specific alleged misconduct, asking the court for declaratory and injunctive relief to clarify the state of the law in advance of a concrete controversy over treatment of an actual resident. The benefit of this type of litigation is that the rights and responsibilities of the respective parties are set out in advance and future violations can be avoided (or at least entered into knowingly rather than through ignorance or inadvertence).

Nursing home staff also may engage in pursuits at the macro or societal level to try to influence or change the law on this subject. Acting singly or through interested organizations, nursing home professionals may lobby the national, or more likely the state, legislatures for statutory reforms that would provide more flexible and sensitive treatment and limitation of treatment options that both protect and respect critically ill nursing home residents. Additionally, as explained earlier, the federal and state Administrative Procedure Acts guarantee individuals and groups the opportunity to attempt to influence the development of regulatory law, and nursing home professionals should not overlook administrative or executive departments of government in lobbying efforts on the limitation of treatment issue. Timely and persuasive provision of information and argumentation may encourage the promulgation of reasonable, clarifying regulations or at the least prevent the promulgation of vague or unreasonable regulatory mandates.

As has been mentioned several times already, qualified legal representation should be obtained by nursing home professionals in many of these various dealings with survey agencies concerning the limitation of life-sustaining medical interventions matter. A note is in order on the selection of legal counsel for this purpose. Just as is true for medicine, the practice of law today is a highly specialized affair. The attorney who handles the tax, real estate, or corporate needs of a nursing home or a physician may or may not be well qualified to negotiate with or litigate against the state health department concerning the limitation of life-sustaining medical interventions for critically ill residents. Ideally (and, unfortunately, attorneys who fulfill this ideal model are not plentiful), a nursing home and its staff should be represented in this context by an attorney who has expertise and experience (a) in administrative law, especially on the state level and with the health department in particular and (b) in patient or resident care issues. Expertise and experience in other phases of health law may be useful, but having handled Certificate of Need, fraud and abuse, staff privileges, or Medicare reimbursement matters does not automatically make one an expert on the legal implications of decision making about life-sustaining medical interventions for the critically ill.

STAFF EDUCATION

It is essential that an accurate, realistic understanding of applicable administrative (as well as statutory and common law) legal requirements and boundaries concerning decisions to limit life-sustaining medical interventions for seriously ill residents be achieved for nursing home administrators and the leaders of their medical, nursing, and social work staffs. It is equally as important, however, that such legal understanding permeate throughout the facility's culture and all of its actors, from the board of trustees to the nursing aides. Undue apprehension of legal consequences can lead to counterproductive decisions and behavior at all levels. Conversely, a degree of legal confidence and security can contribute to an atmosphere of more respectful and compassionate care for residents who are vulnerable both to too little and too much medical intervention.

Accordingly, staff (as well as trustee) education in this area should be a high priority. Regular, repeated, mandatory in-service training programs and self-study opportunities should be developed and put into place. Competent legal professionals should be consulted in this educational process. Consideration should also be given to involving local nursing home ombudsman and resident advocacy groups in clarifying for staff the pertinent issues. The assistance of a resident council and family council in spreading accurate information about the state of the law, and about the particular facility's institutional policies and procedures on the limitation of treatment subject, may be valuable. Finally, where a nursing home operates an Institutional Ethics Committee (Brown, Miles, & Aroskar, 1987; Glasser, Zweibel, & Cassel, 1988), this body and its individual members should play an instrumental role in policy formulation, interchange with the state survey agency, and internal and external education about the permissible limits of decision making in this difficult sphere.

CONCLUSION

When contemplating perplexing ethical issues concerning the possible limitation of life-sustaining medical interventions for critically ill nursing home residents, physicians and others in positions of responsibility for resident care and well-being must be acutely sensitive to the requirements and prohibitions imposed on treatment or nontreatment options by state administrative regulations, and to the possibility of legal and financial sanctions for running afoul of those regulations. Legal ignorance in this area is far from bliss.

By the same token, though, a paralyzing apprehension of perceived regulatory requirements that is based on rumor and speculation rather than accurate information can lead to treatment decisions and actions that violate the wishes and dignity of resident and family and that press counter to the clinical judgment and ethical values of the health care professional and institution. This phenomenon is especially distressing when its genesis is an unreasonable fear to even question the regulatory basis against which the survey agency will hold the facility and its staff accountable.

This chapter offers advice on understanding the nature of administrative law as it affects one area of decision making and on dealing with state agencies that have as their responsibility the enforcement of that administrative law. It is hoped that enhanced knowledge regarding the existence and content, or the nonexistence, of relevant regulations will reduce counterproductive anxiety and encourage productive interaction and better medical decision making for nursing home residents. Where this result is not easily achievable, enhanced knowledge can at least set straight the basis for disagreement between the state and health care professionals and facilitate an orderly and rational resolution of the conflict.

REFERENCES

Brown, B. A., Miles, S. H., & Aroskar, M. A. (1987). The prevalence and design of ethics committees in nursing homes. *Journal of the American Geriatrics Society 35*, 1028–1033.
Caldwell, G. G., Deputy Director, Arizona Department of Health Services. (1989, January 13). Letter on file with author.
District of Columbia Code. (1987). Section 21-2047 (c) (3).
District of Columbia Code. (1989). Section 21-2210 and 2211.

Fuller, E., Director, Bureau of Medical Services/Division of Licensing and Certification/Maine Department of Human Services. (1988, December 28). Letter on file with author.

Gervase, M., Supervisor, Federal Program Certification/New Mexico Health and Environment Department. (1988, December 19). Letter on file with author.

Glasser, G., Zweibel, N. R., & Cassel, C. K. (1988). The ethics committee in the nursing home: Results of a national survey. *Journal of the American Geriatrics Society 36*, 150–156.

Goldberg, S., Director, Licensing, Certification and Standards/Health Facilities Evaluation/New Jersey Department of Health. (1988, December 16). Letter on file with author.

Hamilton, H. K., Assistant Chief, Licensure Section/Division of Facility Services/ North Carolina Department of Human Resources. (1988, December 20). Letter on file with author.

In the Matter of Kathleen Farrell, 108 N.J. 335, 529 A.2d 404 (1987).

Kapp, M. B. (1988). *Legal aspects of health care for the elderly: An annotated bibliography*. Westport, CT: Greenwood Press, chaps. 8 and 9.

New York Official Compilation of Codes, Rules and Regulations, 10 NYCRR. (1988, February 4). Public Health Code Sections 405.42 and 414.23.

New York Department of Health, (1988, March 18). "Do not Resuscitate Orders." Health Facilities Series Memorandum H-13, NH-8, HRF-8, Series 88-24.

Price, D. M., & Armstrong, P. W. (1989). New Jersey's "Granny Doe" squad: Arguments about mechanisms for perfection of vulnerable patients. *Law, Medicine, & HealthCare, 17*, 255–263.

Society for the Right to Die. (1985 & 1988 Supplement). *The physician and the hopelessly ill patient: Legal, medical and ethical guidelines*. New York: Society for the Right to Die.

State of Maryland, (1988, October 17). *73 Opinions of the Attorney General*, Opinion No. 88-046.

7

Case Management Roles in Emergent Approaches to Long-Term Care

John A. Capitman
Margaret A. MacAdam
Ruby Abrahams

INTRODUCTION

Case management can be considered as an administrative service that directs client movement through a series of planned involvements with the long-term care system. It is also an advocacy service that attempts to integrate formal long-term services with care provided informally by family members and friends (Capitman, Haskins, & Bernstein, 1986). Unlike managed care, case management is not limited to functioning within a captitated financial system, such as an HMO, nor is case management limited to coordinating care within a single provider organization. Long-term care analysts have identified a series of variables that help policymakers and practitioners organize and understand differences in case management programs. These variables examine such areas as program goals, staffing patterns, case management tasks, and scope of authority (Capitman, Haskins, & Bernstein, 1986; Austin, 1983). Increased availability and changes in design of care coordination programs may require development of additional concepts for describing and analysing the factors that determine the relationships between case managers and their clients.

The proliferation of case management programs can be traced to a number of trends in public and private sector health care policies. New health care financing incentives such as prepayment and capitation have combined with health care delivery changes to increase interest among hospital systems in long-term care services coordinated by case management. Recently, a private market for long-term care through insurance policies and related vehicles has emerged, and attention has been directed to the infrastructure requirements of these ventures (Firman, 1988; Entmacher & Weil, 1988).

Public policy is changing in response to political and social pressure to expand the range of options for frail elders. The Medicaid home- and community-based care waivers and new applications of Federal Title III and Title XX monies have produced long-term care coordination systems at some level of development in most states (Laudicina & Burwell, 1988; Lipson, Donohoe, & Thomas, 1988; Omata et al., 1989). A number of states are in the process of allocating state funds to statewide systems for community-based home care programs which include case management as a central feature. Further there are now numerous proposals for major expansions in federal-level public financing of long-term care. Almost all of the legislative proposals to increase long-term care coverage under the Medicare program for example include case management as a covered benefit.

To date, there has been little information on the differences between case management services resulting from these policy, financial, and organizational changes. Public and private financing proposals recognize neither the emergent diversification of care coordination approaches, nor the diversity of long-term case management mechanisms being used in extant public and private systems. There is little basis for characterizing the consequences of new settings for care coordination programs on the relationships between case managers and clients or their informal care givers.

In this chapter we use three case studies to illustrate the variations in case management programs that are developing under the new incentives. We look at the case management service in a large state-funded case management and in-home care program; the Social Health Maintenance Demonstration, an HMO with expanded coverage for long-term care using insurance financing principles; and in a hospital that is responding to competition and to PPS pressures to discharge elders as quickly as medically appropriate. In each case, we describe the larger programmatic setting in which case management is embedded, the procedures and criteria for establishing eligibility for receipt of managed long-term care, unique aspects of case management practice, and the special issues and challenges facing care managers in each program.

CASE STUDIES

Case Management in the Massachusetts Home Care Program

Managed at the state level by the Executive Office of Elder Affairs, the Massachusetts Home Care Program (HCP) is operated at the local level by 27 nonprofit Home Care Corporations (HCCs), each of which covers a specific area of the state. The goal of HCP is to assist elders to "secure and maintain independent living in a home environment."

The HCP delivers case management and 15 other direct services, ranging from companionship to skilled nursing and other certified home health services to frail elders. With the exception of case management, services are purchased from private service provider agencies in each HCC area. The HCP is linked to 7 other state programs for the elderly: congregate housing, adult protective services, nursing home preadmission screening, home- and community-based waiver services for Medicaid recipients, respite care, emergency shelter, and Medicare and Medicaid-covered home health services. As well, 21 of the 27 HCCs are also designated Area Agencies on Aging with strong connections to elderly nutrition and other services funded under Title III of the Older Americans Act. Funding for the Home Care Program is available from state appropriations, supplemented by Medicaid payments through the home and community-based care waiver program and sliding fee revenue. For fiscal year 1989, the total HCP appropriation was $126 million of which 98% came from state funds and the remainder from the Medicaid program. In June 1989, the caseload was 43,300 elders or about 5% of the state's 60+ populations (Norman, 1989).

Targeting

Massachusetts residents aged 60 or more with at least 2 instrumental activities of daily living deficits are accepted into the HCP if they meet the financial eligibility criteria and have unmet needs for service. Financially, elders qualify for state-supported care if they receive SSI, Medicaid, or have annual incomes below $12,532 (1 person family) or $17,752 (2 person families). These criteria are intended to identify a population with greater risk for nursing home use than the general aged population, but the program does not intend to limit services to only those likely to enter a nursing home quickly without extended care. If service appropriations are exhausted before the end of the fiscal year, new applicants, with fewer service needs are put on waiting lists and/or current clients may have their service levels reduced. Priority is given to clients with any ADL deficits or more severe IADL problems.

Several studies document the success of the program in serving frail and vulnerable elders. In 1981, Branch, Callahan, and Jette found that the HCP targeted services to elders with characteristics associated with vulnerability and increased risk of institutionalization. A latter study found that the targeting success had been maintained over a 5-year period (Branch & Stuart, 1984). As shown in Table 7.1, the HCP population had changed only slightly by 1988. A greater proportion of clients were over 85 years old, but the proportions of female, widowed, and clients living alone remained very

TABLE 7.1 Comparisons of Home Care Client Characteristics in 1979 and 1988

	1979[1]	1988[2]
Age	%	%
65–74	31	26
75–84	49	47
85+	20	31
Gender		
Male	19	19
Female	81	81
Marital status		
Currently married	17	16
Widowed	66	66
Other	17	17
Living arrangement		
Lives alone	71	73
Spouse only	14	15
Other combination	15	12
Functional impairment level*		
4–7 ADLs		8
2–3 ADLs		15
7–9 IADLs		47
4–6 IADLs		28
2–3 IADLs		7

*No functional impairment level data are available for 1979.
Source: [1]Branch et al. 1981; [2]MacAdam & Yee, 1988.

similar (MacAdam & Yee, 1989). It appears that the program has been successful in selecting low income elders with characteristics associated with vulnerability and risk of nursing home admission.

Case Management Practice

Case managers perform a variety of tasks in the program including determining financial and service eligibility, assessment, care planning, service authorization, monitoring, reassessment, and redetermination of eligibility. Program regulations specify timelines and procedures by which each task is to be accomplished and detail client rights to appeal or protest case manager decisions.

Table 7.2 presents the characteristics of the case management work force. In June 1988 the 27 HCCs employed about 620 case managers. Ninety percent of them were generic case managers: They performed all of the tasks of case management. The average caseload of 68 cases was higher than the state guideline, 65 cases per worker. These HCP workers were relatively young, inexperienced women, with low salaries, who were likely to leave their jobs after 1–2 years. About one-fifth had been in their jobs less than 6 months, and 54% for more than a year. The 1988 annual salary range was

TABLE 7.2 Case Manager Characteristics

	%
Age	
21–29	40
30–39	22
40–49	19
50–59	11
60+	8
Gender	
Males	12
Females	88
Length of time as HCP case manager	
1–6 months	21
7–12 months	25
13+ months	54
Education	
Less than high school	6
High school	3
Bachelors degree	70
Masters	12
Other	9
Previous case management experience	
Yes	20
No	80
Salaries (full-time case managers only)	
$16,100–16,999	58
$17,000–17,999	24
$18,000–21,500	18
Second jobs (full-time case managers only)	
Yes	32
No	68

Source: MacAdam & Yee, 1988.

$16,100 to $22,550. Not surprisingly, one-third of the case managers had a second job (MacAdam & Yee, 1989).

HCP case managers do not take full advantage of the rich array of services available to meet client needs in most Massachusetts communities. As shown in Table 7.3, the vast majority of clients (83%) receive homemaker services. Clients who might have benefited from day care, specific chore services, companionship, transportation or even personal care and skilled nursing are in general receiving the same services as those who do in fact require homemaker care. Over time, there have been some shifts in the service utilization patterns. For example, proportionately more clients are receiving homemaker services and fewer are receiving heavy chore services than in earlier analyses. The average care plan cost ranged from $1700 to $4200 per year in 1989.

Issues for This Model

One of the concerns of policymakers is that a broadly defined long-term care program will be overwhelmed with elders and their families seeking assistance. The experience in Massachusetts does not support that concern. The vast majority of clients have IADL impairments only and relatively few are severely functionally impaired or medically complex. Far fewer than the national estimates of 18% of the elderly population with functional disabilities are being served in the HCP (Manton, 1988). Program data support the conclusion that elders seek out the program because they need it, not because it is available.

On the other hand, the provision of service to a broad range of elders in a public program with politically determined funding has implications for the staffing and delivery of case management. The HCP case management service is suffering from high turnover of staff due to low salaries because the state's priority has been to channel as many resources as possible to direct

TABLE 7.3 Comparison of Services by Utilization in 1979 and 1988

	% Clients Receiving the Service	
Service	1979[1]	1988[2]
Homemaker	69	83
Personal care	*	13
Heavy chore	24	8
Transportation	19	16
Home delivered meals	*	20

*Not available in HCP in 1979
Source: [1]Branch et al., 1981; [2]MacAdam & Yee, 1988.

service rather than care management. Most staff lack professional training in nursing or social work or experiences as a case manager at the time of hiring and are not likely to remain in the job beyond two years.

In addition to work force recruitment and retention issues, it appears that the case management service suffers from a "cookie cutter" model of service delivery. In spite of the differences in impairment levels, living arrangements, and access to informal support across the caseload, by regulation all clients are expected to receive the same amount of case management. The end result is that some elders are probably receiving more case management than they need while others are not receiving enough. Further, in spite of a rich array of services available to case managers, most continue to rely on homemaker services to meet client needs. The service utilization pattern seems to follow from the targeting criteria.

Unlike other case management programs that are designed to serve a subset of the functionally impaired population with nursing home diversion as an explicit goal, the Massachusetts program responds to the relatively straightforward needs of moderately impaired elders. The complex requirements of severely impaired or medically unstable elders can receive a limited HCP response at best. As the size of the program has grown, however, the state has added features to enhance services for the more frail. Program coverage of home health and personal care and staff assigned to facilitate service delivery for hospitalized elders are new features of the HCP to better meet the needs of medically unstable and acutely ill clients. In the future, the challenge for large welfare programs with generous admissions policies will be to continue to serve the moderately impaired while adequately serving chronically ill and medically unstable elders.

Case Management in the Social/HMO

The four Social/Health Maintenance Organization (SHMO) programs (in Portland, Oregon; Long Beach, California; Minneapolis, Minnesota; Brooklyn, New York) have now been in operation for four years as a national demonstration sponsored by the Health Care Finance Administration (HCFA). There are four essential features to the SHMO model that allow it to consolidate the health and long-term care delivery system at all levels: provider, population, finances, and risk (Leutz et al., 1986).

1. A sponsor takes responsibility for bringing the range of acute and chronic care services offered by the plan into a single delivery system.
2. The plan enrolls a membership that is representative of the community: well and functionally disabled Medicare elders are eligible. Three of the four sites have used a queuing technique whereby applicants have been

put on waiting lists to keep the case mix similar to the distribution of impairment in the community.

3. The plan is financed on a prepaid capitation basis by the monthly premiums of individual members and Medicare: Medicaid participates in payment for those who qualify.

4. The SHMO is at risk for medical care, short-term nursing home care, and long-term home care service costs with the organization taking responsibility for meeting its own budget even when losses are incurred.

Table 7.4 shows some of the key characteristics of the four SHMO settings. The Kaiser SHMO is an add-on benefit within a large established HMO. Seniors Plus (Minnesota) results from a partnership between an HMO and a comprehensive long-term care provider, both well established in the community. Senior Care Action Network (SCAN) is a broker case management agency, working in close association with a community hospital and its medical group (a newly formed Independent Practice Association). Elderplan, sponsored by an established geriatric facility, also developed a new HMO, linking with a medical group practice and contracting with several community hospitals.

The sites provide all services currently covered under Medicare, and in addition, a core long-term care benefit package that extends skilled nursing home and skilled home health beyond Medicare and also includes intermediate care facilities, therapies, and in-home personal care homemaker services. Supportive service such as adult day care, respite services, medical transportation, and personal emergency response systems are covered as well. Table 7.4 shows the annual extended care benefit available for enrollees at each site.

Targeting

The process for intake and determination of eligibility for extended care is similar across the sites. New members complete a self-report Health Status Form (HSF), which is reviewed in the case management unit, when they join the plans and yearly thereafter. Case managers telephone the enrollee or family care giver if there are problems reported. A comprehensive in-home assessment is scheduled if the client appears to need and qualify for extended care. Intake into case management for continuing enrollees occurs through referral from physicians, hospitals, other providers, or self/family (Leutz et al., 1988).

Eligibility criteria for receipt of expanded care services and case management differ slightly across the sites. At two sites (SCAN and Elderplan) qualification for the benefit depends on meeting the Medicaid "nursing home

TABLE 7.4 Social/HMO Site Characteristics

	Kaiser Permanente Oregon	Seniors plus Minnesota	Scan Health Plan California	Elderplan New York
Site sponsor(s)	Medical Care Program	Group Health Inc. Ebenezer Society (partners)	Senior Care Action Network	Metropolitan Jewish Geriatric Network
Type of sponsor(s)	Large established HMO	HMO and comprehensive LTC agency	Case management brokerage agency	Comprehensive LTC agency
Type of S/HMO	New benefit program	New benefit program	New HMO	New HMO
Annual LTC benefit	$12,000	$6000	$7500	$6500
Monthly premium	$57.85	$24.50	$24.95	$36.47
Total enrollment[1]	5479	3030	3041	5145
% Nursing home certifiable (NHC)[2]	10.6%	7.6%	6.9%	4.8%
% Receiving care plans[3]	4.4%	8.6%	13.8%	2.6%

[1]Enrollment as of February 1989.
[2]As of December 1988.
[3]As of December 1987. (The percentage for SCAN includes both the severely and moderately impaired served under the LTC benefit at that time. In 1988, SCAN changed its eligibility criteria to include only the severely impaired. The reduced percentage with care plans is not yet available.)

Source: S/HMO Consortium Management Data Set.

certifiable" (NHC) criteria of their respective states. Kaiser developed its own NHC criteria based on items from Oregon's Medicaid placement requirements for nursing home applicants. In all three of these sites, extended care services were not offered to all members who qualified as NHC, but only to those who were judged to need services. Seniors Plus also uses Medicaid nursing home criteria, but members who "in the case manager's judgment are at risk of becoming NHC" may qualify as well. Prior to mid-1988, SCAN also offered care plans to some severely and moderately disabled members who did not qualify as NHC, based on perceived unmet needs. Table 7.4 shows the range across sites in the proportion of members who qualify as NHC and who were offered care plans through the early months of 1988.

Case Management Practice

The case management unit at each site is staffed mainly by individuals with nursing or social work backgrounds. Case management supervisors usually have an advanced degree, and all programs require that staff have relevant training and clinical experience. Salaries are generally competitive with other public and private sector opportunities for gerontological clinicians in the plans' cities. All case managers determine members' eligibility for the benefit, perform comprehensive in-home assessments, develop care plans with the member and family, and authorize extended care services and then monitor and adjust care plans as necessary over time. The average caseload per case manager in the SHMO ranges from 40 to 50 cases at Kaiser, up to 70 cases at Seniors Plus, 50 cases at Elderplan, and 37 cases at SCAN, reflecting differences in case management practice.

A major goal of case management in the SHMO is to facilitate integration of acute, post-acute, and extended care services. Variations in the organizational arrangements that link services influence the integrative roles of SHMO case managers. At Kaiser, case management system seeks integration of extended care into the preexisting practices of a large HMO, without duplicating the responsibilities of existing medical and post-acute providers. Discharge planning and post-acute home care are the responsibility of Kaiser's hospital planners and home health agency. The SHMO case managers authorize only expanded benefit services but work closely with these other units for clients who require ongoing skilled services. By contrast, Seniors Plus case managers take full responsibility for authorization of all post-acute and extended care. Even more of the medical system responsibilities have been assumed by case managers at SCAN and Elderplan where there were no preexisting care coordination mechanisms. Because their new medical groups were not experienced in HMO norms of practice, their case management units include utilization review/discharge planning nurses in addition to long-term care case managers. (Abrahams et al., 1989; Yordi, 1988).

Care Planning and Service Use

Two different approaches to the benefit structure influence care-planning practice. At three sites (Kaiser, SCAN, Elderplan) the annual benefit is prorated to a monthly cap. The case manager negotiates with the enrollee and family to develop a plan that meets the member's needs within the monthly cap. Case managers at these three sites can go up to the limit of the monthly benefit and then, if appropriate, reduce services later as the client situation stabilizes. There is more flexibility in varying the intensity of services at the fourth site (Seniors Plus), where case managers work within the annual benefit cap, with no defined monthly limit. Seniors Plus case managers can prescribe an intensive level of services for short periods of time around episodes of acute illness, or exacerbations of psycho-social situations. When the client situation has stabilized, services are reduced to a level that is sustainable within the annual cap. Even given these differences across sites, it has been found that most care plans are well within and often below the annual benefit level.

Table 7.5 shows the mix of initial care plan service packages at three Social/HMO sites during 1985–1988. These packages include skilled (Medicare criteria) and paraprofessional services, both in institutions and in the community. At all three sites, the frequency with which skilled and paraprofessional services are mixed is relatively high compared with prior long-term demonstrations (Capitman, 1989). Use of institutional, or institutional with community services ranges from 11% to 39% of the care plans analyzed; use of skilled community, with or without paraprofessional community services, ranges from 18% to 24% of these care plans; use of paraprofessional and

TABLE 7.5 Social/HMO: First Month Care Plans:
Service Packages 1985–1987 (percentages)

	Kaiser (n = 574)	Seniors Plus (n = 461)	Scan (n = 708)
SNF/ICF only	26.0	3.3	5.5
SNF/ICF and community	13.4	8.0	9.2
Community:			
Adult day care	2.4	6.5	3.0
Skilled and paraprof.	23.5	13.2	4.4
Skilled only	0.5	5.4	9.6
Paraprof. only	33.4	30.6	34.6
Support services	NA	1.7	5.7
Transportation only	0.7	31.2	28.0

Source: S/HMO Consortium data. Includes skilled services prescribed but under Medicare capitation and under the LTC benefit. Durable medical equipment is excluded. Data not available for Elderplan.

community support services only ranges from 33% to 40%. Adult day care, used most at Seniors Plus, may involve both skilled and paraprofessional care. Transportation only services are used at Seniors Plus and SCAN in somewhat less than one-third of their initial care plans.

Greenlick et al. (1988) examined the use of short-term nursing home placement, as part of care plans designed to keep the enrollee in the community. Among enrollees receiving services under the benefit, most had received services at home. Among those using a nursing home, 58% of the placements were short-term and designed to keep people in the community with 41% of these placements for post-acute convalescence, 10% for a medical flare-up, and 7% for respite or care giver crisis (Greenlick et al., 1988).

Issues Related to this Model

The SHMOs have attempted to integrate acute and long-term care financing and delivery for a diverse aged population to an extent that has not been attempted in prior efforts. Such consolidation of service delivery in the context of limited long-term care benefits presents a broader range of challenges for case management than were explored by prior programs that focused on coordination of community-based paraprofessional services. As described above, the sites have developed alternate approaches to intervening in transitions into illness and disability, and from prepaid to ongoing fee-for-service or Medicaid-financed long-term care. They have all sought to manage initial use of extended care services, and where organizationally feasible have expanded case management authority to post-acute services. The clinical and economic implications of the differences in case management roles in the consolidation of acute and long-term care have yet to be fully articulated or assessed.

Only the On Lok program in San Francisco's Chinatown and North Beach neighborhoods, and replications under development across the country provide a point of comparison with the SHMOs since they consolidate financing and most aspects of services delivery. On Lok, however, has served a relatively small, mostly Medicaid-enrolled, nursing home level of care population, whose primary needs are for long-term care. On Lok does not manage transitions into illness and disability since all of its members are already at the nursing home level of care, nor do care managers and clients wrestle with a benefit limited in time and intensity. Evaluations of the On Lok model are promising though somewhat inconclusive because of problems with the design and implementation of the internal evaluation (Capitman, Haskins, & Bernstein, 1986; Weissert, Cready, & Pawelak, 1988).

As a reflection of the integration of acute and long-term care financing, and the goal of spreading risk across an insured population, the SHMOs have been faced with balancing the perceived affordability of the plan to consumers with adequate coverage of chronic care services. The principal mechanisms for limiting extended care expenditures have been targeting and care management for those who do qualify. Sites made different choices on whether to target only the severely impaired, or to include some of the moderately impaired as a prevention strategy aimed at limiting medical care expenditures. Case managers at sites with narrower criteria have expressed concerns about unmet needs among members who do not qualify, but neither economic nor clinical support for the preventative strategy has been developed.

In order to keep the plans consumer price competitive with existing HMOs for the aged that do not offer long-term care, the SHMO long-term care benefit has been modified over time. For example, initially Kaiser offered 100 days of nursing home coverage beyond Medicare, but in the past year, this has been reduced to 30 days. This nursing home benefit can provide short-term post-acute and respite stays to help stabilize patient and family situations for continued community service but this benefit does not provide for longer stay nursing home needs. These benefits were never intended to provide adequate coverage for ongoing very intensive packages of home care. The SHMO can extend the time before long-term users spend down to Medicaid, but it does not eliminate that need for all members. A major issue for case managers in this model is balancing clinical judgments of need, consumer preferences for both asset protection and services, and broader plan needs for limiting service prescription.

Case Management at South Shore Hospital and Medical Center

South Shore Hospital and Medical Center, a small community hospital (156 beds) serving the southern portion of Miami Beach, Florida, was one of 24 participants in the Robert Wood Johnson Foundation's Program for Hospital Initiatives in Long-Term Care from 1984 until 1988 (Capitman et al., 1988; MacAdam et al., 1989). The hospital receives ongoing support from the Foundation for innovations in geriatric care management. South Shore's diverse neighborhood features a dense concentration of the old-old. The elder residents of this community have been described as challenged by multiple chronic illnesses, low income status, and relatively meager public financing for long-term care. Nursing home care is in short supply, while the confusing array of community care providers is often difficult to access. At the same time, the health care market in metropolitan Miami is highly competitive: there are many acclaimed medical centers, hospital occupancy rates are low, and prepaid health plans for the elderly have been marketed actively.

South Shore has sought to distinguish itself as a provider of services for the aged and chronically disabled. The hospital serves as a geriatrics and rehabilitative medicine teaching, practice, and research site for the University of Miami medical school; is a research site in several national programs such as the Veterans Administration adult day care demonstration; and has strong linkages with a variety of institutional and community long-term care providers. A grant from the Robert Wood Johnson Foundation allowed the hospital to diversify its outreach activities and strengthen the geriatric medical and rehabilitative services offered to in-patients and clinic users (DeVito & Zubkoff, 1985).

A form of case management is at the core of South Shore's model geriatrics program. The Geriatric Assessment and Planning (GAP) Program provides comprehensive assessment services to all elder in-patients. For those patients who require continuing care, service planning, service arrangement, and monitoring are also provided by professional staff and peer volunteers. GAP care management is not open-ended. The typical duration of case management involvement is less than 2 months, with small subsamples followed to 3 or 6 months. Case managers attempt to ensure linkage with needed services and so pass the baton of responsibility for long-term service coordination to appropriate community agencies. Additional services, including care giver education, distribution of printed materials on accessing community care, and offering educational and other supports to community care providers supplement this explicit focus on managing the transition between hospital and community.

The GAP program and associated services do not alter the financing or overall organization of long-term care delivery. Clients are only able to access those community services for which they can pay out of pocket or that are covered by public payors. The hospital neither authorizes nor directly manages delivery of discrete services. It has no financial or organizational control of service provision for case management praticipants.

Case Management Practice

The central feature of the GAP program is the integration of comprehensive assessment and planning for continuing care into the normal processes of inpatient care at South Shore Hospital. All in-patients over age 65 receive a comprehensive assessment around the time of admission, and those who need community services receive additional assessment during the course of the hospitalization. The goals of the at-admission assessment include identifying potential obstacles to effective provision of acute care and beginning discharge planning. Subsequent assessments are more oriented toward identification of individuals who will require follow-up in the community after discharge, or whose plan will involve a complex array of services.

While functional assessments are generally performed by registered nurses on the wards, other components of the assessment and discharge plan are completed in conjunction with professional nursing and social work staff in the discharge planning and continuing care office. Depending on the complexity of the discharge plan and the agencies to whom the patient is being referred, service arrangement may be conducted by clerks or clinical staff, all of whom have professional training and significant experience. Salaries at South Shore are competitive with other area hospitals. As shown in Table 7.6, about one-third of the individuals who were assessed did not receive a care plan: it was determined that they would not require post-acute services.

All referrals are verified with the receiving agencies within a few days to ensure that the prescribed care has been initiated and that any special requirements have been taken in account. Because of restricted supply of intermediate care and supportive housing beds and sparse public funding for personal care, homemaker, adult day care, and related community chronic care servcies, GAP staff report frequent frustrations in completing "linkage" between post-acute patients and service providers. Severe medical and technical restrictions on Medicare-reimbursed home health and nursing home care also result in the eventual rejection of many Medicare certified home health referrals. Table 7.6 shows that nonetheless, almost one-third of elders assessed by GAP received certified home health services. Nursing home care and noninstitutional chronic care modalities were featured in smaller proportions of the plans eventually implemented by the receiving agencies. It is noteworthy that even with the reported difficulties in acquiring post-acute services for GAP participants, higher proportions received post-acute servcies than is typical for Medicare beneficiaries (Manton & Hausner, 1987; Gornick & Hall, 1988).

TABLE 7.6 Services Received After Hospital Discharge: South Shore Hospital 1986 GAP Participants

Service	% of Discharges* ($N = 2452$)
Nursing home care	18
Home health care	33
Attendant/supervisor	18
Personal care/homemaker	19
Home-delivered meals	2
Assistance with chores	4
Equipment/supplies	2
No care plan	32

*Total may exceed 100%.
Source: Evaluation of the Robert Wood Johnson Foundation Program for Hospital Initiatives in Long-Term Care, 1987 Survey, Brandeis University.

The program also responds to difficulty in securing community care for South Shore hospital patients by contacting them directly after discharge. "Fast follow-up" monitoring is conducted within a few days of leaving the hospital for selected patients (about 12% of those with discharge plans in 1986 and 1987) by the clinical coordinator for continuing care. Criteria for receipt of fast follow-up have varied over time, in response to the staff perceptions of the situations that in the absence of case management intervention are most likely to result in hospital recidivism, nursing home use, or other negative outcomes. For example, in 1987, follow-up was conducted with patients characterized by confusion or severe functional disability and living alone, or functional disability and leaving the hospital against medical advice. These criteria have been reassessed and modified throughout the course of the program. These patients are monitored on a frequent basis for up to 3 months or until they have been successfully linked with a community care provider.

Some of the patients selected for fast follow-up also meet the criteria for "tracking" that include formal assessment at 3, 6, and 12 months after discharge. Criteria for tracking are 2 or more ADL limitations or selection for fast follow-up and subsequent failure to link the patient with an adequate community care provider. About 11% of those with discharge plans in 1986 and 1987 were reassessed 3 months post-discharge, with far fewer included in subsequent reassessments. Tracking has provided primarily research information, but has also permitted the hospital to stay involved in ongoing medical and chronic care utilization decisions by targeted patients.

Issues Related to This Model

While the South Shore Hospital care management program has not been evaluated from the perspectives of cost-effectiveness or clinical efficacy, it has a number of features in common with the geriatric assessment unit and geriatric assessment team concepts that have been tested with mixed results within the Veterans Administration medical centers (Rubenstein, et al., 1984; Saltz, et al., 1988; Becker, et al., 1987) and in civilian hospitals (Barker, et al., 1985). Rubenstein and colleagues found that transferring complex inpatients to a sub-acute unit that offered comprehensive medical assessment, rehabilitative services, discharge planning, and transition follow-up dramatically reduced total hospital and nursing home use. But Barker et al. (1985) and Becker et al. (1987) found that a program that offered comprehensive medical assessment and discharge planning without the specialized sub-acute unit, or post-discharge monitoring had no such effects. All three studies did note changes in inpatient treatment patterns. An assessment of the efficacy of the South Shore GAP model is needed.

Several other issues have been raised by the South Shore Hospital experience. The hospital has noted increases in the number of severely disabled elders transferred or directly admitted for inpatient care and fears that such patients may be "dumped" because of the specialized geriatric program. Increased admissions of such patients if they tend to have longer stays than less disabled patients with comparable admitting diagnoses could over time hurt the financial position of the hospital. Nonetheless, the potential for more efficient discharge and avoidance of quicker than expected readmission of Medicare patients would seem to justify the relatively meager costs of the GAP program.

The South Shore experience also underscores the need for active participation by medical providers and payors in the development of services and funding sources for community-oriented geriatric care: A sizable proportion of the elders leaving this hospital required services beyond those generally covered by Medicare and also were judged to require assistance in gaining access to these services. Transition management services were only partially effective in overcoming these systemic barriers to adequate provision of post-acute and chronic care. Passing the baton of responsibility for continuing care is only possible to the extent that a community provider is able and willing to receive the referral.

DISCUSSION

Care coordination programs have emerged in a broad array of acute and chronic care delivery systems for the aged. As demonstrated by the three programs described, the goals and practices of case management differ dramatically across settings. These differences can further elucidate the program design variables identified in earlier studies (Capitman, Haskins, & Bernstein, 1986; Austin, 1983). Most notably, a new perspective on the variability in targeting procedures and criteria is suggested by these examples. At the same time, the addition of coordinating services to new financing and delivery systems also suggests 2 additional parameters for characterizing programs: medical system linkage and focus of accountability. The care coordination models developed in new long-term care systems suggest that differing relationships between case managers and clients or their informal caregivers are associated with these program design factors.

Targeting Procedures and Criteria

The procedures for identifying potential case management participants and criteria for determining their eligibility in programs such as Channeling, Medicare and Medicaid demonstrations, and current Medicaid home- and community-based care programs attempt to limit services to the "who but for" population (Capitman, 1989; Weissert, Cready, & Pawelak, 1988). At least in theory, all of these efforts focus case management and expanded services on individuals who but for the availability of community services on an ongoing basis would need long-term custodial nursing home care. In implementing traditional targeting goals, the case manager is a representative of the system of care: a gatekeeper who may continue to work with only those clients for whom offering the new services appears to influence use of institutional care.

This approach ignores the extreme diversity of medical and functional conditions and socioeconomic situations among long-term care users (Capitman, 1989). Recent findings from analyses of national data sets on long-term care (Liu, Manton, & Liu, 1989; Manton, 1988; Morrissey, Sloan, & Valvona, 1988) suggest four major types of target groups for chronic care coordination: post-acute patients making transitions from acute to chronic care settings, patients with complex and changing medical and long-term care needs, medically stable community residents with moderate to severe needs for personal care and home management assistance, and medically stable individuals with minimal to moderate needs for home management assistance.

Consistent with this broader conceptualization of need for long-term care, all of the programs described have targeting goals that explicitly recognize that rehabilitative and maintenance services may be needed by the aged and disabled independent of their efficacy in substituting for institutional care. The Massachusetts home care program currently serves medically stable individuals with modest needs for homemaker/personal care services but stable health conditions: The range and scope of covered direct and care coordination services have only recently been modified to meet the needs of the medically unstable, but targeting and case management practice have not yet shifted focus to include these elders. By contrast, the SHMO provides prepaid community care to individuals with either stable functional disabilities or complex medical and functional conditions. Even though SHMO expanded care criteria reference host state nursing home admissions criteria, targeting procedures and criteria are primarily intended to ensure member access to prepurchased services without exceeding the overall plan's medical and long-term care resources. SHMO extended care is targeted to individuals in transition, the medically unstable with functional disabilites, and the chronically severely disabled. The South Shore GAP program is focused on those elders requiring assistance in acquiring post-acute care: it is targeted to the transitions group.

Case managers function as representatives of the system of care in implementing each of these targeting goals, but the systems they represent are not geared primarily to nursing home diversion and minimizing overall long-term care costs. Targeting services to all clients with even moderate disabilities, as in the HCP, implies that case managers rarely are faced with hard choices related to eligibility. As shown below, the challenge in this context is more related to ability to offer adequate services and coordination. Similarly, in South Shore, some transitional care is potentially available to a wide range of patients leaving the hospital. Targeting is aimed at identifying those who need short-term assistance in accessing post-acute and ongoing community care. The case managers' challenge is to identify individuals for whom care coordination will make a difference in length of stay and delay of readmission. By contrast, SHMO case managers face challenges similar to those in traditional diversion program, in that they can work only with a limited subpopulation. The potential for conflict between the roles of client advocate, long-term care gatekeeper, and coordinator of alternative services intended to reduce medical care use may be pronounced for SHMO case managers when assessing the eligibility of clients who are at the edges of eligibility.

Medical System Linkage and Responsibility

The organizational linkages between community-oriented long-term care coordination programs—even those sponsored by hospital systems—and medical care providers have been tenuous and strained in most cases (Kemper, Applebaum, & Harrigan, 1988; Capitman, 1989; Capitman et al., 1988; Kane & Kane, 1987). Medicare-certified home health agency services have been the exception to this pattern since they share funding sources with acute care and in principle, home health is directed by physicians. Referral by a physician has also been required in Medicaid community care programs, but this medical preauthorization does not ensure ongoing communication or sharing of responsibilities for patient care. Most state-based long-term care systems are like the Massachusetts program in that case managers have no direct involvement with medical and acute care arrangements, no systematic access to information on medical services being provided to clients, and no formal mechanism for ongoing coordination between home care services and those financed through the Medicare program. These minimal organizational links with medical care providers reflect a perspective that sharply differentiates the responsibilites and potential contributions of "social" and "medical" care givers (Omata, et al., 1989).

Both the SHMO and South Shore's GAP demonstrate the potential for rather different organizational relationships and associated concepts of the relative responsibilities of acute care and other providers. In the SHMO, long-term care coordination is intimately linked to hospital and post-acute care provision and there are formal machanisms for ongoing bidirectional communication between case managers and medical care providers. While there are variations across sites, the underlying assumption in these arrangements is that case management is charged with encouraging efficient and responsive health plan service provision by coordinating these dual responsibilities.

The South Shore Hospital GAP program demonstrates how this same philosophy can be manifest in the fee-for-service delivery system. The GAP program allows for active participation by interns and nursing staff in preparing for reentry to the community during an acute care episode. Thus not only post-acute services but also in-hospital interventions are aimed at minimizing inpatient length of stay, and maximizing the potential for independent living after leaving the facility. Planning, arranging, and managing both post-acute care and the transition to ongoing community care or independent living have been adopted as the responsibility of the acute care system in this project. It is important to note, however, that this philosophical shift did not result in changes in physician practice, but in the orientation of the hospital system.

Focus of Accountability

In most cases, case management programs have been analyzed within the context of demonstration programs. The primary focus of accountability has been on implementation of proscribed research protocols and meeting sponsor requirements. As case management programs are increasingly adopted by state governments and private provider groups, however, the focus of accountability shifts to payers, consumers, and other health and social service providers. In each of the programs described here, the focus of accountability has direct implications for case managers' relationships with clients and their informal caregivers.

For the Massachusetts HCP, program accountability has been to state government and the legislature, rather than consumers or a broader professional community. During state fiscal crises, HCP allocations may be inadequate to respond to the demand for care. As a result, HCP agencies have either closed intake of all new clients, dramatically reduced service levels for current clients, or both. These actions are not based on consumer demand, nor are they responsive to professional assessments of need. Such agency behavior, however, significantly alters the roles of care managers as they become representatives of an apparently arbitrary welfare system rather than client advocates. Staffing patterns for case management have also ignored broader professional standards by using inexperienced and minimally trained workers for even the most clinically complex assessment and care planning functions.

As private organizations, at risk for losses associated with utilization and costs for health and long-term care services that exceed expectations, and dependent for revenue on consumer premiums, the SHMOs have demonstrated primary accountability to their memberships. Organizational survival and meeting obligations to members require that the plans remain financially viable, price competitive with HMOs that do not offer long-term care benefits, and sensitive to consumer preference for home rather than institutional care. Restrictions in nursing home benefits, changes in targeting criteria, changing relationships with providers, and other program adjustments have most often reflected responsiveness to marketing and member satisfaction issues. Case managers may experience less conflict between their roles as representatives of the plan and client advocates in care coordination than they do in eligibility determination. Client advocacy, counseling, and helping clients to use benefits for which they qualify in the most efficient and effective manner are in the best interest of the health plan.

The South Shore Hospital GAP is primarily accountable to the hospital and its professional staffs. The program seeks to reduce hospital length of stay through adequate discharge planning and transitional care management. These efforts to encourage efficient discharge are needed not so much as a response to consumer demand or payer requests, but so that the hospital with its high proportion of complex elder patients can survive under prospective payment by Medicare. At the same time, South Shore has come to view its mission as a partnership with community agencies in meeting the needs of elders in the south Miami Beach area. In this context, the case manager's role has similarities to those of Channeling basic site staff, in that they have no direct control over the community service system, but try to act as client advocates by developing cooperative professional and agency relationships. It is professional skills and this network of relationships that the case manager can offer to clients.

Implications for Long-Term Care Policy

While there is growing consensus that case management alone does not ensure efficient or cost-effective provision of long-term care, almost all proposals for public and private financing of an improved delivery system include case management as one tool in utilization control and quality assurance. Some analysts have suggested that other long-term care delivery system features such as prospective, case-mix and outcome adjusted reimbursement, service differentiation, and linkages between services and housing may be equally important tools in meeting these goals (Weissert, Cready, & Pawelak, 1988; Kane & Kane, 1987). Yet the experience of new generation long-term care systems suggests that the capacity of case management units to aid in the search for efficiency and excellence is at least partially determined by broader program goals and arrangements.

As the variety of long-term care organizational settings and goals continues to grow, new variants on the present roles and structures of case management programs may be expected to emerge. The experiences of HCP, the

SHMOs, and South Shore Hospital all suggest that the relationships between case managers, elder clients, and care givers both formal and informal are also modified by new program designs. Future research should seek to understand the factors shaping case management services, and how differing approaches are related to the efficiency and clinical efficacy of long-term care.

REFERENCES

Abrahams, R., Capitman, J., Leutz, W., & Macko, P. (1989). Variations in care planning practice in the Social/HMO: An exploratory study. *The Gerontologist, 29*, 725–736.

Austin, C. D. (1983). Case management in long term care: Options and opportunities. *Health and Social Work, 8*, 16–30.

Barker, W. H., Williams, T. F., Zimmer, J. G., VanBuren, C., & Vincent, S. J. (1985). Geriatric consultation teams in acute hospitals: Impact on back-up of elderly patients. *Journal of the American Geriatrics Society, 33*, 422–428.

Becker, P. M., McVey, L., Saltz, C., Feussner, J., & Cohen, H. (1987). Hospital-acquired complications in a randomized controlled clinical trial of a geriatric consultation team. *Journal of the American Medical Association, 257*, 2313–2317.

Branch, L., & Stuart, N. (1984). A five year history of targeting home care services to prevent institutionalization. *The Gerontologist, 24*, 387–391.

Capitman, J. A., Haskins, B., & Bernstein, J. (1986). Case management approaches in coordinated community-oriented long-term care demonstrations. *The Gerontologist, 26*, 398–404.

Capitman, J. A., Prottas, J., MacAdam, M. A., Leutz, W., Westwater, D., & Yee, D. (1988). A descriptive framework for new hospital roles in geriatric care. *Health Care Financing Review*. 1988 Annual Supplement. HCFA Pub. No. 03275. Office of Research and Demonstrations. Health Care Financing Administration, Washington, DC: U.S. Government Printing Office.

Capitman, J. A. (1990). Policy and program options in community oriented long-term care (pp. 357–388). *Annual Review of Geriatrics and Gerontology Vol. 9*. New York: Springer Publishing Co.

DeVito, C. A., & Zubkoff, W. (1985). The role of the acute care hospital in long-term care: A model program on South Miami Beach. *Journal of the Florida Medical Association, 72*, 258–262.

Entmacher, P. S., & Weil, J. B. (1988). Long term care insurance: An industry perspective. *Pride Institute Journal of Long Term Health Care, 7*, 25–28.

Firman, J. P. (1988). Long-term care insurance: Consumer issues for an emerging industry. *Pride Institute Journal of Long Term Home Health Care, 7*, 3–8.

Gornick, M., & Hall, M. J. (1988). Trends in medicare use of post-hospital care. *Health Care Financing Review: Annual Supplement*, 27–38.

Greenlick, M. R., Nonnenkamp, L. L., Gruenberg, L., Leutz, W., & Lamb, S. (1988). The S/HMO demonstration: Policy implications for long term care in HMOs. *Pride Institute Journal of Long Term Health Care, 7*, 15–24.

Kane, R. A., & Kane, R. L. (1987). *Long-term care: Principles, programs, and policies*. New York: Springer Publishing Co.

Kemper, P., Applebaum, R. A., & Harrigan, M. (1987). Community care demonstrations: What have we learned? *Health Care Financing Review. 8*, 87–100.

Laudicina, S. S., & Burwell, B. (1988). A profile of Medicaid home and community-based care waivers, 1985: Findings of a national survey. *Journal of Health, Politics, and Law, 13,* 525–546.

Leutz, W. N., Greenberg, J. N., Abrahams, R., Prottas, J., Diamnond, L. M., & Gruenberg, L. (1986). *Changing health care for an aging society: Planning for the social health maintenance organization.* Lexington: Lexington Books.

Leutz, W. N., Abrahams, R., Greenlick, M., Kune, R., & Prottas, J. (1988). Targeting expanded care to the aged: Early SHMO experience. *The Gerontologist, 28,* 4–17.

Lipson, D. J., Donohoe, E., & Thomas, C. (1988). *State financing of long-term care services for the elderly.* Washington DC: Intergovernmental Health Policy Project, George Washington University.

Liu, K., Manton, K. G., & Liu, B. M. (1989). Morbidity, Disability, and Long-Term Care of the Elderly: Implications for Public and Private Policies. Working paper #3773-03: The Urban Institute, Washington DC.

MacAdam, M., & Yee, D. (1989). Providing high quality services to the frail elderly: A study of homemaker services in greater Boston. Final Report to the Farnsworth Foundation, Sept. 1989.

MacAdam, M., Capitman, J., Yee, D., Prottas, J., Leutz, W., & Westwater, D. (1989). Case management for frail elders: Results from the Robert Wood Johnson Foundation's program for hospital initiatives in long-term care. *The Gerontologist, 29,* 737–744.

Manton, K. G. (1988). A longitudinal study of functional change and mortality in the United States. *Journal of Gerontology: Social Sciences, 43,* S153–S161.

Manton, K. G., & Hausner, T. (1987). A multidimensional approach to case mix for home health services. *Health Care Financing Review, 8,* 37–54.

Morrisey, M. A., Sloan, F. A., & Valvona, J. (1988). Medicare prospective payment and posthospital transfers to subacute care. *Medical Care, 26,* 685–699.

Norman, A. (1989). Home care goes flat. *The Older American, 14,* 2.

Omata, R., Pendleton, S., Capitman, J., & Leutz, W. (1989). A nationwide survey of state long-term care infrastructure. Working paper: Bigel Institute for Health Policy, Brandeis University.

Rubenstein, L. Z., Josephson, K., Wieland, G. D., English, P. A., Sayre, J. A., & Kane, R. L. (1984). Effectiveness of a geriatric evaluation unit: A randomized clinical trial. *New England Journal of Medicine, 311,* 1664–1670.

Saltz, C., McVey, L. J., Peter, M. B., John, R. F., & Harvey, J. C. (1988). Impact of a geriatric consultation team on discharge placement and repeat hospitalization. *The Gerontologist, 28,* 344–350.

Weissert, W. G., Cready, C. M., & Pawelak, J. E. (1988). The past and future of home- and community-based long-term care. *The Milbank Quarterly, 66,* 309–388.

Yordi, C. L. (1988). Case management in the social health maintenance organization demonstrations. *Health Care Financing Review: 1988 Annual Supplement,* 83–88.

8

The Institute of Medicine Study: Improving the Quality of Nursing Home Care

Catherine Hawes

In October 1983 the Health Care Financing Administration signed a contract with the Institute of Medicine (IOM) of the National Academy of Sciences for a study of nursing home quality and regulation. As a result, the IOM formed a Committee on Nursing Home Regulation whose charge was to undertake a study that would "serve as a basis for adjusting federal policies and regulations governing the certification of nursing homes so as to make those policies and regulations as appropriate and effective as possible" (IOM, 1986). The Committee's conclusions and recommendations, reported in *Improving the Quality of Care in Nursing Homes* (IOM, 1986), are generally considered to be the foundation of the nursing home reforms contained in the Omnibus Budget Reconciliation Act of 1987 (OBRA).

This chapter discusses the IOM Committee's study and recommendations, the OBRA reforms, and the likely effects on nursing homes and the residents who live there. These reforms, together with changes in the federal certification survey process as a result of *Smith* v. *Heckler*, 747 F.2nd 583 (10th Cir. 1984), represent the most significant reforms in the way the federal government regulates nursing homes since the inception of Medicare and Medicaid. They also hold the promise of dramatically improving the quality of care and life experienced by individuals who reside and receive care in nursing homes.

NURSING HOME REGULATION: 1960s THROUGH THE 1980s

Nursing homes entered the 1980s with a regulatory process that nearly all observers viewed as inadequate. States promulgate health and safety standards that all nursing homes must meet in order to receive an operating

147

license. However, the content of the licensure laws, the effectiveness of the inspection system, and the resources devoted to enforcement vary significantly from state to state. Until the passage of Medicare and Medicaid, there were no federal standards for nursing homes, and regulation was largely a state responsibility. However, the regulation in most states was widely viewed as weak and ineffective in ensuring quality.

The passage of Medicare and Medicaid in the mid-1960s dramatically changed the financing of long-term care, and with the flow of federal dollars came federal regulations. These too, however, failed to remedy fundamental quality problems. The original Medicare nursing home standards, promulgated for "extended care facilities" (ECFs), were not extended to skilled nursing facilities participating in the Medicaid program because so few homes could meet those standards. Instead, 1967 amendments to the Social Security Act authorized two new categories of nursing homes—skilled nursing facilities (SNFs) and intermediate care facilities (ICFs)—with different standards of care. As the Medicare program continued to limit its spending on nursing home care, and fewer and fewer Medicare beneficiaries received Medicare coverage for their stays in nursing homes, the role of Medicaid-certified SNFs and ICFs became more critical.

The development of Medicaid certification standards for SNFs (conditions of participation) and ICFs (standards of care) was fraught with controversy. The Congress and consumer advocates sought strict standards that would ensure the health and safety of residents. Further, they felt strong federal standards were essential to state reforms. Existing licensure standards were highly variable across states (with some having strong and some very weak standards); however, the laws generally were poorly enforced. Thus, the general view of reformers was that strict federal standards were also essential to improving state regulation, since any reforms in state standards were likely to follow key elements of federal standards.

Providers, on the other hand, resisted the concept that stringent regulation by government would ensure desirable quality, viewing the proposed standards as too rigid. States feared the costs of stringent standards. And nearly everyone was concerned about both the ability of many (perhaps even most) homes to meet strict standards and also the willingness of states and the federal government to insist that homes do so. As a result, the final SNF regulations were not issued until 1974, with ICF standards following in 1976.

Although it had taken years to develop final regulations for nursing homes participating in the Medicare and Medicaid programs, the standards finally issued by HEW in the mid-1970s were widely viewed as inadequate. In 1975, the U.S. Senate Committee on Aging estimated that at least 50% of the nation's nursing homes were substandard, that is, having one or more life-threatening conditions present (U.S. Senate, 1974). A study of nursing home quality conducted by the Department of Health Education and Welfare

(HEW—now the Department of Health and Human Services) found serious and widespread deficiencies. Based on inspection of facilities in 47 states and interviews with 3458 residents, HEW found overdrugging of residents, extensive medication errors (as much as 80% of all medications were improperly administered), inadequate medical attention, insufficient diets, and widespread failure to provide needed therapies (U.S. DHEW, 1975). States that investigated nursing homes, such as New York with its special investigation by the Moreland Act Commission, also found serious quality problems (New York State Moreland Act Commission, 1975; 1976).

As a result of the scandals about quality and the consistent criticism of the Medicare and Medicaid regulatory systems, substantial effort was expended on developing meaningful reforms during the Carter administration. For example, after considerable study, HEW proposed elevating compliance with residents' rights to the status of a Condition of Participation for the Medicare and Medicaid programs. Additionally, HEW recommended a single stronger set of standards for SNFs and ICFs and that care planning requirements be consolidated into a single condition, with the additional requirement that each nursing home have interdisciplinary assessment and care planning teams (e.g., Chow, 1977). However, the department promulgated formal regulations for only one of these reforms (the elevation of residents' rights) before the change from the Carter to Reagan administration. The Reagan administration promptly rescinded the new regulation on residents' rights, shelved the other recommendations, and undertook its own review of the Medicare and Medicaid regulations.

In May 1982 the Health Care Financing Administration (HCFA) of the department proposed a number of reforms to the regulations governing nursing homes that participate in the Medicare and/or Medicaid programs. These new reforms were generally considered in line with the Reagan administration's announced intention of reducing government intervention in the market and freeing industry from unnecessary regulation, as well as a direct response to nursing facility providers' complaints about the rigidity of the existing regulations. The proposed changes, for example, would have eased the requirement of at least annual inspections of all homes, and they abandoned enhanced regulations developed but not finally enacted by the Carter administration.

Consumers, groups representing the elderly, and advocates for nursing home residents, as well as many state regulatory agencies, opposed HCFA's proposed reforms. They argued that HCFA's proposals failed to address the fundamental flaws in nursing home regulation and would further erode what they viewed as already inadequate quality. This opposition and the controversy it engendered persuaded Congress to intervene. In the fall of 1982, Congress prohibited implementation of any HCFA nursing home proposals and mandated a HCFA study of how to improve nursing home regulation. That led to the HCFA contract with the IOM for its study.

THE IOM COMMITTEE AND ITS STUDY

The IOM selected a committee of 20 individuals with substantial and varied experience in long-term care to direct the 2-year study. The Committee was led by Dr. Sidney Katz, who developed the Katz Scale for measuring individual functional status in the activities of daily living. The committee included individuals with training in medicine, nursing, social work, health law, economics, health services research, public administration, and policy analysis and with experience as nursing home operators, consumer advocates, regulators, care providers, and researchers. The committee included:

Sidney Katz
Associate Dean of Medicine
Brown University

Carl E. Adams
Director
National Health Corporation

Allan Beigel
Professor of Psychiatry
University of Arizona

Judith F. Brown
Vice President of Professional Services
ARA Living Centers

Patricia A. Butler
attorney

Iris Freeman
Director
Nursing Home Residents' Advocates

Barry J. Gurland
Director
Center for Geriatrics and Gerontology
Columbia University

Charlene Harrington
Associate Professor
School of Nursing
University of California at San Francisco

Catherine Hawes
Senior Policy Analyst
Research Triangle Institute

Rosalie A. Kane
Professor
School of Social Work and Center for
   Health Services Research
University of Minnesota

Judith R. Lave
Professor
Graduate School of Public Health
University of Pittsburgh

Maurice I. May
Chief Executive Officer
Hebrew Rehabilitation Center for Aged

Dana L. Petrowsky
Chief, Division of Health Facilities
Iowa Department of Health

Sam Shapiro
Professor, Department of Health Services Administration
Johns Hopkins University

Peter W. Shaughnessy
Director
Center for Health Services Research
University of Colorado

June L. Sides
Consultant
Regency Health Centers, Inc.

Helen L. Smits
Associate Vice President for Health Affairs
University of Connecticut

David Alan Wagner
Vice President for Planning and Marketing
Trimark Corporation

Bruce C. Vladeck
President
United Hospital Fund of New York

May Louise Wykle
Associate Professor
Frances Payne Bolton School of Nursing
Case Western Reserve University

The committee divided into four working groups, with IOM professional staff assigned to each.[1] One group concentrated on issues related to defining and measuring nursing home quality, particularly in the context of a regulatory system. A second group focused on processes for monitoring nursing home performance, particularly certification surveys and inspection of care. The third group's work included reimbursement, bed supply, and other issues, such as training and professional certification or licensure, as they relate to nursing home quality. The fourth group focused on the role of consumer advocacy and management incentives as mechanisms for enhancing nursing home quality.

The committee and its workgroups set about four basic tasks. The first was to determine the status of quality of care and life in the nation's nursing homes. The second was to examine the existing regulatory system, identifying its strengths and weaknesses. Third, the Committee sought to determine what the state of the art was in defining, measuring, and assuring quality. Finally, the committee was charged with making recommendations designed to improve nursing home regulation. The committee endeavored to meet these various charges through a variety of activities, including:

- 5 public hearings across the country;
- interviews with regulators, ombudsmen, consumer advocates, nursing home owners and staff, trade associations, legislative staff, and others who are knowledgeable;
- case studies of regulation in 6 states;
- visits to nursing homes;
- a mail survey of regulatory agencies in 50 states plus the District of Columbia;
- review of 15 state nursing home investigatory commission reports and HCFA and congressional reports and hearings over the preceeding decade, as well as review of research;
- special conferences and workshops with invited papers by experts on such topics as quality assessment, Medicaid reimbursement policies and effects on quality, bed supply and effects on quality and regulation, staffing, consumer role in assuring quality, enforcement of regulations, and management incentives; and
- commissioned papers on numerous special topics related to improving nursing home quality.

THE IOM COMMITTEE'S CONCLUSIONS

The Committee announced 4 basic conclusions, based on the study findings and the knowledge and experience of the members:

[1]David Tilson (Staff Director), Robert Burke, Mike McGeary, Peter Reinecke, Susan Sherman, and Jane Takeuchi.

1. Quality of care and quality of life in many nursing homes are not satisfactory.
2. More effective government regulation can substantially improve quality in nursing homes. A stronger federal role is essential.
3. Specific improvements are needed in the regulatory system.
4. There are opportunities to improve quality of care in nursing homes that are independent of changes in the Medicaid payment policies or bed supply (IOM, 1986, pp. 21–22).

Inadequate Quality of Care and Life in Nursing Homes

Over the nearly quarter of a century of the Medicare and Medicaid programs, there have been hundreds of scandals about inadequate care and conditions in nursing homes and scores of reports faulting state and federal regulatory systems for these widespread failures. However, many providers, regulators, and consumer advocates concur that conditions have improved over the last 20 years. Many factors have combined to produce better nursing homes, including regulation (such as the life safety code, staffing requirements, and training), innovations in the survey process, advances in geriatrics and gerontology and increasing sophistication. Despite these improvements over the dire conditions found in the 1950s, 1960s and even the 1970s, the committee found that serious quality problems persist.

Public testimony at committee hearings, state and federal reports about deficiencies, recent research studies, newspaper exposés, and the committee's own case studies and visits to nursing homes revealed widespread inadequacies in quality of care and quality of life. For example, state investigations reviewed by the committee found:

- in Virginia, nursing homes had an average of 23 deficiencies per home in minimum health and safety standards (Virginia, 1978);
- in Missouri, 25% of the nursing homes failed to meet minimum health standards (Missouri, 1978);
- in Texas, 33% of the facilities violated minimum dietary standards (Texas, 1977), and a subsequent study of 113 Texas facilities found 25% had inadequate interior maintenance (e.g., cracked peeling paint, water leaks, broken windows) and 33% had offensive odors (Texas, 1979);
- in Ohio, 25% of the facilities spent less on food than the USDA estimated as the *minimum* cost of a diet adequate to meet nutritional needs of older persons and an investigatory commission estimated between 15 and 20% of the facilities were seriously substandard (Ohio, 1978, 1979).

Unfortunately, these findings were not limited to only a few states. While there were improvements in many nursing homes and while most nursing homes met at least minimum standards, studies found that quality of care varied widely from facility to facility (Mech, 1980; Ohio, 1979). Life-threatening conditions persisted in a minority of homes, and even in adequate homes, there were care problems and inadequate attention to residents' quality of life. Studies in California and Missouri found evidence of neglect and abuse leading to premature death (San Jose *Mercury News*, May 1986; Wood & Pepper, 1988). These studies and others also found overuse of psychotropic drugs and physical restraints; inadequate medical care and therapies; lack of appropriate attention to restorative care, residents' psychosocial well-being, and mental health; insufficient activities; and infringements of residents' rights were problems across the country (California, 1982; Colorado, 1977; Connecticut, 1976 & 1980; Florida, 1981; Garibaldi, Brodine, & Matsumiya, 1981; Kane et al., 1979; Himmelstein, Jones, & Woolhandler, 1983; Irvine, Van Buren, & Crossley, 1984; Ray et al., 1980; Vladeck, 1980).

In essence, the evidence presented to the committee demonstrated that while many homes were found to provide excellent care and a majority at least acceptable care, appalling conditions still occur in a sizable minority of homes. Moreover, serious inadequacies exist in many nursing homes, and improvements are needed in most homes. Subsequent to the committee's analysis, a study by the General Accounting Office found that numerous homes continued to operate year after year with the same or similar violations and suggested that the norm of care was declining during the 1980s, along with reductions in resources devoted to regulation at both the federal and state levels (U.S. GAO, 1987). Thus, the IOM Committee and subsequently the Congress concluded that in terms of what is both possible and desirable in nursing homes, improvements in quality of care and quality of life are needed. As the committee observed:

> These observations do not mean that the picture of American nursing homes is entirely gloomy or that the regulatory efforts of the past decade have been entirely unsuccessful. Today, many institutions consistently deliver excellent care. Good care can be observed in all parts of the country; it exists under widely varying reimbursement systems and all types of ownership. Such facilities serve both as evidence that overall performance can be improved and as markers for how that improvement can be accomplished. (IOM, 1986, p. 4)

Inadequate Regulation

Like prior studies, the IOM Committee concluded that many of the substandard conditions in nursing homes were able to occur because of failures in public policy, particularly in the regulatory system governing nursing homes (Arkansas, 1978; Bardach, 1983; California, 1983; Connecticut, 1980;

Florida, 1981; Illinois, 1984; Michigan, 1981; Missouri, 1978; New Jersey, 1978; New York, 1975). A regulatory system has three basic components: the standards or criteria used to specify what a nursing home must do to provide acceptable care; the monitoring process by which the regulator can determine whether homes are in compliance with standards; and the mechanisms used to ensure compliance with standards. Like other prior studies, the IOM Committee found all three components of federal regulation of nursing homes to be inadequate.

The standards required of homes participating in the Medicare and Medicaid programs were widely faulted for four basic failings. First, the standards represented "minimums" the facility had to meet, and many argued that those minimums, particularly in requirements on staffing, mental health care, and residents' rights, were too low to define and assure acceptable quality. Second, states criticized the federal standards for a lack of clarity on key items, such as that staffing must be "adequate to meet the needs of residents." This ambiguity left surveyors with too little formal guidance and too much latitude for individual judgement, a situation that contributed to inconsistencies among surveyors and difficulties in enforcing survey findings.

The third major criticism was that the standards focused almost solely on structural criteria and the "inputs" that facilities must provide. The implicit assumption was that if a facility met these standards, it had the capacity to provide appropriate care—and that capacity would translate into the actual provision of appropriate care. As a result, both the standards and the surveys based on them relied too much on a facility's paper compliance with standards covering issues such as staffing levels, door widths, documentation of medication passes, and records of patient care. Yet neither the standards nor the survey addressed what actually happened to the resident on a day-to-day basis. Of the nearly 600 items on the certification survey, only a handful required direct observation of the residents, and neither the standards nor the survey focused on resident outcomes. Thus, for example, the facility's record about a resident's care and condition ("resident was groomed and bathed") took precedence over the clear physical evidence of dirty, unkempt hair, an unwashed body and torn, soiled clothing (Ohio, 1978; New York, 1976).

Finally, the standards were criticized for adhering too closely to a medical model of long-term care. The committee argued that while nursing home residents require expert medical assessment and care, the current standards not only fail to ensure that, they ignore many other important aspects of high quality long-term care. As the New York Moreland Act Commission (1976) argued, the existing regulations did not capture the essential requirements of nursing facilities as *homes*.

The IOM Committee saw these failings manifested in several concrete ways. The committee argued that the standards failed to attend to resident outcomes and to specifying clearly the processes of care that would lead to improved resident outcomes. In addition, the committee found substantial evidence that both physical and chemical restraints were being used inappropriately, that is nontherapeutically, in many nursing homes, and that existing standards did not address these issues. Finally, the committee concluded that federal certification standards failed to address adequately several critical aspects of quality, including residents' rights, psychosocial well-being, and other elements of quality of life.

The inadequacies in the standards were mirrored in the survey process which was geared to measure compliance with those standards. However, the survey process was also criticized on several additional counts. In addition to focusing too much on paper compliance and requiring little observation of the actual care and condition of residents, the surveys occurred on such a predictable schedule (or were actually announced in advance) that few observers expressed any confidence that the conditions observed during an annual survey were representative of what occurred in many facilities during the remaining 360 days of a year. Particularly in homes with a reputation of providing poor care, the practice of presurvey "clean-up, fix-up and staff-up" for the three weeks around the annual survey schedule were reported as common occurrences. Further, for the most part, homes with few problems receive nearly the same type and frequency of inspections as homes with a history of poor care and deficiencies.

The survey process was also viewed as ineffective because of inconsistency among the surveyors in the licensure and certification agencies, as well as inconsistency and lack of coordination between that agency and others responsible for a range of inspections of nursing homes. Finally, nearly half the states that conducted investigations during the 1975–1985 decade reported both inadequate resources for staffing and also for training of survey staff.

The committee also concluded that remedies for noncompliance and enforcement of standards were another weak component in the regulatory system. Even if the standards and monitoring components of the federal regulatory system had been ideal, the ineffectiveness of the enforcement mechanisms would impede the government's attempts to ensure facility compliance with standards. The basic problem with the enforcement component of the system was that it relied almost solely on termination of the facility's Medicare/Medicaid provider agreement (or "decertification") as a sanction for noncompliance. In effect, this was the "atomic bomb" approach to enforcement—a sanction considered too harsh to be used for all but the most serious deficiencies but, for a variety of reasons, seldom used even for those.

Facilities recognized that the government was reluctant to use its main sanction and decertify providers. Moreover, even when the government undertook termination of a provider agreement (decertification), the facility could postpone the action for long periods of time through a series of legal appeals. Further, if a facility came into compliance on the last day of the last possible appeal, punitive action, including decertification, was typically dropped. Whatever the effect on facilities with a history of either good or mediocre performance, the message of this enforcement system to "bad actors" was that there was little the Medicaid program could or would do to ensure that poor facilities would correct deficiencies and maintain compliance. Thus, the committee, like other studies, found facilities with a history of poor care and noncompliance had little incentive to meet standards for more than a few days or weeks at any given time; moreover, such bad actors continued to operate year after year, virtually without penalty.

THE IOM COMMITTEE'S RECOMMENDATIONS AND OBRA '87

While the committee concluded that there were serious and widespread inadequacies in both quality of care and quality of life and in the federal regulation of nursing homes, it also concluded that these situations were amenable to improvement. The committee argued that some improvement in quality will continue to come about as a result of increasing professionalism and skill among providers. Additional improvements in quality will come with research and increasing knowledge about effective interventions for the chronic diseases and disabilities that are experienced by residents in nursing homes. However, the committee also argued that improvements in the regulatory system were essential to improving and assuring more uniform quality of care, and the committee made a number of concrete recommendations for how this could be accomplished. And the Congress largely concurred with these recommendations.

The members of Congress and their staff, who had been largely responsible for pressuring the administration to conduct a study of how to improve nursing home regulation, maintained their commitment to enhancing quality and the effectiveness of Medicare and Medicaid regulations. When the committee reported its findings and recommendations, several members of Congress responded with bills encompasing some of the recommendations. Congressmen Waxman (D-CA) and Pepper (D-FL) and Senators Mitchell (D-MA) and Heinz (R-PA), in particular, introduced extensive reform bills. These came together in the nursing home reform package included in the Omnibus Budget Reconciliation Act of 1987 (OBRA). This package contained the vast majority of the committee's recommendations and represents the most substantial changes in both standards and the regulatory process since the inception of federal funding and regulation of nursing homes.

Regulations

The committee's first set of recommendations addressed regulatory criteria— the standards of performance expected of facilities that wish to participate in the Medicare and Medicaid programs. The committee made 9 major recommendations about specific changes in the existing standards, and OBRA '87 mandated most of them. First, as the Committee recommended, the regulatory distinction between SNFs and ICFs is abolished. The 2 classes of homes and standards were originally intended to serve different resident populations—at least in terms of nursing and rehabilitative care needs. However, the committee found that states had largely used this nominal distinction between SNFs and ICFs to set differential Medicaid payment rates and control their expenditures. In practice the distinction between whether a facility is a SNF or ICF often means little in terms of the actual mix of residents and their care needs, as well as in terms of the staff resources needed to provide appropriate care.[1] Thus, the committee and Congress concluded that only one set of standards is needed and that given the increasingly complex and serious mix of diseases, disabilities, and needs among residents, the new standards should be based on the generally stronger SNF conditions of participation.[2] In particular, a registered nurse should be on duty at least one shift each day in every facility.

The IOM Committee and Congress also concurred about the importance of resident assessment as the foundation of both improvements in the quality of care and life provided to residents and also in the regulatory system. As the committee noted,

> Providing high-quality care requires careful assessment of each resident's functional, medical, mental, and psychosocial status . . .[T]he development of individual plans of care clearly depend on resident assessment. (IOM, 1986, p. 74)

Beginning in October 1990, each nursing home participating in the Medicare or Medicaid program must assess residents on admission and at least annually thereafter using a uniform assessment instrument. The assessments are to be updated quarterly, as well as upon any significant change in a resident's functional status. Moreover, Congress gave HCFA very specific directions to develop a *comprehensive* assessment system. OBRA specified that

[1]For example, data from the Medicare and Medicaid surveys in 1981 show that of 427 certified facilities in Iowa, 402 were ICF only. In Oklahoma, 354 of the 363 homes are ICFs. In California, on the other hand, only 36 of 1184 homes are ICFs (IOM, 1986, p. 356). As the committee observed, it is "highly improbable" that this variation in the certification status of homes is associated with genuine differences in the state's population and residents' requirements for services (IOM, 1986, p. 73).

[2]In OBRA and the newly issued Interpretive Guidelines issued by HCFA, the term "conditions of participation" has been replaced by "requirements."

the resident assessment system must consider the multidimensional strengths and needs of residents and cover a wide range of domains relevant to appropriate care planning.

HCFA entered into a contract for the development of the resident assessment system with Research Triangle Institute and its subcontractors, the Hebrew Rehabilitation Center for Aged, Brown University, and the University of Michigan (Hawes et al., 1988). HCFA charged the project team with developing an assessment system that focuses on factors affecting residents' functional status and that will guide care planning in facilities. While developing an assessment that guides care planning is the primary project task, the team has also been directed to develop a plan for creating a database from the resident-specific information. This resident-specific information, with baseline and change measures of resident status, will facilitate the development of outcome norms, criteria for evaluating facilities, and a resident-focused survey process.

The committee and Congress also concurred on the importance of focusing the attention of providers and regulators on the quality of life experienced by residents, as well as making the regulations more resident-centered and outcome-oriented. New requirements, comparable in importance to the old conditions of participation, were added on quality of care, quality of life, and residents' rights. They clarify the government's expectation that each resident is to receive high quality of care to assure their physical, mental and psychosocial well-being. Further, the new requirements recognize and detail expectations about specific residents' rights, autonomy, the environment, and other aspects of quality of life. OBRA specified 18 areas to be included in the quality of care requirement, and the Interpretive Guidelines for surveyors developed by HCFA clarify the requirements, addressing such process issues as assessment, care planning, and service provision (appropriate treatment, restorative care, and prevention) in such key areas of care as decubitus, urinary continence, activities, psychosocial well-being, use of restraints, use of psychotropics, falls, range of motion, and activities of daily living.

Training of nursing assistants or aides in nursing facilities was also a focus of both committee and congressional attention. Beginning in October 1990 all nurse's aides must complete a state-approved training course and demonstrate their competence prior to providing hands-on care to residents. In OBRA 1989, which included technical amendments to OBRA '87, Congress permitted states to waive competency evaluations for aides who have worked for the same nursing home employer for 24 consecutive months. Further, OBRA '89 delays the 75-hour training requirement of OBRA '87. Now, states are directed to deem aides as trained and qualified those who, prior to July 1989 have received 60 hours of training (including 15 hours of inservice) or received 100 hours of training and demonstrated their competence in some way. There is little disagreement with the concept that aides ought to receive training and demonstrate competence in basic care giving prior to providing hands-on care to residents. However, as discussed in the next section, many aspects of implementing this recommendation have generated significant controversy and illustrate the difficulty of achieving reform and high quality of care.

The committee also addressed a number of other issues that met with mixed success in Congress. The committee and OBRA both addressed such issues as social work staffing, although OBRA's requirements were less than the committee's recommendations. The Congress also did not adopt the IOM Committee's recommendation that federal law prohibit nursing homes from setting different standards or criteria for admission, transfer, discharge, and services to residents based on their source of payment. Thus, the discrimination experienced by individuals whose care is paid for by the Medicaid program remains to be addressed.

One of the more difficult aspects of the committee's deliberations was the issue of cost—the price tag of the recommendations. The committee members discussed this issue and their role in this regard at considerable length. Clearly, the committee recognized the existence of the 1980s changed political climate and its pressing fiscal realities. On the other hand, the committee was charged with making recommendations for improving the quality of nursing home care and the effectiveness of regulation. It was not charged with estimating costs nor, more importantly, with deciding what trade-offs were appropriate. Those decisions are intensely political—issues of values, policy priorities, and political will. In essence, the committee felt that these issues were largely outside its proper domain. The committee viewed its task as one which demanded careful, responsible consideration of a variety of policy alternatives and the selection of those for which there was widespread consensus. It also felt a responsibility to recommend that Medicare and Medicaid rates be adjusted to reflect any new requirements that would produce new costs for providers, as well as recommending more funds for the states to enhance their regulatory systems. Congress carefully considered the costs of all its mandates, and OBRA specified that Medicare and Medicaid payment for nursing home care should be adjusted, if necessary, to cover new costs associated with OBRA regulations.

Monitoring Nursing Home Performance

The IOM and OBRA also addressed issues related to making the survey or inspection process more effective, including making the timing of surveys less predictable. Further, the survey process will include both a "standard" and an extended survey. The basic idea is that the standard survey is resident-oriented and focuses not on the capacity of the home to provide acceptable care but instead on its actual performance. Rather than spending days examining nursing home records, the standard survey is to focus on key indicators of process and outcome quality. Interviews with residents and observation of their condition and care are important elements of the standard survey. Only if a facility "fails" the standard survey process would it be subjected to an extended survey. (That extended survey examines both process quality and structural features of the home's operation in some detail, on the assumption that failure to provide acceptable quality in terms of key quality indicators is associated with a failure in the structural aspects of the facility's organization. In addition, a sample of all facilities will also receive an extended survey each year.) The goal of the two-tiered survey process is to use the standards survey (which uses resident-focused, outcome and process quality measures to evaluate nursing home performance) as the usual process. Then the presumably lengthier and more comprehensive extended survey process would be used only for those facilities with apparently serious problems.

The committee and Congress agreed that state survey agencies should not be responsible for certifying that state-owned facilities are in compliance with Medicaid standards. Finally, the IOM Committee issued a number of other recommendations designed to strengthen the state survey agencies capacity and to produce more reliable and consistent surveys. Some were mandated in OBRA, while others have been adopted by HCFA. One important reform, for example, involves enhanced federal funding for the survey activities related to OBRA. The committee also recommended much more extensive training for surveyors to increase the validity and consistency of surveyors' decisions. HCFA's Health Standards Quality Bureau has expended considerable effort on this and on the Interpretive Guidelines, working also with clinical experts, consumer advocates, and other groups participating in a Quality of Care Coalition to develop meaningful Interpretive Guidelines and training materials on such key elements as residents' rights and environmental assessments. The HCFA-funded resident assessment project is also charged with developing protocols and training materials to assist surveyors in evaluating the accuracy of assessments and adequacy of care plans. The purpose of this process is to enhance the consistency of surveyor judgements.

Enforcing Compliance with Federal Standards

The IOM Committee consistently viewed the regulatory system as a "three-legged stool," that is, one which relies on equally strong components of standards, inspections/monitoring, and enforcement. Without any one of those three, the system would fail. Thus, the committee and Congress concurred that the federal government and states should have (and use) a range of "intermediate" sanctions for addressing noncompliance among nursing facilities. These enforcement mechanisms include a ban preventing new admissions to the facility, civil fines, and the imposition of receivership, under which the facility is operated by a court-appointed receiver until life-threatening conditions can be corrected or all residents can be safely moved.

Other IOM Committee Recommendations

While the Congress and HCFA incorporated many of the committee's recommendations, some that went beyond the Medicare and Medicaid certification system have yet to be formally incorporated in government long-term care policy. Most significantly, the committee's recommendations for strengthening the ombudsman program have not been implemented. In addition, some issues the committee identified as requiring additional study have yet to be addressed by the Department of Health and Human Services.

The committee recommended that DHHS undertake a study to design a system for acquiring and using resident assessment data. This is being done as part of the HCFA-funded project to develop a uniform resident assessment system (Hawes et al., 1988).

The committee also recommended further study of Medicaid payment policies and how they can be structured to enhance quality of care. The committee found that prior research findings were insufficient to generate recommendations about how to structure Medicaid payment policies. To date, the research funded by HCFA has been promising but not met the goals of the IOM Committee. HCFA's Office of Research and Demonstrations has funded a demonstration of case mix payment systems, with an emphasis on the effects on quality of care (Cornelius, 1989). HCFA also funded a broader comparison of alternative payment systems that focused on the effects of prospective payment systems compared to those in which the payment is case mix–adjusted (Schlenker, 1988); however, this study concentrated primarily on effects on case mix and cost with much less attention to and adequate measures of quality. Thus, the prior study has insufficient information about effects on quality, and the new demonstration, while focusing directly on quality, will be examining only one type of payment system. Therefore, additional study is needed.

The committee also examined the effect of nursing home bed supply on quality and the effectiveness of regulation. However, the relationship between bed supply and quality is hardly clear, and the regulators' argument that enforcement of regulations was difficult in conditions of tight bed supply often seemed more self-serving than a real limitation. In addition, the issue of bed supply and quality is complicated by its relationship to the other complex, interrelated issues, such as developing a continuum of home and community-based services and controlling long-term care costs. Thus, the committee felt uncomfortable about making policy recommendations on this issue without the benefit of additional, well focused studies. To date, HCFA has not funded such studies.

THE LIKELY EFFECT OF THE
NURSING HOME REFORMS

The IOM recommendations are clearly the most comprehensive reforms to date in the Medicare and Medicaid programs and will undoubtedly have a significant effect on quality of care and quality of life for nursing home residents. Implementation of most of the IOM recommendations and OBRA mandates will not occur until October 1990; thus, we have not yet had an opportunity to observe their effects on quality of care and life. However, early field tests of the new resident assessment system have found that nurses using the system have discovered new information about residents, information they find very relevant to good, individualized care planning and believe will improve quality of care (Morris et al., 1990). Indeed, some facilities participating in the field test altered residents' care plans as a result of what they discovered from the assessments. To those working on the assessment system, this is an exceptionally encouraging early result and suggests the system may indeed achieve its goal of improving quality. Others, such as consumer advocates, are confident that many of the other IOM and OBRA provisions will have positive effects on the performance of both homes and regulatory agencies.

Despite general consensus about the importance of the reforms and their likely beneficial effect on quality of care, there are some serious problems with the IOM recommendations and OBRA reforms. First, the IOM study and OBRA recommendations did not address factors that appear to be important to achieving uniformly high quality of care for nursing home residents. Some of these omissions may limit the effectiveness of the reforms that have been adopted. Second, some of the IOM recommendations and OBRA reforms were poorly thought out and have provisions that may limit the effectiveness of the reforms. Third, there may be inadequate funding attached to the reforms to assure their successful implementation; this is an issue involving both real fiscal constraints and the political will and commitment of Congress and the state governments, which bear much responsibility for implementing and enforcing federal legislation. Fourth, the regular operations and normal imperatives of regulatory agencies may impede effective implementation of the reforms. And finally, there is continuing political opposition to many of the reforms.

The IOM recommendation and OBRA reform requiring training of nurse's aides illustrates the problem of inadequacy in the design of a reform. Because nursing assistants provide more than 80% of the hands-on care of residents, having trained and competent aides is clearly essential to high quality of care and quality of life for nursing home residents. However, implementing this without addressing adequate pay and working conditions, as well as other factors that would reduce staff turnover for these critical personnel, is clearly problematic. Further, the implementation of this reform has been fraught with controversy and problems. There is no provision addressing payment for the training, and many observers argue that it is inequitable to ask individuals who earn little more than minimum wage to pay for the training; moreover, such personnel may not be able to forego income from working while they are taking the training course. In addition, the issue of competency testing has raised serious questions about how to address the issue of aides who are not literate and those for whom English is not a first language. Finally, in some states, there has been a battle between agencies, such as the Health Department and Education Department, over which has the authority to certify training courses and competency tests for the nursing assistants. Such problems point not only to the problem of policymakers omitting important considerations from the recommendations and legislation but also to the difficulty of successfully implementing policies.

Unfortunately, factors that may curtail the effectiveness of the IOM recommendations and OBRA reforms are not limited to aide training. For years, observers have argued that nursing home care was the most troubled and troubling segment of the health care sector, experiencing significant problems in access, quality and cost, as well as financing. The IOM study and its recommendations, as well as Congress in OBRA '87, addressed only one aspect of these complex and interrelated problems. The fundamental issue of access problems for both individuals with heavy care needs (especially for high technology care and for dementia patients with problem behaviors) and also for those who rely on Medicaid remain largely untouched by federal public policy, despite the IOM Committee's recommendations.

The IOM Committee also did not address issues of cost, financing, and payment for nursing home care. These issues were outside the direct charge of the Committee and considerably beyond the scope of the HCFA contract. Nevertheless, they are clearly related to quality issues. The committee did examine the effects of Medicaid and Medicare payment systems on quality. While there is what appears to be unequivocal evidence about the perverse incentives and quality problems with some types of systems (e.g., "flat rate" payment systems), the evidence about what produces good or improved care is much less clear. Further, the committee did investigate the relationship between cost and quality, and the empirical evidence suggests the relationship is positive but very weak (Schlenker, 1984; Hawes & Phillips, 1986).

While the result needs careful interpretation, it does point up the difficulty of improving nursing home quality with simple (or simplistic) interventions.

The persistent concern that some states do not provide a Medicaid rate that is sufficient to pay for adequate quality of care remains a major issue, whatever the characteristics of the payment system. Given the lack of evidence for how to improve quality with changes in payment systems and/or rates, the committee chose to recommend further study; however, as noted, the type of systematic comparisons and evaluations called for are not being funded. And unless and until public policy can adequately grasp and use one of the potentially most important mechanisms for affecting nursing home performance, quality improvements may be more difficult to achieve.

Financing long-term care is also a major unresolved issue and one clearly beyond the scope of the IOM study. Most proponents of improved financing mechanisms for nursing home care support financing reforms because of the difficulties most older and disabled persons face in coping with the high cost of long stays in nursing homes and the problems of relying primarily on a public welfare system (Medicaid) as a means of providing public financing. This system requires the elderly to become impoverished before receiving any assistance, provides financing mainly for institutional rather than home and community-based care, and consumes so much of the Medicaid program's funds that it threatens the benefits designed for other recipients— poor children and their mothers. In addition, the access problems faced by Medicaid recipients—and the general conclusion that facilities with high Medicaid censuses provide poorer quality of care—make this a pressing issue, independently of concerns about the impoverishment of the elderly who need long-term care (Hawes & Phillips, 1986; Phillips & Hawes, 1987; IOM, 1986). While the IOM Committee did address the later issue (as one related to quality) with its recommendation for a ban on discrimination against Medicaid recipients, as noted earlier, the Congress did not concur.

The issue of nursing home costs also arises in relation to the resources available to and used by state and federal agencies to regulate nursing homes. The IOM Committee made a number of concrete recommendations about enhancing regulatory capacity and resources, but it is unclear that these will be adequately translated into public policy. Despite the offer of an enhanced federal "match" (the ratio of federal dollars from HCFA to match state dollars for approved activities) to states for implementing OBRA, regulatory agencies in many states remain understaffed. Moreover, many are expressing serious reservations about their ability to implement OBRA reforms (Simmons, 1990). Further, there is concern about the ability and willingness of the federal government to provide sufficient training and support for state surveyors, as well to monitor their performance.

Some state Medicaid agencies are also concerned about the consequences of OBRA implementation for Medicaid costs (Parker, 1989). While the

Congress directed that Medicare and Medicaid rates be adjusted to reflect new costs associated with new OBRA requirements, some Medicaid directors have expressed reservations about actually increasing Medicaid expenditures on nursing homes in a time of fiscal constraints. Reports from the nursing home industry assert that some Medicaid directors have said privately that homes will have to sue the state (under the Boren Amendment provisions) if they want higher rates for OBRA implementation (Klejbuk, 1990). Many observers argue that such fiscal constraints on the Medicaid program threaten the ability of nursing homes and the state regulatory agencies to implement both the letter of OBRA and the spirit of IOM recommendations.

While these limitations are important, there is also clear evidence that many individuals and agencies are dedicated to implementing these reforms and improving the quality of care and life experienced by nursing home residents. Moreover, though limited, the reforms recommended by the IOM and enacted by the Congress *are* major advances in long-term care. Even if limited by the factors discussed above, their effect will be to improve quality. Further, those dedicated to reform in long-term care are encouraged by these reforms, viewing them as the most important yet enacted and a sound foundation for further improvements.

REFERENCES

Arkansas General Assembly. (1978). *Nursing Home Study, 1978: Evaluation of State Regulation, Volumes 2 and 3*, The Legislative Joint Performance Review Committee, Little Rock, Arkansas.

Bardach, E. (1983, October). Enforcement and policing. Paper presented at the Association of Public Policy and Management, Philadelphia.

California Auditor General, Department of Health Services. (1982). *Long-Term Care Facilities*. Sacramento, CA.

California Commission on State Government Organization and Economy. (1983, August). *The Bureaucracy of Care: Continuing Policy Issues for Nursing Home Services and Regulation*. Sacramento, CA: State of California.

Chow, R. K. (1977). Development of a patient appraisal and care evaluation system for long–term care. *The Journal of Long-Term Care Administration*, 5, 12–17.

Colorado Attorney General's Office. (1977). Report of the Attorney General Concerning the Regulation of the Nursing Home Industry in the State of Colorado.

Connecticut, Governor's Blue Ribbon Nursing Home Commission. (1976). Report of the Blue Ribbon Committee to Investigate the Nursing Home Industry in Connecticut. Hartford, CT.

Connecticut, Governor's Blue Ribbon Nursing Home Commission. (1980). Report of the Blue Ribbon Committee to Investigate the Nursing Home Industry in Connecticut. Hartford, Connecticut.

Cornelius, J. Office of Demonstrations and Evaluations, Health Care Financing Administration, Baltimore, Maryland. (1989). Personal communication with author about the design of HCFA demonstration on case mix payment systems and quality.

Covert, A., Rodrigues, T., & Soloman, K. (1977). The Use of Mechanical and Chemical Restraints in Nursing Homes. *Journal of the American Geriatrics Society, 25*, 85–89.

Florida Department of Health and Rehabilitative Services, Office of the Inspector General (1981, September). *Nursing Home Evaluative Report.* Tallahassee, FL

Garibaldi, R. A., Brodine, S., & Matsumiya, S. (1981, September). Infections in Nursing Homes: Policies, Prevalence, and Problems, *New England Journal of Medicine, 305*, 731–735.

Harrington, C. & Grant, L. (1985). Nursing Home Bed Supply, Access, and Quality of Care. Unpublished paper, University of California Aging and Health Policy Center, San Francisco, CA.

Hawes, C., Morris, J., Mor, V., Fries, B., Phillips, C., & Drugovich, M. (1988). Development of a Resident Assessment System and Database for Nursing Home Residents. Proposal submitted to the Health Care Financing Administration. Research Triangle Park, North Carolina: Research Triangle Institute.

Hawes, C. & Phillips, C. (1986). The Changing Structure of the Nursing Home Industry and the Impact of Ownership on Quality, Cost, and Access. In Gray, B. (Ed.), *For-Profit Enterprise in Health Care.* Washington, DC: National Academy Press.

Himmelstein, D. U., Jones, A. A., Woolhandler, S. (1983, August). Hypernatremic Dehydration in Nursing Home Patients: An Indicator of Neglect. *Journal of the American Geriatrics Society, 31*, 466–472.

Howard, J. (1977). Medication Procedure in a Nursing Home: Abuse of PRN Orders. *Journal of the American Geriatrics Society, 25*, 83–84.

Illinois Legislative Investigating Commission. (1984). *Regulation and Funding of Illinois Nursing Homes.* Springfield, Il.

Institute of Medicine. (1986). *Improving the Quality of Care in Nursing Homes.* Washington, DC: National Academy Press.

Irvine, P. W., Van Buren, N. & Crossley, K. (1984, February). Causes for Hospitalization of Nursing Home Residents: The Role of Infection. *Journal of the American Geriatrics Society, 32*, 103–107.

Kane, R. (1981, October). Assuring Quality of Care and Quality of Life in Long-Term Care. *Quality Review Bulletin, 7*, 3–10.

Kane, R., Kane, R., Kleffel, D., et al. (1979). *The PSRO and the Nursing Home, Volume 1: An Assessment of PSRO Long-Term Care Review.* Report submitted to the Health Care Financing Administration, U.S. Department of Health, Education, and Welfare, under contract No. 500-78-0040.

Klejbuk, C. (1990). Pennsylvania Association of Non-Profit Homes for the Aging. Personal communication with author.

Linn, M. W. (1974). Predicting Quality of Patient Care in Nursing Homes. *The Gerontologist 14*, 225–227.

Linn, M. W., Gurel, L., & Linn, B. S. (1977, April). Patient Outcome as a Measure of Quality of Nursing Home Care. *American Journal of Public Health 67*, 337–344.

Mech, A. B. (1980, March). Evaluating the Process of Nursing Care in Long-Term Care Facilities. *Quality Review Bulletin 6*, 24–30.

Michigan Department of Public Health (1981). Division of Health Facilities Certification and Licensure Management and Operations Review. Report to the Bureau of Health Care Administration, Plante and Moran, Consultants, Inc., Lansing, Michigan.

Michoki, R. J., & Lamy, P. P. (1976, July). The Problem of Pressure Sores in a Nursing Home Population: Statistical Data. *Journal of the American Geriatrics Society 24*, 323–328.

Miller, M. B. (1975, August). Iatrogenic and Nursigenic Effects of Prolonged Immobilization of the Ill Aged. *Journal of the American Geriatrics Society 23*, 360–369.

Miller, M. B., & Elliott, D. F. (1976, March). Errors and Omissions in Diagnostic Records on Admission of Patients to a Nursing Home. *Journal of the American Geriatrics Society*, 106–116.

Minnesota Senate and House Select Committee on Nursing Homes. (1976, January). Final Report, Minnesota State Legislature, St. Paul, MI.

Missouri State Senate, Health Care Committee. (1978). *Nursing and Boarding Home Licensing in Missouri*. Jefferson City, MI.

National Citizens Coalition for Nursing Home Reform. (1985). *A Consumer Perspective on Quality Care: The Residents' Point of View*. Washington, DC.

New Jersey State Nursing Home Commission. (1978). *Report on Long-Term Care*. Trenton, NJ.

New York State Moreland Act Commission. (1975). *Regulating Nursing Home Care: The Paper Tigers*.

New York State Moreland Act Commission. (1976). *Long-Term Care Regulation: Past Lapses, Future Prospects*.

Ohio Nursing Home Commission. (1978). *A Program in Crisis: Interim Report*. Ohio General Assembly, Columbus, OH.

Ohio Nursing Home Commission. (1979). *A Program in Crisis: Blueprint for Action, Final Report of the Ohio Nursing Home Commission*. Ohio General Assembly, Columbus, OH.

Parker, P. (1989). Interagency Board on Quality Assurance, Minneapolis, MI. Personal communication with author.

Phillips, C., & Hawes, C. (1987). Discrimination by Nursing Homes Against Medicaid Recipients: The Potential Impact of Equal Access Legislation on the Industry's Profitability. Contract report to the American Association of Retired Persons, Washington, DC.

Ray, W. A., Federspiel, C. F., & Schaffner, W. (1980, May). A Study of Anti-Psychotic Drug Use in Nursing Homes: Epidemiological Evidence Suggesting Misuse. *American Journal of Public Health, 70*, 485–491.

San Jose Mercury News. (1986, November 9–12). No Place to Die: California's Nursing Homes, la.

Schlenker, R. E. (1984, November 10). *Nursing Home Reimbursement, Quality, and Access—A Synthesis of Research*. Prepared for the Institute of Medicine Conference on Reimbursement, Anaheim, CA.

Schlenker, R. (1988). Center for Health Services Research, University of Colorado Health Sciences Center, Denver, CO. Personal communication with author.

Simmons, M. (1988). President, Association of Health Facility Licensure and Certification Directors, Denver, Colorado. Personal communication with author.

Smith v. Heckler. (1984). 747 F. 2nd 583 (10th Cir.).

Texas Nursing Home Task Force. (1979). *Report on Nursing Homes to the Attorney General of the State of Texas*. Austin, TX.

Texas Senate, Subcommittee on Public health and Welfare, Office of the Attorney General of the State of Texas. (1977). Report on Texas Nursing Homes to John Hill, Attorney General. Austin, TX.

U.S. Department of Health, Education and Welfare, Office of Nursing Home

Affairs (1975, July). Long-Term Care Facility Improvement Study: Introductory Report. Washington, DC.

U.S. Department of Health and Human Services. (1981). Health Standards Quality Bureau, unpublished analysis of 1981 (Medicare and Medicaid Automated Certification Survey) data, Washington, DC.

U.S. Senate, Special Committee on Aging. (1974). Subcommittee on Long-Term Nursing Home Care in the United States: Failure in Public Policy. Washington, DC: U.S. Government Printing Office.

Virginia Joint Legislative Audit and Review Commission (1978, March 28). Long-Term Care in Virginia: The Virginia General Assembly, Richmond, VA.

Vladeck, B. (1980). *Unloving Care*. New York, NY: Basic Books.

Waxman, H., Klein, M., & Carter, E. (1985). Drug Misuse in Nursing Homes: An Institutional Addiction? *Hospital and Community Psychiatry, 36*(8), 886–887.

Wood, T., & Pepper, M. (1988, May 29–June 3). How Safe A Haven? *Kansas City Star*.

9

The Impact of Nurse Practitioners on the Care of Nursing Home Residents

Judith Garrard
Robert L. Kane
Edward R. Ratner
Joan L. Buchanan

With the growth in the number of elderly in the population and increasing concern about the quality of care in nursing homes, one solution has been to introduce a new type of health professional in the health care delivery system, the nurse practitioner (NP). The concept of the geriatric nurse practitioner (GNP) was developed in the early 1960s to fill a perceived void in clinical attention and quality of care of nursing home elderly (Ebersole, 1985). Although much has been written about the need, role, training, and expected impact of the nurse practitioner working with the elderly in nursing homes, only 6 research studies have been completed in which the NP's impact has been empirically examined. In this chapter, we will begin with a general discussion of the issues involved in studying quality of care of nursing home elderly, followed by a brief overview of these 6 studies. We will then concentrate on the findings of these studies, with a focus on the impact of this new kind of health professional and a discussion of factors that might enhance or limit the impact of the NP* on quality of care of elderly nursing home residents.

---

*Unless otherwise specified, the term, nurse practitioner (NP), will be used to refer to both the NP and the geriatric or gerontological nurse practitioner (GNP). Since the majority of nurse practitioners are female, the pronoun, she, will be used throughout this chapter to refer to NPs and GNPs of either sex.

STUDYING QUALITY OF CARE

The intent of a nursing home is not only to provide treatment and supportive health care for frail or incapacitated individuals, but also to maintain a residence which substitutes for the homes they have left. Because of this dual purpose, a nursing home has elements of both an acute care hospital and a hotel, with the potential of an extended or permanent living arrangement. A variety of factors have been examined in considering the impact of the nurse practitioner on the resident in such an environment. These include: case mix of those admitted, the clinical services they received once admitted, evidence of quality of care in the nursing home, the morale or satisfaction by the residents, and their discharge outcomes.

The results of research on quality of care can be expected to vary depending on which groups of nursing home residents are studied, either new admissions to the facility or residents who have lived there over a period of time. Compared to elderly residents with one or more years in a nursing home, those newly admitted have been shown to be relatively younger, clinically sicker, with fewer diagnoses of dementia or congestive heart failure, but with more diagnoses of hip fracture or cancer, and more likely to either die or be discharged (in presumably better condition) soon after entering the nursing home (Garrard et al., in press). New admissions also include greater proportions of males, who in turn have a greater likelihood that a younger able-bodied spouse will be available to help during the nursing home stay or to facilitate earlier discharge home. Alternatively, long stay residents are survivors of whatever brought about their admission to the nursing home in the first place, although they did not improve sufficiently in either their condition or their circumstances to be discharged back to the community. This group of long stayers are older, consist of proportionately more women, have often outlived their spouse or family, and are more likely to have exhausted their financial resources (Liu & Manton, 1983). In contrast to the new admissions, the long stayers tend to have more chronic disabilities which might place practical limitations on the feasibility of improvement in activities of daily living, and they tend to suffer in greater numbers from dementia (with accompanying behavioral problems for staff or family members) or mental illness (thus necessitating greater need for psychoactive drugs). Given the contingencies within each group, the opportunity to demonstrate the NP's impact on the functional status, medication use, or behavioral aspects could be a function of which group was studied. Most of the earlier research projects concentrated on long stay residents, with only the more recent studies differentiating between the long stayers and the new admissions.

In addition to taking subject group into account, some of the methodological factors that might be important in detecting the impact of an NP include the length of the study period, the kinds of measures used to assess functional status, and whether or not change attributed to an NP was compared to that of a control or comparison group. In other words, an evaluator might find it relatively easy to detect improvement in functional status in a new admission cohort because a large portion of such a group is very likely to improve anyway; the key to such a comparison would be to ask how much more improvement was found compared to a similar group of new admissions who were not under the care of an NP.

Two issues concerning the residents studied also need to be taken into account: sample size and sample selection. In some of the earlier studies, the number of subjects was small, but included all who participated in the program; in others, the numbers were larger, but consisted of a subset of all those who were enrolled in the intervention. If a random sampling strategy was used to select these subjects (for either the experimental or the comparison groups), then some of the major issues about a representative sample were addressed.

Finally, the variables used to assess the NP's impact on quality of care must take into account the goals of the program being studied. For example, if one of the criteria used to assess quality of care was reduction in psychotropic drugs, but the program under which the NP was hired did not focus on medication use, then she might not be expected to have much more than general impact.

OVERVIEW OF RESEARCH STUDIES

The six studies that have been conducted over the past 15 years have varied by the role of the nurse practitioner, the number of subjects in the study, whether or not new admissions or residents were studied, geographic location of the nursing homes, methodological design, data collection instruments, and type of data examined. These differences, summarized in Tables 9.1, 9.2 and 9.3 can be described as follows.

Salt Lake City Study

The earliest study described an evaluation of a project intended to improve direct patient service and staff education that emphasized therapeutic rather than custodial care (Kane et al., 1976). Thirteen intermediate-care (ICF) nursing homes in Salt Lake City were randomly assigned to one of three combinations of health professionals: (1) a team consisting of an NP responsible for primary care of the patients, with consultive backup by a physician and a clinical pharmacist; (2) a second combination in which a social worker was added to the NP–MD/pharmacist team; and (3) a "modified" control group in which the existing provision of medical care by an MD was facilitated by the addition of a social worker, but not the inclusion of an NP

TABLE 9.1 Characteristics of Evaluation Studies of NP or GNP Impact on Care of Elderly in Nursing Homes—Program Implementation

Study	Intervention	Employment of NP/GNP
Salt Lake City Study Kane, Jorgensen, Teteberg, Kuwahar, 1976	NP with MD and clinical pharmacist consultation NP and SW with MD and clinical pharm. consultation SW with traditional MD model	Employed by medical school department
Boston Study Master, et. al., 1980	NP/PA as primary care provider with MD supervision	Employed by medical group
VA Study Wieland, et. al., 1986	GNP as primary care provider with MD supervision; backup by interdisciplinary team	Employed by VA
TNHP Study Shaughnessy, Kramer, Hittle, 1988	Affiliations between nursing homes and academic nursing programs	Affiliation
Mt. States Study Kane, et. al., 1989	GNP as nursing direct service provider	Employed by nursing home
Massachusetts Study Kane, et. al., Forthcoming	NP/PA as primary care provider with MD supervision	Employed by medical group

Notes: NP—Nurse practitioner; GNP—Geriatric nurse practitioner; PA—Physician assistant; VA—Veterans Administration; NH—Nursing home.

or a pharmacist. Enrollees ($n = 497$) in the health care plan by the Department of Community and Family Medicine of the University of Utah College of Medicine were the recipients in these three variations of health care delivery (Kane, Jorgensen, & Pepper, 1974). Evaluation of this program focused on 283 residents who participated during the five-quarter data collection period. The majority of these residents were Medicaid recipients, with a mean age of 68. Using a posttest only design, quality of care was assessed through a retrospective record review over a period of 6 months or more following the introduction of each of these 3 teams. Data collection was from 1972 to 1974, a period prior to either the mandatory review of medications by phrmacists (Kidder, 1987) initiated in 1978 or the Medicare prospective payment system for reimbursement of hospital inpatient care begun in 1984. The variables examined in this study consisted of changes in patients' functional status, behavior, medications, and hospital use and costs.

TABLE 9.2 Characteristics of Evaluation Studies of NP or GNP Impact on Care of Elderly in Nursing Homes

Study	Number of Subjects in Groups				Methodological Design					Data Collection			Subject Characteristics	
	NP/GNP	NH	Exper.	Control	New Admits Studied Separately	Pre-post Design	Random Assign. of Intervention	Random Sampling of Subjects in N.H.	Record Review	Interviews with Residents	Other Data Collection	Length of Data Col. Period (in Months)	Percent Female	Average Age
Salt Lake City Study Kane, Jorgensen, Teteberg, & Kuwahar, 1976	—	13	283	—	no	no	yes	no	yes	no	—	18	—	median: 68
Boston Study Master, et al., 1980	3	10	358	—	no	no	no	no	yes	no	patient encounter form	12	63	mean: 75
V.A. Study Wieland, et al., 1986	2	1	60	91	yes	yes	no	all included	yes	yes	clinical assessment	4	E: 2% C: 9%	mean: E: 68 C: 71
TNHP Study Shaughnessy, Kramer, & Hittle, 1988	—	12	2741	2240	yes	yes	no	yes	yes	no	Medicare & Medicaid data	12	—	mean: 80
Mt. States Study Kane et al., 1989	record review: 30 interview: 5	60 10	record review: 4854 interview: 428	4884 420	yes	yes	no	yes	yes	no	interviews with GNPs, directors of nursing & N. H. adminstrators	record review: 12–24 interview: 12	—	record review: Mean: 81–85 interview: 80–82
Massachusetts Study Kane, et al., Forthcoming	—	170	1324	1327	yes	yes	no	no	yes	no	Medicare & Medicaid cost data	18	76–80	mean: 82–85

Note: E—experimental; C—control.

TABLE 9.3 Characteristics of Evaluation Studies of NP or GNP Impact
on Care of Elderly in Nursing Homes

Study	Categories of dependent variables	
Salt Lake City Study Kane, Jorgensen, Teteberg, Kuwahar, 1976	medications mental status functional status behavioral financial mortality	
Boston Study Master, et al., 1980	diagnosis NP/PA visit frequency hospital use financial	
VA Study Wieland, et al., 1986	mental status functional status pt. satisfaction discharge outcomes	
TNHP Study Shaughnessy, Kramer, & Hittle, 1988	facility characteristics diagnosis medications mental status	functional status behavior hospital use financial discharge outcomes
Mt. States Study Kane, et al., 1989	faculty characteristics diagnosis medications mental status functional status behavior	hospital use financial pt. satisfaction discharge outcomes interviews with GNP, DON, NH Admin.
Massachusetts Study Kane, et al., Forthcoming	diagnosis medications mental status functional status	behavior hospital use financial outcomes discharge outcomes

Boston Study

The second study described a project in which physicians in the Urban
Medical Group, a multi-specialty group practice, and mid-level practitioners
collaborated in an effort to improve the quality of health care delivery to
inner city residents living in a variety of settings, including nursing homes.
(Master et al., 1980). The aspect of this project concerned with nursing

homes included the assessment of 358 Medicaid recipients in 10 nursing homes. In this project, the group practice's 3 nurse practitioners and physician assistants (NP/PA) functioned as primary care providers for nursing home residents with supervision by 5 primary care physicians under a fee-for-service arrangement with the state Medicaid office. The NP/PAs were responsible for patients at a variety of nursing homes and averaged 30–35 nursing homes visits per week, with a case load of approximately 120–130 residents. The evaluation consisted of a posttest only, no control group design in which nursing home data were collected prospectively over a representative 1 year study period (1977–1979). Project-designed encounter forms were used, supplemented by record reviews that provided information about the residents' demographic and clinical characteristics and hospitalizations. The major variables of interest in this study were hospitalization rates, length of stay, and case load capacity of the NP/PAs.

VA Study

This study was an evaluation of an academic nursing home program initiated in 1984 at a California Veterans Administration (VA) facility (Wieland et al., 1986). Two GNPs were appointed full-time to the staff of the nursing home which was attached to the VA medical center. The GNPs were responsible for day-to-day patient management, with supervision by staff physicians and input from an interdisciplinary team; internal medicine house staff were also assigned to this unit. Each GNP was responsible for approximately 30 patients per week. A pre–1982-83/post–1984-85 quasi-experimental design was used in which subjects were not randomly assigned to the experimental (N = 60 subjects) and control (N = 91 subjects) groups. A distinction was made between new admissions and long stay residents; however, the new admissions were not treated as a cohort; rather, they were defined as long stayers if their nursing home stay was beyond 4 months. Over 90% of the sample were male, with a mean age of 68–71 years; there was no restriction on lower age limit in the enrollment of subjects in this study. Data were collected using a standardized interview form, supplemented by retrospective record review. Within each pre-post period, subjects were followed over a 4-month study period. Outcomes were recorded at the end of 1 year or upon discharge, whichever was first. The major dependent variables in this study included changes in the subjects' functional status, satisfaction, morale, hospitalization, cost, and discharge outcomes.

Mountain States Study

The fourth study was a comprehensive evaluation of the role of the GNP as a nursing home employee in nursing homes located in 8 Mountain States (AZ, CA, CO, ID, WA, OR, MT, NM) (Kane et al., 1989a). Over the 10 years of this project (1976–85), a registered nurse from each of 113 nursing homes received university-based training in geriatric nursing and returned to each of their original facilities with the goal of improving direct patient care and staff education. The impact of the GNP's intervention was assessed in a study which included 30 of the nursing homes with GNPs compared to 30 matched comparison homes. The study used a quasi-experimental design with pre-post, experimental comparison groups; it was not possible to assign subjects randomly to groups nor treatments to nursing homes. Random samples of new admissions and of residents were drawn from each of the 60 nursing homes. Pre-post data were collected using a retrospective record review of 5752 new admissions and 3191 residents (Kane et al., 1989b). The mean age of these subjects was 81–85 years; payment source was not a factor in the selection of these subjects. In addition. an interview study in a subset of 10 of the nursing homes (5 experimental; 5 control) was conducted on a post-only basis with 525 new admissions and 323 residents (Garrard et al., 1990). Interviews were also conducted separately with GNPs, directors of nursing, and nursing home administrators in the 30 experimental homes (Kane, R. A. et al., 1988; Radosevich et al., 1990). The major dependent variables included changes in functional status, case mix, extent of provider attention, medications, discharge outcomes, and quality of clinical care in 7 tracer conditions (diabetes, congestive heart failure, hypertension, fever, urinary incontinence, feeding, and confusion). Hospital utilization and costs (Buchanan et al., 1989) were also examined.

The Teaching Nursing Home Program (TNHP)

The fifth study was an evaluation of the Teaching Nursing Home Program, a demonstration project from 1982 to 1987 designed to enhance care of nursing home residents through affiliations between schools of nursing and nursing homes at 11 sites located in 8 states and the District of Columbia (Shaughnessy, Kramer, & Hittle, 1988). In the evaluation of this project, a pre-post, experimental comparison group design was used, with retrospective record reviews over a 1-year study period in 6 teaching nursing homes ($n = 2,741$ subjects) and 6 comparison facilities ($n = 2240$ subjects). (Shaughnessy & Kramer, 1989) Additional prospective data were collected using an "after only" design to supplement the retrospective data. The 6 experimental nursing homes, located in Ohio, Oregon, Wisconsin, and Nebraska, constituted a convenience sample, with matching of comparison homes on the basis of general characteristics (Number of beds, occupancy rate, length of stay, percent Medicare and Medicaid days, hospitalization affiliation, type of ownership, and state), rather than a one-to-one match. Within each of these 12 nursing homes, 2 groups of subjects (≥60 years or older) were selected randomly: new admissions (enrolled over a 1-year period) and residents already living in the home. The individuals in the resulting sample had a mean age of 80–81 years and used multiple payment sources to finance their nursing home stay. The major variables studied included case mix, hospitalization rates, community discharge rates, cost of nursing home care and quality of care using process measures and patient status outcomes.

Massachusetts Study

Recently, an evaluation was completed of the Massachusetts Nursing Home Connection demonstration program on the use of NPs and PAs as primary caregivers of elderly in nursing homes (Kane et al., in press). This demonstration project was a statewide extension of the Urban Medical Group model described in the Boston study (Master et al., 1980). In this demonstration project, 16 medical groups, 185 nursing homes, and over 3000 patients under the care of these provider groups had enrolled in the program by 1989; the greatest proportion of patients were under the care of the Urban Medical Group. Initiated in 1984 with continuation through 1990, the goal of this program was to improve the quality of care of nursing home elderly who were Medicaid and Medicare eligible. NP/PAs were hired, supervised, and paid by the medical groups. Demonstration waivers allowed: (1) Medical groups to bill Medicare and Medicaid for NP/PA services to nursing home elderly, and (2) removed restrictions on the number of reimbursed visits per month by either the NP/PA or the supervising physicians. Within the program, all provider visits (NP, PA, MD) were reimbursed at the same rate. Because the demonstration aimed to test whether the program of the Urban Medical Group (see Boston Study, above) could be replicated by other provider groups, the evaluation of the Massachusetts project was limited to nursing home residents under the care of the 15 new medical groups. Patients ($n = 1324$) enrolled with the new provider groups in this waiver program over an 18-month period (January 1985 to June 1986) were subjects in this evaluation. Matched control subjects ($n = 1327$) were drawn from the population of 20,009 patients in nondemonstration nursing homes during the same time frame (Buchanan et al., 1989b). Patients were matched on patient characteristics, prior medical care use, time in nursing home, and nursing home characteristics. Data were collected through retrospective record reviews (using the same record review form as in the Mt. States study) based on a pre-post design with residents ($n = 2087$) and a post-only design with new admissions ($n = 564$). The cost component of the evaluation relied on Medicare and Medicaid claims data. Dependent variables in this study included case mix, hospitalization rates, community discharge rates, quality of care using process measures and patient status outcomes, and medical services expenditures.

IMPACT OF THE NP ON ELDERLY
IN NURSING HOMES

In summarizing the results of these 6 studies, we begin by focusing on the measures in which the NP has been found to have the most consistent and favorable impact, and then shift the focus to variables in which there is less evidence in any of the studies of the hoped for success. Then we examine factors that might enhance or limit the NP's impact on elderly in nursing homes.

Hospitalization Rates

Nursing home elderly under the care of an NP have a lower hospitalization rate than comparable groups without an NP. This finding, consistent in all 6 of the empirical studies reported to date, has been found whether the elderly studied were a cross-section of residents of the facilities (Kane et al., 1976; Master et al., 1980) or a cohort of new admissions (Wieland et al., 1986; Shaughnessy, Kramer, & Hittle, 1988; Kane et al., 1989a; Kane et al., in press), the latter of which tends to be hospitalized more frequently because they are often clinically more unstable (Garrard et al., in press). This NP impact has also been reported across many different types of nursing homes, private, for-profit, public, attached to a medical center, free standing, or Veterans Administration facility. This reduction in rates of hospitalization could be attributed to one of several competing explanations: more timely or better quality of care which prevented the need for subsequent hospitalization, or the substitution of clinical care and supervision by the NP in the nursing home for care which otherwise would have been provided in an acute care setting, or the denial of hospital services that were needed but not provided. These six studies suggest that either of the first two explanations is probably the most viable. None of the studies reported adverse outcome or process measures when quality of care of NP patients was compared to quality delivered in control groups.

Cost Effectiveness of the NP

In each of these studies, NPs were expected to enhance the amount of medical attention that patients received. In most cases, this resulted in increased use of some medical and ancillary services, especially in areas of restorative care. In all of these studies, the added costs of this increased medical attention were more than offset by the reduction in costs due to lower hospitalization rates. The Teaching Nursing Home Program found a significant overall cost reduction (Shaughnessy, Kramer, & Hittle, 1988); other studies reported either lower costs for NP patients without tests of statistical significance (Master et al., 1980; Kane, Jorgensen, & Pepper, 1974) or, alternatively, significant cost reductions that were limited to some subsets of patients (Buchanan et al., 1989a).

Impact on Quality of Care

Although cost is an important consideration in any change in the delivery of health services, an equally (and possibly more) important consideration is the impact of such a change on the quality of care of the patient. One of the major difficulties in evaluating quality of care is that of operationally defining its different facets. Three of the most frequently used measures in these studies have been changes in residents' functional status, medication use, and reduction in inappropriate or disruptive behavior.

Functional status generally refers to the resident's ability to care for him- or herself or to accomplish some of the basic tasks of daily living such as bathing, dressing, going to the toilet, transferring, continence, and feeding. Although each of these abilities is assessed individually, the results can also be combined to describe an overall measure of functional status, e.g., an activities of daily living (ADL) dependency score. (Katz et al., 1963). In 5 of the 6 studies (Kane et al., 1976; Wieland et al., 1986; Shaughnessy, Kramer, & Hittle, 1988; Kane et al., 1989b; Kane et al., in press) in which functional status of nursing home elderly was studied, the NP was found to have had a favorable impact on 1 or more of the ADL measures of elderly under her care. Improvements in overall measures of functional status were reported for a cross-sectional sample of elderly in 2 of the studies (Kane et al., 1976; Wieland et al., 1986). In the two other projects which differentiated between long stay residents and new admissions, the new admissions with an NP showed greater improvement over time than a comparable group without an NP in transferring and dressing, but no difference in toileting, bathing, continence, or feeding. No impact was found on functional status of the long stay residents under the care of an NP in either of these two later studies (Kane et al., 1989a; Kane et al., in press).

Another measure of the impact of the NP on quality of care of nursing home residents has been to study the medications residents receive. The results of such a study can be difficult to interpret since both the addition as well as the reduction of certain medications for specific individuals can signal a beneficial impact. Furthermore, the NP's impact on medication use is often indirect since she has independent prescriptive authority in only 4 of the 51 states (Swart, 1983). In none of these 6 studies was there a detailed analysis of the appropriateness of drug utilization and changes in medications; however, several did examine whether or not there were changes in medications, which might indicate that some attention was being given to this issue. A favorable impact due to an NP and pharmacist team was reported in one study of a cross-section of residents living in the nursing homes in terms of reduced drug utilization (Kane et al., 1976), although no statistical comparisons between NP and non-NP groups were described. In 2 later studies, the presence of an NP had no effect on changes in the use of 6 groups of drugs used frequently by nursing home elderly in either a new admissions cohort or cross-sectional samples of residents living in the nursing homes (Kane et al., 1989a; Kane et al., in press). The 6 drug groups in these studies included antipsychotic/neuroleptics, sedative-hypnotics, antidepressants, digoxin, and diuretics.

Changes in behavior, especially the reduction of disruptive behaviors, have also been used to examine whether or not the NP has had a beneficial effect on the residents plagued with such problems, as well as the quality of the environment for the other residents. Only 2 studies have examined this issue (Kane et al., 1989a; Kane et al., in press), and both found that elderly residents under the NP's care did not improve along this dimension at any greater rate than residents who were not being seen by an NP. In both of these projects, new admissions and long stay residents were studied separately.

Case Mix of New Admissions

Over the past 2 decades, individuals entering nursing homes have been admitted in increasingly sicker condition (Sekscenski, 1987), possibly due to the competition for nursing home beds and regulations about their use, and possibly also due to more recent changes in the funding of acute care in hospitals known as the diagnosis related groupings (DRG) system (Shaughnessy & Kramer, 1990). With the development of a new health practitioner especially trained to better manage the day-to-day care of clinically frail residents, the nursing homes might be more willing to accept or even recruit sicker patients. Thus, over time, this potential might result in even sicker elderly and their families gravitating to those physicians or nursing homes that offered the services of an NP. Such a possibility was explored in in 2 of the studies. The case mix of 2 groups of elderly new admissions (those with and without an NP) were compared before and after the addition of the NP. The results were mixed: In the Mt. States study in which the NP was a nursing home employee, there was no difference. Although the more recent admissions were clinically sicker than those admitted in earlier years (reflecting the nationwide trend), those under the care of the NP were no sicker than those in nursing homes without the services of an NP. The TNHP, based on affiliations between nursing homes and academic nursing programs, found similar changes over time; however, here the increases over time in functional disabilities were moderately greater in those homes with affiliations.

Morale or Satisfaction of Elderly

Two studies (Wieland et al., 1986; Garrard et al., 1990) examined residents' morale or satisfaction with the care they received in the nursing home and the findings produced mixed results. One of the studies of male VA elderly found a significant improvement in morale over a 4-month period (Wieland et al., 1986) which they attributed to the presence of the NP; however, this could have been due to a Hawthorne effect, that is, due to the excitement and positive expectation of participating in a new program, of which the NP was a part. The other study assessed both satisfaction over a 1-year period, but found no differences in the improvement by the NP group over the non-NP group in either new admissions or long stayers. (Garrard et al., 1990)

Discharge Outcomes

The NP's impact on outcomes at the end of specified study periods have been examined in all of the studies. These outcomes included death and discharge to the community. Some of the studies reported a reduction in mortality rate (Wieland et al., 1986) where others did not (Kane et al., 1989a; Kane et al., in press). Of the 2 studies in which discharge of the elderly to the community in a presumably better condition was examined, there was no difference between the experimental and the comparison groups.

ISSUES AFFECTING POTENTIAL IMPACT

Training of the NP

Factors that have a potential effect on the impact of the NP include training, role, and reimbursement. A major controversy in the training of the NP has been whether the educational program has been based on the continuing education model or the master's degree. To be admitted to the continuing education programs, the applicant had to be a registered nurse with an associate diploma, baccalaureate, or higher degree; the master's degree programs required that the RN hold a baccalaureate. The more recent NP programs have all been at the master's degree level. The NPs evaluated in these 6 studies have been graduates of both types of programs, and no research has been reported to date in which graduates of these 2 levels of training have been systematically compared.

Beyond the issue of which training program is preferable, the ongoing success of any of these programs depends upon the establishment of a core of trained personnel dedicated to careers in long-term care, settings that traditionally do not command high salaries. Only one study, the Mt. States study, systematically examined career paths of the GNPs in this project. This analysis concluded that the Mt. States project, which used the continuing education model, had successfully developed such a commitment among its trainees (Radosevich et al., 1990). In the Massachusetts project, NP interviews suggested that this program, which included predominantly master's prepared NPs, would not be as successful in developing NPs with a commitment to careers in long-term care (Kane, R. A., 1989). Wages, which were markedly higher in the Massachusetts study, were noted to be inadequate to retain these master's-prepared NPs in this role. Most of the NP and GNP programs are now evolving into master's level training and the continuing education model is in the process of being phased out. This decision within the nursing profession may leave nursing homes, which historically have offered much lower salaries, at a competitive disadvantage.

Role of the NP

The role expectations of the NP have also varied. Although the NPs and GNPs in these 6 studies have in common a background in nursing, the system within which they have been employed and/or reimbursed has probably had a considerable impact on the roles they have assumed. Some of the variations described in these 6 studies include the NP as an employee of the nursing home or a medical group, as a salaried employee, or as an affiliate of the nursing home. Theoretically, the NP could also function as an independent practitioner without supervision by an MD; however, under current legal restrictions on clinical practice, such an alternative has not been feasible.

Conceivably, an NP's impact on the quality of care of nursing home elderly could differ depending on her role. As a nursing home employee, the NP available to residents and staff on a full-time basis could be responsible for preadmission screening, provide continuity of care to all in the facility, and facilitate discharge planning. Some of the expectations, as well as the *perceived* advantges and disadvantages of the NP as a nursing home employee have been described elsewhere (Kane, R. A. et al., 1988; Radosevich et al., 1990). When hired by the physician with the opportunity for third party reimbursement, the NP could also provide the same types of clinical services to nursing home elderly, but is more likely to focus on billable services in the medical model with less attention to traditional areas of nursing care (Kane, R. A., 1989). Since most physicians have patients located at more than one nursing home, the NP employed by a medical group would probably not be available in the same nursing home on a full-time basis and would therefore be less likely to supervise or provide daily on-site care to the extent that a nursing home employee would. Alternatively, the MD-employed NP might have the logistical advantage in coordinating the care of nursing home elderly who are in transition to, as well as in, different components of the long-term care system, including the acute care hospital, nursing home, home health care, adult day care, or hospice. In one of the 6 studies (Kane et al., 1989a) the model evaluated was that of the NP as a nursing home employee; 2 of the studies evaluated the NP as an employee of a medical group (Master et al., 1980; Kane et al., in press); two were evaluations of the NP as a salaried employee by either a medical school department or the VA (Kane et al., 1976; Wieland et al., 1986), and one was of a nursing school affiliation model (Shaughnessy, Kramer, & Hittle, 1988) Although no study has compared the effectiveness of different NP roles, the results of these 6 studies do not provide enough information to permit us to conclude that one role was better than any of the others in terms of either quality of care or cost effectiveness. In fact, the impact of these role and/or employment variations was remarkably homogeneous.

Reimbursement of the NP

Reimbursement for NPs continues to be an issue of concern not only within the nursing profession, but throughout the health care system. In late 1989, Congress passed legislation (PL101-239) which authorized Medicare reimbursement for nurse practitioner visits to nursing home residents. This same law, while continuing to mandate physician supervision of NPs, removed requirements for on-site supervision of NPs but only for patient care in nursing homes. Reimbursement was set at 85% of the physician rate. Similar legislation (PL99-509) governing physician assistants was passed in 1986. Many in the nursing profession continue to argue that the requirements for physician supervision should be dropped and that NPs should be allowed to practice and bill Medicare independently. Their dissatisfaction with this model stems in part from the concern that it promotes a strictly medical approach to patient care and ignores the unique and important contribution that the nursing profession provides.

SUMMARY

The results of these and other reports,[*] about the impact of the NP on nursing home elderly, have shown consistently that elderly under the care of an NP have lower rates of hospitalization and this reduction offsets costs from increased use of other services, whether the NP is a nursing home employee, a physician employee, a salaried member of a system, or an affiliate. Five of the 6 (Kane et al., 1976; Wieland et al., 1986; Shaughnessy,

[*]See entire issue of the *Journal of Long-term Care Administration* 11 no. 3 (Fall 1983).

Kramer, & Hittle, 1988; Kane et al., 1989a; Kane et al, in press) studies reviewed have contrasted combined NP-MD teams with comparison groups that included routine care by the residents' physicians. Although most of the quality of care and outcome variables did not show consistent improvements in quality, the absence of negative findings clearly demonstrates that the addition of the NP is an important contribution to primary care delivery in nursing homes. In all of these studies to date, the effectiveness of the NP as a primary care provider with physician backup is an good as, and in some areas better than, the traditional provision of care by physicians alone.

ACKNOWLEDGMENT

This chapter was prepared by Dr. Garrard under a Special Emphasis Research Career Award in behavioral geriatrics (1K01-AG-000434-02) from the National Institute on Aging.

REFERENCES

Buchanan, J. L., Arnold, S. B., Bell, R. M., Witsberger, C., Kane, R. L., & Garrard, J. (1989a). The financial impact of nursing home based geriatric nurse practitioners: An evaluation of the Mt. States Health Corporation GNP Project. Santa Monica, CA: The RAND Corp. #R-3694-HCFA/RWJ.

Buchanan, J. L., Kane, R. L., Garrard, J., Bell, R. M., Witsberger, C., Rosenfeld, A., Skay, C., & Gifford, D. (1989b). Results from the evaluation of the Massachusetts Nursing Home Connection Program. Santa Monica, CA: The RAND Corporation, #JR-01.

Garrard, J., Kane, R. L., Radosevich, D. M., Skay, C. L., Arnold, S, Kepferle, L., McDermott, S., & Buchanan, J. L. (1990). Impact of geriatric nurse practitioners on nursing home residents' functional status, satisfaction, and discharge outcomes. *Medical Care*, 28, 271–283.

Garrard, J., Kane, R. L., Ratner, E. R., Chan, H.-C., Makris, L., & Buchanan, J. L. (Paper submitted for publication). Differences between admissions and residents in nursing homes.

Ebersole, P. (1985). Geriatric nurse practitioners past and present. *Geriatric Nursing*, 6, 219–222.

Kane, R. A., Kane, R. L., Arnold, S., Garrard, J., McDermott, S., & Kepferle, L. (1988). Geriatric nurse practitioners as nursing home employees: Implementing the role. *The Gerontologist*, 28, 469–477.

Kane, R. A. (1989). Perceptions of GNPs, nursing home administrators, directors of nursing, and physicians. Paper presented at the annual meeting of the Gerontological Society of America, Minnneapolis, MI.

Kane, R. L., Jorgensen, L. A., & Pepper, P. (1974). Can nursing-home care be cost-effective? *Journal of the American Geriatrics Society* 22, 265–272.

Kane, R. L., Jorgensen, L. A., Teteberg, B., & Kuwahar, J. (1976). Is good nursing-home care feasible? *JAMA* 235, 516–519.

Kane, R. L., Garrard, J., Skay, C. L., Radosevich, D., Budhanan, J. L., McDermott, S., Arnold, S., & Kepferle, L. (1989a). Effect of a geriatric nurse practitioner on the process and outcomes of nursing home care. *AJPH* 79, 1271–1277.

Kane, R. L., Garrard, J., Buchanan, J. L., Arnold, S., Kane, R. A., & McDermott, S. (1989b). The geriatric nurse practitioner as a nursing home employee: Conceptual and methodological issues in assessing quality of care and cost effectiveness. In Mezey, M. D., Lynaugh, J. E., & Cartier, M. M. (Eds.), *Nursing Homes and Nursing Care: Lessons from the Teaching Nursing Homes.* New York: Springer Publishing Co.

Kane, R. L., Garrard, J., Buchanan, J. L., Rosenfeld, A., Skay, C. L., & McDermott, S. (in press). Improving primary care in nursing homes. Paper submitted for publication.

Katz, S., Ford, A., Moskowitz, R., Jackson, B., Jaffee, M., & Cleveland, M. (1963). The index of ADL: A standardized measure of biological and psychological function. *JAMA*, 195, 914–919.

Kidder, S. W. (1987). Cost-benefit of pharmacist conducted drug-regimen reviews. *The Consultant Pharmacist*, 394–398.

Liu, K., & Manton, K. G. (1983). The characteristics and utilization pattern of an admission cohort of nursing home patients (I). *The Gerontologist* 23, 92–97.

Master, R. J., Feltin, M., Jainchill, J., Mark, R., Kavesh, W. N., Rabkin, M. T., Turner, B., Bachrach, S., & Lennox, S. (1980). A continuum of care for the inner city: Assessment of its benefits for Boston's elderly and high-risk populations. *New England Journal of Medicine*, 302, 1434–1440.

Radosevich, D. M., Kane, R. L., Garrard, J., Skay, C. L., McDermott, S., Kepferle, L., Buchanan, J. L., & Arnold, S. (in press). Career paths of geriatric nurse practitioners employed in nursing homes. *Public Health Reports.*

Sekscenski, E. S. (1987). Discharges from nursing homes: Preliminary data from the 1985 National Nursing Home Survey. *Advance Data from Vital and Health Statistics*, no. 142. National Center for Health Statistics (NCHS). DHHS Pub. No. (PHS) 87–1250. Hyattsville, MD: Public Health Service.

Shaughnessy, P. W., Kramer, A. M., & Hittle, D. F. (1988). The teaching nursing home experiment: Its effects and implications. Study Paper 6. Denver, CO: Center for Health Services Research, University of Colorado Health Sciences Center.

Shaughnessy, P. W., Kramer, A. M. (1989). Trade-offs in evaluating the effectiveness of nursing home care. In Mezey, M. D., Lynaugh, J. E., & Cartier, M. M. (Eds.), *Nursing Homes and Nursing Care: Lessons from the Teaching Nursing Homes.* New York: Springer Publishing Co.

Shaughnessy, P. W., & Kramer, A. M. (1990). The increased needs of patients in nursing homes and patients receiving home health care. *New England Journal of Medicine* 322, 21–27.

Swart, J. C. (1983). The role of the nurse practitioner. *Journal of Long-term Care Administration* 11, 19–22.

Wieland, D., Rubenstein, L. Z., Ouslander, J. G., & Martin, S. E. (1986). Organizing an Academic Nursing Home: Impacts on Institutionalized Elderly. *JAMA*, 255, 2622–2627.

10
Home Care:
Measuring Success

William G. Weissert

If home care for the elderly were a privately marketed product similar to movie theater tickets, there would be no need to ask, How shall we measure success? The answer would be obvious: Satisfied consumers would demand more of the product and providers would prosper. If consumers were not satisfied, demand would drop and providers would go bankrupt. But these rules of market economics apply in only a limited way when the product is a publicly subsidized social service such as health care (Pauly, 1983) where the argument has been made that the public has a stake in guaranteeing access to care for everyone (Daniels, 1985).

The success of home care (home health, homemaker, day care, respite, and other health and social services delivered at home or in the community) for the elderly may be measured in a number of ways. Employing Donnebedian's (1980) perspectives on evaluating success in terms of outcome, process, and structure, a reasonable starting point is to ask, "Has home care succeeded in improving outcomes, including increased longevity, improved physical or mental functioning, or increased satisfaction or morale of the patient or informal caregiver?"

OUTCOME MEASURES OF SUCCESS

For most measures of outcome, effects have been negligible. Drawing upon evidence synthesized by Weissert, Cready, and Pawelak (1988) from the 27 home and community care demonstration projects of the past 3 decades (Table 10.1), the accumulated results show that use of home care has not proved to be of significant measurable efficacy in helping patients live longer, function better, or experience fewer restricted activity days. Longevity may

Research for this chapter was supported by a grant from the PEW Charitable Trusts of The PEW Memorial Trust. Views are those of the author.

**TABLE 10.1 Home and Community-based Long-term Care
Demonstration Projects, 1959–1989**

Project	Interventions	Eligibility Criteria
Continuity in Care (1959–63)*	Nurse home visits	Indigent geriatric rehab. hosp. discharge
Continued Care (1963–71)*	Nurse home visits	Rehab. hosp. discharge
BRI Project Service (1964–66)*	Case management and ancillary services	Noninstitutionalized mentally impaired with no informal caregiver
Congestive Heart Failure (1964–66)*	Nurse home visits	Chronic congestive heart failure, outpatient hosp. clinic visits
BRH Home Aide (1966–69)*	Home aide visits	Geriatric rehab. hosp. discharge
Highland Heights (1970–76)	Housing	Functionally impaired or medically vulnerable
Chronic Disease (1971–76)	Interdisciplinary team home visits	Amb. care facility patient or hosp. discharge
Worcester (1973–75)*	Case management and non-Medicaid–covered home services	Noninstitutionalized and primarily receiving informal care, or institutionalized with discharge potential
Section 222* Day Care (1974–77)	Adult day care services	In need of health care services to restore or maintain fuctional ability
Homemaker (1974–77)	Homemaker services	Hosp. discharge in need of health care services to restore or maintain functional ability
Health Maintenance Team (1975)*	Nonskilled nursing and nurse home visits	Chronically ill or disabled needing nonskilled care
Wisconsin CCO/ Milwaukee (1975–79)*	Case management and non-Medicaid–covered home services	At risk of institutionalization
Alarm Response (1975–80)	In-home alarm response system	Medically vulnerable or functionally impaired public housing tenant who lives alone

TABLE 10.1 (Continued)

Project	Interventions	Eligibility Criteria
Georgia (1976–80)*	Case management and non-Medicaid–covered home services	Previously institutionalized nursing home applicant, or certified as Medicaid eligible for nursing home care
Triage (1976–81)	Case management and non-Medicare–covered services	Unstable condition (medical/social problems, poor informal support, or environmental or financial problems)
Chicago (1977–80)	Interdisciplinary home visits	Homebound, ADL impaired
On Lok (1978–83)	Case management and non-Medicare–covered services	Qualified for skilled or intermediate nursing home care
Project OPEN (1978–83)*	Case management and non-Medicare–covered services	Cognitively aware with medical problem, needing function assistance
Home Health Care Team (1979–82)*	Interdisciplinary team home visits	Chronically disabled or terminally ill and homebound with informal care available
NYC Home Care (1979–84)	Case management and non-Medicare–covered services	Chronically ill with functional needs
San Diego (1979–84)*	Case management and non-Medicare–covered home services	Requires assistance to remain at home, risk of institutionalization, or needs nontraditional long-term care
Florida Pentastar (1980–83)*	Case management and non-Medicaid–covered home services	Risk of institutionalization and in need of project services
Nursing Home Without Walls Downstate (1980–83)	Case management and other non-Medicaid–covered home services	Medicaid eligible for nursing home care
Upstate (1980–83)	Case management and other non-Medicaid–covered home services	Medicaid eligible for nursing home care

TABLE 10.1 (Continued)

Project	Interventions	Eligibility Criteria
South Carolina (1980–84)*	Case management and other non-Medicaid–covered home services	Preadmission screening determined Medicaid eligible nursing home applicant
Channeling* Basic (1980–85)	Case management and limited gap-filling services	2 or more ADL impairments, 3 IADLs, or 1 IADL and 2 IADLs with unmet need
Financial (1980–85)	Case management and other home care services	2 or more ADL impairments, 3 IADLs, or 1 IADL and 2 IADLs with unmet need
Acute Stroke (1981–83)	Interdisciplinary team home visits	Victim of acute stroke
ACCESS Medicare/ Private Pay (1982–86)	Case management skilled nursing home and/or non-Medicare–covered home care services	Needs 90+ days of skilled nursing care
Medicare/ Medicaid (1982–86)	Case management skilled nursing home and/or non-Medicare–covered home care services plus non-Medicaid–covered home care services	Needs 90+ days of skilled nursing care
Post-Hospital Support (1983–85)	Case management and interdisciplinary home visits plus services for care givers	Hosp. discharge with problem expected to last 1 yr and qualified for skilled nursing care and has informal care giver

Note: *These studies were randomized, controlled trials; others were nonrandomly selected comparison groups.
Source: Adapted from Weissert, W. G., Cready, C. M., & Pawelak, J. E. (1988).

sometimes be affected, but evidence was tenuous. Counting the 4 studies which examined effects in 2 discrete samples, the total number of studies reviewed was 31. Of those, 28 measured the impact of home care on survival. Half found positive and half found negative impacts. When results were significant (only 8 studies), they were usually positive. However, half (14) of the studies found no significant impacts due to home care. Some studies (6) did not report level of significance.

The effects of physical functioning appear to be negligible. Physical functioning was measured by activities of daily living (ADL), restricted activity days and other measurements. From the total of 31 studies, 26 measured ADL functioning. About half found positive impacts due to home care. Only 7 studies found statistically significant impacts, and again, these were split almost evenly between positive (3) and negative (4) impacts. Similar patterns existed for other measures of physical functioning.

Most psychosocial outcomes, as measured by mental functioning, life satisfaction, social activities, and social interactions, were likewise rarely statistically significant. Though often the direction of findings was predominantly positive, effect sizes were usually very small and transient— lasting only 6 to 12 months despite continued use of home care (Weissert, Cready, & Pawelak, 1988).

Impacts on informal care givers (usually measured as life satisfaction, satisfaction with patient care, or stress) were usually small and nonsignificant, but uniformly positive in direction. Performance by the informal social support network appears to have been substantially unaffected by receipt of expanded formal home care—good news for policymakers concerned that paid care would drive out unpaid care.

In short, from the perspective of outcomes, home care has achieved quite limited success—accomplishing little with respect to objective measures of patient health status, but possibly improving life satisfaction of patients and family care givers by small transient amounts.

Why so little success in the outcomes domain? One obvious explanation is that health and medical care evaluations usually don't show much when the events studied (death, functional status change) are relatively rare in the population (Fuchs, 1974; Grannemann & Pauly, 1983; Benham & Benham, 1975; Newhouse & Friedlander, 1980; Brook et al., 1983; and DesHarnais et al., 1987). Benefits are either not produced or are missed because we have not appropriately matched patients to appropriate outcome expectations. What we need are clinically relevant subgroups of patients who might be successfully treated to ameliorate the specific health risks which they face. While home care use is nominally controlled by patient-specific care plans, both the interventions and the research have been directed to populations that are quite heterogeneous with respect to their specific risks of adverse outcome and their potential for tractability.

In other words, there is a great tendency in home care to assume that patients need pretty much the same thing and are likely to improve in pretty much the same way regardless of important differences in the specific health risks which they may face at a given point in time. Greater potential for achieving success might lie in separating the home care population into groups of individuals who face different risks (e.g., chronic physical function decline; postacute physical function rehabilitation potential; mental decline;

death and family bereavement; satisfaction decline; breakdown of informal care giver support network; hospital readmission; nursing home admission or extended stay; etc.) and treating them in accordance with ameliorating those specific risks.

Research has not yet succeeded in disaggregating the home care population into such groups. When it does, care plans can be tailored to these groups' specific needs, outcomes can be evaluated in terms of avoiding the specific health risks which they face, and resource inputs might be limited to those expected to produce the appropriate outcome. Such an approach would greatly increase statistical power in research studies and is consistent with the findings of several of the recent studies of health and medical care efficacy which have tended to show benefits only in certain subgroups facing rather immediate risks of specific adverse outcomes (Hadley, 1982; Laurie et al., 1984; Keeler et al., 1985; Ware et al., 1986), and with Wennberg's (1985) view that we need much more specific research on the effectiveness of specific medical procedures for specific types of patients.

Strategies for making this match must start with profiles of who is at risk of various adverse outcomes such as death, nursing home admission long stay, hospital admission, readmission or long stay, failure to achieve functional potential, declining life satisfaction, or care giver burnout. Considerable work has already been done on profiling patients at risk of death, hospital admission, and nursing home entry (Boulier & Paqueo, 1988; Campbell et al., 1985; Heinemann, 1985; Branch & Jette, 1982; Cohen, Tell, & Wallack, 1986; Greenberg & Ginn, 1979; Morris, Sherwood, & Gutkin, 1988; Weissert & Cready, 1989b; Cafferata, 1987; Coulton & Frost, 1982; Evashwick et al., 1984). These tools should be used and others developed to estimate patients' risks for each type of outcome.

PROCESS MEASURES OF SUCCESS: EFFICIENCY

When home care first moved to the public agenda in the early 1970s the emphasis was not on outcomes but rather on efficiency. The claim was widely made that it would be a cost-effective substitute for nursing home care. As a consequence, the purpose of home care was to save money by serving patients more efficiently. Results on this point have been uniformly negative (Weissert, Cready, & Pawelak, 1988). While home care does provide a substitute for nursing home care for some patients, for most patients it serves as a complement to existing health care services. Most patients who use home care would not have been in a nursing home without it. Hence their additional costs of home care more than offset the savings produced by keeping a few patients out of nursing homes. Consequently, home care has not proved to be a cost-effective substitute for institutional care.

Surprisingly, cost increases have not been particularly large, however, averaging somewhere between 15 and 20% over the past three decades (Weissert & Cready, 1989a). This leads to the question: Could home care be delivered more efficiently so that it might move closer to a break-even point?

This potential appears to be worth exploring for one important reason: Most of the ways in which home care could be made more efficient appear to be traceable to better management practices which in turn might result if better data were available for management decision making.

The following formula for net costs of home care tells the story: Net costs = savings minus new spending, where savings refer to avoided nursing home and hospital care and new spending is for outpatient services and new home care services. (The value of patient benefits may also be added to the equation, but is very difficult to quantify.)

In essence this formula means that the better job home care does of targeting services to patients at high risk of long nursing home stays or hospital admission—and the better job it does of avoiding those admissions or shortening stays—the more savings are generated that can be used to offset the new costs of home care and other outpatient services used by home care patients.

Conversely, if home care patients are given cheaper home care services or fewer of them, new home care costs are reduced and therefore more limited success in generating savings from avoided inpatient care is required.

How well has home care succeeded in targeting patients at risk of long nursing home admission, avoiding those admissions as well as hospital admissions, and reducing lengths of stay? And how well has use of home care been controlled to make it as efficient as possible?

Results are mixed. Typically, among the studies reviewed, about one-fourth or one-fifth (depending upon whether or not results are weighted by study population size) of home care patients would have entered a nursing home without home care, and they would have had a length of stay of about 4 months, resulting in a per capita cost of $3059. By decreasing admissions by approximately one-fourth and length of stay by about 11%, home care was able to decrease the per capita cost of nursing home care by just under a half (46%). In addition hospital admissions are typically relatively high among home care patients, but they tend not to be much afffected by home care, nor do lengths of stay drop by much. Detailed results are presented in Weissert and Cready (1989a). Therefore, while some savings are produced on these institutional use reductions, they tend to be offset by large spending on home care (Weissert & Cready, 1989a).

One of the reasons for such large home care spending appears to be a lack of consensus on home care utilization guidelines. Like all health care use, much of home care use is stochastic and defies explanation by health services researchers. But further analysis (in progress by the author and colleagues) of utilization patterns from the National Long-term Care Channeling Evaluation suggests that there is substantial room for development of clinical guidelines for utilization control, especially to decrease intensity of use after the patient and family care giver have effectively adapted to the care giving role. If home care suffers the same diminishing returns typical of most other inputs in life including health care (Fuchs, 1974), one might expect a systematic effort to reduce frequency, intensity and skill level of home care to decline after a few months of care. Yet patterns of home care use tend to show little of this diminishing level of use with time.

Likewise, lack of clinically relevant subgroups, discussed above as potentially important to enhanced outcomes, also are likely to be of great importance to utilization decisions. Care planners might be willing to work within a break-even budget constraint if they had the discretion and knowledge to tailor their resource spending to patients' potential to benefit.

In short, while home care has not yet been sufficiently successful in terms of efficiency to actually cost less than existing options, achievement of that goal may be closer today than it was a decade ago when home care treatment groups cost 60 to 70% more than their control groups (Weissert, Wan, Livieratos, & Katz, 1980; Weissert, Wan, Livieratos, & Pelligrino, 1980). Needed are some better clinical tools for selecting patients, including identification of those at risk of institutionalization and other adverse outcomes, and some clinically appropriate utilization control guidelines capable of achieving maximum benefit at minimum cost.

A shift in the home care cost research agenda from whether or not home care is cost-effective to how to make it cost-effective might greatly enhance its prospects for future success in the process of home care.

POLITICAL SUPPORT AND RATIONALES, QUALITY ASSURANCE MECHANISMS, AND ACCOUNTABILITY

Because it is not simply a private good, but one that must rely upon public subsidy, the ultimate measure of home care's success may have little to do with either outcomes or efficiency. If home care could garner sufficient political support to ensure a steady and adequate source of public payment, it would "succeed" in one important sense, efficiency, outcome issues not withstanding.

Yet, one must ask why that has not happened already? Why have the states or Congress not funded broad-based eligibility for home care for the aged? Current federal funding for home care comes from a variety of fragmented and niggardly sources including Medicare, Medicaid, Social Services Block Grant, Older American's Act, Veteran's Administration, and a variety of state and locally funded programs.

Such small fractions of the larger health care spending probably reflect more than anything else concerns over potential to exacerbate runaway budget deficits. Failure by an overwhelming vote in Congress of the Pepper bill last year—which would have extended home care to all elderly suffering dependency in at least 2 activities of daily living—appeared to reflect "sticker shock" at its $50 billion per year price tag.

But another reason for insufficient funding may be that home care has not succeeded in establishing a sufficiently strong rationale for itself. What is needed is a good enough reason to provide home care that society is willing to do it even at the cost of doing less about some competing worthy social goals. What comes to mind here is the floundering position in which home care finds itself when its two major claims of purpose (cost savings and improved outcomes) are substantially or wholly taken away by an overwhelmingly consistent body of research findings showing few benefits and negative savings.

Though home care advocates continue despite the contrary evidence to claim outcome and efficiency benefits, currently neither claim carries much weight among those familiar with the home care demonstration project findings, including federal budget staff, congressional committee staff and most state Medicaid directors. There is simply no way that home care can be convincingly sold to well informed policy analysts on the basis that it will save money. Arguing outcome benefits means citing small and transient satisfaction benefits and reduction of unmet needs without consequent change in health status.

Two alternative rationales have been less well developed. The first is that home care serves primarily not the patient but the informal (e.g., family) care giver. Satisfaction benefits were higher among informal care givers than patients in the recent National Long-term Care Channeling Evaluation (Kemper, 1988; Applebaum et al., 1988). Second, home care now appears to be rationed on the basis of price, irrespective of need—a notion which seems to fly in the face of the purpose of Medicare: to remove price as a barrier to equal access to health care by the elderly.

Certainly the assertion that home care in its various forms (respite, day care, homemaker aide, etc.) can take the burden off the care giver is a point that has been made. But the notion that the real client is the informal care giver has been advanced by few home care commentators (Hendrickson, 1988). Clearly society has an important stake in keeping the family care-giving network in place. Replacing it rather than supplementing it with formal care would be enormously expensive.

Indeed, employers have begun to recognize that workplace efficiency may be enhanced by programs which support family care givers in the work force. Recent developments such as employer-supported family relations counsel-ors and the American Association of Retired Persons—Travelers Insurance Company's survey of care-giving among its work force (Opinion Research

Corporation, 1988) demonstrate that there is substantial potential to marshal support in the future around home care's role in freeing the employed informal care giver from burdens which may interfere with work force productivity. The potential is enchanced by the steady increase in labor force participation among the group which has the highest potential for becoming informal care givers—females. A recent national survey of adult day care family care givers found that one-fourth of them were in the labor force (Weissert et al., in press). It takes no soothsayer to anticipate that use of home care services will increase in the future as a means of freeing informal care givers to go to work. While a true cost-effectiveness analysis from the employer's perspective might show that home care costs more than it saves in lost productivity, firms may nonetheless be forced to provide this benefit option if they are to compete successfully for top female employees. If firms want to avoid this expense, one way would be to support government subsidy of care giver relief programs such as home care.

What makes this especially relevant is that it offers a rationale for providing home care to a subgroup of home care patients for whom improved outcomes other than care giver relief are not relevant.

The necessity of public subsidy if equity' of access is to be achieved represents another important potential rationale for public payment for home care. Preliminary and as yet unpublished research by the author and colleagues suggests that among patients who are dependent in activities of daily living, use of home care increases with income. This suggests that it is currently rationed on the basis of price and ability to pay, not need. This is the opposite of the Medicare dream of equal access to health care among the aged.

No doubt this finding reflects the deliberately restrictive eligibility requirements of Medicare—the program under which most middle-class elderly would be likely to qualify. Medicare covers home care only for patients who qualify as homebound, need a skilled service, and need it only intermittently—typically for no more than 3 weeks. Except for incidental help with bathing, eating, and dressing of a skilled-care patient, aide services are not covered. This effectively excludes most nonacute elderly patients from eligibility for home care services under Medicare. Indeed, home care advocates have recently accused the Health Care Financing Administration of deliberately adopting a policy of more aggressive denials of home care applications (United States Senate, 1988)—a response to increased home care use following implementation of Medicare's prospective payment system for hospitals. Even the limited Medicare benefit currently authorized is thought to be less available in rural areas (United States Senate, 1988).

Again, if home care were theater tickets, few would care that it appears to be rationed on the basis of income and geography. But it is not. Instead, comparing across a subgroup with obvious commonality of need— dependency and lack of social support—price and where they live make differences in who gets care and who does not. The contemporary philosopher John Rawls would regard such a policy as unjust (Daniels, 1985) because it fails to serve the interests of this very disadvantaged social group: dependent elderly and their informal care givers. Whether or not a sufficient number of congressmen and senators would agree remains to be seen, but in the past, equity has been a venerated rationale for public intervention.

Prospects for achieving success in obtaining broader and less fragmented public subsidy of home care on the basis of equity of access and relief of informal care givers might be further enchanced if the suggestions made above for improved home care process were heeded: If home care were delivered efficiently, to those well defined groups of patients or their informal care givers most likely to benefit in specific ways, the cost might be brought down and the benefits brought up so that an argument based upon equity of access to some of society's most disadvantaged members might be persuasive.

Home care might also improve its potential for garnering political support if it were able to make a better case for assured quality of care and accountability to patients, families, and payors. At present, quality assurance in the home care field is almost entirely at the structural level—audits to determine that care was authorized and documented as having been delivered. Presentations at a recent Department of Health and Human Services (DHHS)–sponsored conference on home care quality assurance (DHHS, 1988) made it clear that few standards for measuring quality exist, few mechanisms are in place to enforce standards other than by paper review, and patients typically have little protected opportunity for redress if the quality of the care they receive is substandard. Considering that aides are typically entry level workers, untrained or minimally trained, and unsupervised for much of their work day, the vulnerable population they serve would seem especially in need of oversight, assurance, and accountability mechanisms. Arguing the need for training of home care aides, a recent United States Senate (1988) report cited results of a 1987 survey by the National League for Nursing which showed that most home health aides were untrained in tasks likely to be asked of them in caring for elderly patients (e.g., 30% did not know what to do if a patient stopped breathing). Home care does not appear to have succeeded in developing the necessary structures to assure quality and accountability.

CONCLUSIONS

Home care produces minimal measurable outcome benefits; it costs more than it saves; it lacks a clear purpose in light of its minimal outcome and efficiency benefits; it is not well targeted to subgroups for whom level and mix of inputs can be weighted against expected outcome benefits; it has failed to garner sufficient political support to provide broad and unfragmented reimbursement; it lacks appropriate mechanisms for quality assurance and patient accountability guarantees; and it is available only on an inequitable basis. In these senses home care appears not to have succeeded by many of the standards which might reasonably be applied.

On the other hand, it has become more efficient and shows the potential with better management of actually breaking-even or coming very close. It shows potential to benefit more patients if appropriate subgroups are served and their outcomes well specified and measured.

In turn such subgroups and their appropriate outcomes—including for example informal care giver relief—could provide home care with an appropriate purpose—or in the economist's argot "objective function." An additional rationale for public intervention may be available by appeal to an equity-of-access argument based upon Medicare's objectives and indications of price and geographic rationing. Its shortcomings in terms of aide training and the need for quality assurance and patient accountability mechanisms have now been recognized and are likely to see improvement efforts in the near future.

In short, home care has not yet succeeded in outcome, process, or structural goals. It's advocates need first to figure out who should get it, how much they should get, and what the care is supposed to accomplish. As this happens, it may come closer to achieving another objective: publicly subsidized equity of access to those who need it.

REFERENCES

Applebaum, R. A., Christianson, J. B., Harrigan, M., & Schore, J. (1988). The evaluation of the national long-term care demonstration: The effect of channeling on mortality, functioning, and well-being. *Health Services Research, 23,* 143–159.

Benham, A., & Benham, A. (1975). The impact of incremental medical services on health status, 1963–1970. In R. Anderson, J. Kravitz, & D. W. Anderson (Eds.), *Equity in Health Services: Empirical Analysis of Social Policy* (pp. 217–228). Cambridge, MA: Ballinger.

Boulier, B. L., & Paqueo, V. B. (1988, May). On the theory and measurement of the determinants of mortality. *Demography, 25,* 249–263.

Branch, L., & Jette, A. (1982). A prospective study of long-term care institutionalization among the aged. *American Journal of Public Health, 72,* 1373–1379.

Brook, R. H., Ware, J. E., Rogers, W. H., Keeler, E. B., Davies, A. R., Donald, C. A., Goldberg, G. A., Lohr, K. N., Masthay, P. C., & Newhouse, J. P. (1980). Does free care improve adults' health? *New England Journal of Medicine, 309,* 1426–1433.

Cafferata, G. L. (1987). Marital status, living arrangements, and the use of health services of elderly persons. *Journal of Gerontology, 42,* 613.

Campbell, A. D., Diep, C., Reinken, J., & McCosh, L. (1985). Factors predicting mortality in a total population sample of the elderly. *J Epidemiol Community Health, 39*, 337–342.

Cohen, M., Tell, E., & Wallack, E. (1986). Client-related risk factors of nursing home entry among elderly adults. *Journal of Gerontology, 41*, 785–792.

Coulton, C., & Frost, A. K. (1982). Use of social and health services by the elderly. *Journal of Health and Social Behavior, 23*, 330.

Daniels, N. (1985). *Just Health Care*, D. I. Wikler, (Ed.). New York: Cambridge University Press.

DesHarnais, S., Kobrinski, E., Chesney, J., Long, M., Ament, R., & Fleming, S. (1987, Spring). The early effects of the prospective payment system on inpatient utilization and the quality of care. *Inquiry*, 7–16.

Donnebedian, A. (1980). *The Definition of Quality and Approaches to its Assessment: Explorations in Quality Assessment and Monitoring, Vol. 1.* Ann Arbor, MI: Health Administration Press.

Evashwick, C., Rowe, G., Diehr, P., & Branch, L. (1984). Factors explaining the use of health care services by the elderly. *Health Services Research, 19*, 357.

Fuchs, Victor, R. (1974). *Who Shall Live?* New York: Basic Books.

Grannemann, T. W., & Pauly, M. V. (1983). *Controlling Medicaid Costs: Federalism, Competition and Choice* (Chapters 1–3, pp. 1–29). Washington, DC: American Enterprise Institute.

Greenberg, J., & Ginn, A. (1979). A Multi-variate Analysis of the Predictors of Long-Term Care Placement. *Home Health Services Quarterly, 1*, 75–79.

Hadley, J. (1982). *More Medical Care, Better Health?* Washington, DC: The Urban Institute Press.

Heinemann, G. (1985). Negative Health Outcomes Among the Elderly: Predictors and Profiles. *Research on Aging, 7*, 363–382.

Hendrickson, M. C. (1988). State Tax Incentives for Persons Giving Informal Care to the Elderly. *Health Care Financing Review*, (Annual Supplement), 123–128.

Keeler, E. B., Brook, R. H., Goldberg, G. A., Kamberg, C. J., & Newhouse, J. P. (1985). How Free Care Reduced Hypertension in the Health Insurance Experiment. *JAMA, 254*, 1926–1931.

Kemper, P. (1988). The Evaluation of the National Long Term Care Demonstration: Overview of the Findings. *Health Services Research, 23*, 1.

Laurie, N., Ward, N. B., Shapiro, M. F., & Brook, R. H. (1984). Termination from Medical—Does It Affect Health? *The New England Journal of Medicine, 311*, 480–484.

Morris, J. N., Sherwood, S., & Gutkin, C. E. (1988). Inst-Risk II: An Approach to Forecasting Relative Risk of Future Institutional Placement. *Health Services Research, 23*, 511–536.

Newhouse, J. P., & Friedlander, L. J. (1980). The Relationship Between Medical Resources and Measures of Health: Some Additional Evidence. *The Journal of Human Resources, 15*, 200–218.

Opinion Research Corporation (1988). A National Survey of Caregivers. Final report for The American Association of Retired Persons and The Travelers Foundation. Washington, DC.

Pauly, M. (1983). Is Medical Care Different? In Greenberg, W. (Ed.), *Competition in the Health Care Sector: Past, Present and Future.* Washington DC: Federal Trade Commission, 19–27.

United States Department of Health and Human Services (1988). Report on the National Invitational Conference on Home Care Quality: Issues and Accountability, Vol. 1. Summary of Proceedings by The Office of the Assistant Secretary for Planning and Evaluation. Washington, DC.

United States Senate (1988). Home Care at the Crossroads. An information paper by the staff of the Special Committee on Aging, United States Senate. 100th Cong., 2d Sess., Serial No. 100-H. Washington, DC.

Ware, J. E., Brook, R. H., Rogers, W. H., Keeler, E. B., Davies, A. R., Sherbourne, C. D., Goldberg, G. A., Camp, P., & Newhouse, J. P. (1986, May). Comparison of Health Outcomes of a Health Maintenance Organization with Those of Fee-For-Service Care. *Lancet, 3,* 1017–1022.

Weissert, W. G., & Cready, C. M. (1989a). A Prospective Budgeting Model for Home and Community-Based Long-Term Care. *Inquiry, 26,* 116–129.

Weissert, W. G., & Cready, C. M. (1989b, October). Toward a Model for Improved Targeting of Aged at Risk of Institutionalization. *Health Services Research, 24,* 485–510.

Weissert, W. G., Cready, C. M., & Pawelak, J. E. (1988). The Past and Future of Home and Community-based Long-term Care. *Milbank Quarterly, 66,* 309–388.

Weissert, W. G., Elston, J. M., Bolda, E. J., Zelman, W. N., Mutran, E., & Mangum, A. B. (in press). *Adult Day Care: Findings from a National Survey.* Baltimore, MD: Johns Hopkins University Press.

Weissert, W. G., Wan, T. T. H., Livieratos, B., & Pellegrino, J. (1980). Cost-Effectiveness of Homemaker Services for the Chronically Ill. *Inquiry, 17,* 230–243.

Weissert, W. G., Wan, T. T. H., Livieratos, B., & Katz, S. (1980). Effects and Costs of Daycare Services for the Chronically Ill: A Randomized Experiment. *Medical Care, 18,* 567–587.

Wennberg, J. E. (1985). On Patient Need, Equity, Supplier-induced Demand, and the Need to Assess the Outcome of Common Medical Practices. *Medical Care, 23,* 512–520.

11
Issues Related to Assuring Quality in Home Health Care*

Catherine Hawes
Robert L. Kane

INTRODUCTION AND OVERVIEW

Improving quality assurance in long-term care is critical. The increasing frailty and impairment of patients, growing concerns about quality, the potential effects of pressures to contain costs, and changes in the structure of the industry have generated considerable attention to the issue of quality assurance. This concern is heightened by the rapid growth in the number of elderly at risk of needing long-term care and by pressures exerted on these programs by policies aimed at the acute care sector. Moreover, these issues are especially compelling in home health care. The vulnerability of home health clients to poor care in an in-home setting, where monitoring of the care provider is difficult, makes developing improved measures of quality and methods for quality assurance particularly critical.

Renewed interest and concern about the quality of care received by the elderly has accompanied the advent of Medicare's prospective payment system for hospitals. This concern initially focused on acute care but expanded to include post-acute care—both in terms of access and quality. In the nursing home sector, heightened public and congressional attention and concern about quality were accompanied by the activities and recommendations of the Institute of Medicine Committee on Nursing Home Regulation (1986) and a law suit (*Smith* v. *Heckler*) to produce significant changes in federal regulation. Similarly new momentum developed for improving regu-

*This chapter was originally prepared for The Institute of Medicine Committee on Designing a Strategy for Quality Review and Assurance in Medicare.

lation of Medicare-certified home health care as a result of recent congressional hearings and the American Bar Association's report, *The Black Box of Home Care Quality* (ABA, 1986). At the same time, the 1987 Omnibus Budget Reconciliation Act (OBRA) regulations for nursing homes provided a model for reforms aimed at home health agencies.

NEED FOR IMPROVED QUALITY ASSURANCE IN HOME HEALTH CARE

A variety of factors have made the topic of quality measurement and assurance for home health care an especially relevant topic. Perhaps the most central concerns are that the elderly needing and receiving in-home care are particularly vulnerable to inadequate care and that current public regulation is poorly equipped to assure the quality of in-home services. As the ABA notes in its "Black Box" report (1986),

> Consumers and their families face an utterly confusing array of changing services, a dearth of information on which to base expectations, and little control over what happens. Even more significant is the in-home location of services that makes their actual delivery essentially invisible and, therefore, largely beyond the easy reach of public or professional scrutiny.

These concerns are heightened by a number of factors including

- increasing need and demand for home health care;
- increasing acuity of patient condition;
- generalized concerns about quality of care for the elderly and specific concerns about the quality of home health care;
- pressure to contain costs, augmenting concerns about access and quality of patient care; and
- concerns about the difficulty of regulating home health care and the adequacy of the current QA system.

Increasing Need for Home Health and Increasing Patient Acuity

> The need for home health care is critical and is growing, and those needing home health care are now more dependent and have more intense subacute needs. As a result, monitoring the quality of care provided in the home is increasingly important.

The long-term care sector in general is experiencing increased need and demand for services. Demographic projections point to continued growth in the number of persons over the age of 65 and, in particular of the "old" old. At the same time, research demonstrates that this population's use of formal health care is significantly higher than that of the general population (Doty, Liu, & Weiner, 1985; Berk & Bernstein, 1985; Liu, Manton, & Liu, 1985). In home health care, this finding holds the users are predominantly elderly (Callahan, 1985) and therefore, increases in the aged population are profoundly felt in this sector. These trends, then, represent a challenge for the formal health care system in general and for home health in particular, in which increased use is clearly linked to beneficiary age (Gornick & Hall, 1988; Callahan, 1985; Leader, 1986; Lave, 1985).

The demographic-driven increase in the need for home health care is accompanied by increasing levels of dependency among patients. Although Medicare home health care is predominantly a response to acute care needs, chronic diseases and disabilities also contribute to the need for in-home health care. While some experts predict increased longevity will not be associated with greater disability and chronicity (Fries & Crapo, 1981) many studies find that the prevalence of chronic disease and disability appears to be increasing at the same rate as the aging of the population (Findley & Findley, 1987; Soldo & Manton, 1985).

Public policies are also contributing to increased demand for home health care as well as to the increased acuity of patient need. Such policies include the liberalization of Medicare's home health benefit and the easing of the restriction on proprietary agencies' participation in Medicare. Under the Omnibus Budget Reconciliation Act (OBRA) of 1980 the 100-visit limitation was eliminated, as were the 3-day prior hospitalization eligibility requirement and the Part B deductible for home health services. And in OBRA 1981, occupational therapy (OT) was included in the services needed to qualify for Medicare eligibility.[*] Similarly, more procedures, such as intravenous therapy and chemotherapy, are being allowed as part of Medicare-reimbursable home health services (Leader, 1986; Wood, 1984).

A variety of other policies are also thought to have contributed to increased demand and patient acuity in long-term care. Nursing home preadmission screening, limits on nursing home bed supply, case management, expanded community-based care, and, in some states, case mix reimbursement systems for nursing homes appear to have accelerated this transformation in patient disability and acuity among nursing home residents and among those receiv-

---

[*]According to Gornick and Hall (1988) if part-time skilled nursing or part-time speech therapy are needed, Medicare can also pay for OT, part-time services of home health aides, medical social services, medical supplies, and durable medical equipment. However when skilled nursing, PT or speech therapy are no longer needed, Medicare will continue to pay for home health if OT is needed.

ing care in other modalities, such as home health care (GAO, 1983; Kane & Kane, 1987; Schneider et al., 1987). In effect, as the use of nursing homes has become more restricted, community-based providers are experiencing a concomitant increase in patient acuity. At the margin at least, some substitution of Medicare home health care for Medicaid- and private pay–funded nursing home care seems to occur (Shaughnessy, Kramer, & Schlenker, 1987).

Medicare's prospective payment system (PPS) for hospitals also seems to have had a significant effect on demand and patient acuity. The general perception is that, under PPS, hospitals have an incentive to discharge patients as soon as medically feasible. However, HCFA's 1985 PPS report to Congress reported no growth in the number of home health visits per person and no increase in discharges to SNFs. And in the 1986 hearings before the U.S. Senate Special Committee on Aging, HCFA officials made much the same argument about the paucity of PPS effects on the need for post-acute care (U.S. Senate–Aging, 1986). Other testimony at that hearing and subsequent empirical analyses (e.g., Gornick & Hall, 1988), however, suggest a strong PPS effect.

Other witnesses noted that changes in Medicare's eligibility and coverage determinations, as well as tight supply of SNF beds and the slight lag in response in Medicare home health services were more persuasive explanations for the lack of increased use of Medicare-covered post-acute care services (U.S. Senate–Aging, 1986; see also Gornick & Hall, 1988, and Benjamin, 1986a, who note significant variations in the number of persons who use home health and in the average number of visits by geographic area). Indeed, other studies have found increases in use of home health and in patient acuity in the post-PPS period, although causality cannot strictly be attributed to PPS (GAO, 1986; Leader, 1986).

In general, due to a variety of factors, average length-of-stay (LOS) among Medicare patients was decreasing in the pre-PPS period in all acute care hospitals. As the UCSF Institute for Health Policy and Aging found (1985) the average LOS of 13.4 days in 1968 dropped to 10.2 days by 1982 and 8.9 days in 1984. However, the rate of decrease accelerated in the post-PPS period, with the average LOS for Medicare patients dropping approximately 1 day between 1983 and 1984 in hospitals without a waiver for PPS implementation (Beebe, Lubitz, & Eggers, 1985)

The significantly declining LOS among Medicare patients may have two effects. First, demand for home health services may increase, as home health care is more easily expanded in response to increased demand than the supply of nursing home beds, and the elderly overwhelmingly prefer to receive long-term care services in their homes rather than in an institutional setting (American Association of Retired Persons, 1984; Groth-Junker, & McCusker, 1983; Harris & Associates, 1982; and McAuley & Blieszner, 1985). Indeed, an increased demand for home health as a result of PPS has been borne out by empirical data. For example, while both PPS and non-PPS areas showed a significant increase in hospital discharge to home health as the system was being phased in, the rate of home health use was stronger in PPS areas (Leader, 1986). Areas in which PPS has been in effect since 1983 experienced the greatest increase in both number of home health visits per client and length of service (Pride Institute Journal, 1986, cited in Leader, 1986).

A second potential effect of significantly declining hospital LOS among Medicare patients is that the patient's condition at the time of hospital discharge may be more acute, requiring more extensive and more sophisticated post-acute care. Those who have been discharged more quickly from acute care hospitals may be more dependent upon salaried care givers coming into their homes and less able to oversee or monitor them (Gelder & Berstein, 1986; Bell, 1987). Several studies suggest such increased dependency is occurring (e.g., Forgy & Williams, 1987). One study comparing patient hospital discharge status in 1981/82 with that in 1984/85 found significant reductions in LOS for 5 DRG categories studied and a small but significant increase in the level of patient dependency at discharge (Coe, Wilkinson, & Patterson, 1986). Other studies suggest an increase in patient dependency has occurred and cite as evidence the significant increase found in the level and scope of home health services provided, particularly increases in skilled nursing services and more advanced technologies, such as IVs, respiratory therapy, and chemotherapy (e.g., Wood, 1984; Harlow & Wilson, 1985; and Taylor, 1986).

Additional studies support the contention that patient acuity and dependency have increased in the last few years. The Institute for Health and Aging at the University of California–San Francisco has received funding to examine several areas of public policy effects on the long-term care sector. One of these studies involved interviews with personnel in 100 home health agencies in 8 states over a 3-year period beginning in 1983. The agencies report an increase in elderly clients, particularly those 75 and older, and they indicate that they are seeing a sicker clientele (Wood, 1984). Similarly the National Long-Term Care Study at the University of Colorado examined changes in case mix in nursing homes and home health agencies between a pre- and post-PPS time period (Shaughnessy, Kramer, & Schlenker, 1987). The Colorado study found significant increases among home health agency patients in dependencies in the activities of daily living (ADLs), instrumental activities of daily living (IADLs) and certain subacute problems after the implementation of PPS.[*] The study also found that home health agency case mix changes were primarily attributable to the more debilitated status of Medicare beneficiaries using home health care (Shaughnessy, Kramer, & Schlenker, 1987).

[*]ADLS include bathing, dressing, grooming, eating, transferring, and toileting. IADLS include such activities as housekeeping, taking medications, telephoning, shopping, and meal preparation.

These findings point to an increasingly critical role for Medicare-certified home health in the post-PPS era of health care. Given the increasing demands for services and the acuity of patient need, issues of cost and of quality become more pressing. Further, as growing demand pushes Medicare costs up, policies designed to contain such cost increases may place even greater pressure on the regulatory system to assure adequate quality.

Concerns About Quality of Home Health Care

There is concern about the ability of the home health sector to respond appropriately and with acceptable quality to the increased demand and acuity of condition among patients.

This concern arises out of 5 related factors. First, although home health care generally enjoys a good reputation, serious questions have arisen about the quality of home health care. Second, state and federal quality assurance systems, where they exist, have at best worked imperfectly, while peer and professional reviews have also been inadequate. Third, the drive to contain program costs may have an adverse impact on quality of care. Fourth, the growth of the proprietary home health sector and of unlicensed agencies may negatively affect quality of care. Finally, the nature of home care means that minimal professional supervision of direct care will occur at the same time that there is heavy reliance on nonprofessional caregivers who work with vulnerable clients.

While the home health care sector has generally enjoyed a more respectable reputation than nursing homes, there do appear to be some problems. The ABA (1986) recently described some of the problems identified by various regulatory officials, providers, advocates, and consumers. They include:

- physical injury of clients (both accidental and intentional);
- worker tardiness or failure to show up or spend the specified amount of time with the client;
- inadequate performance of duties;
- attitudinal problems among workers, including insensitivity, disrespect, intimidation, and abusiveness; and
- theft and financial exploitation.

Recent news reports and anecdotal evidence tend to support the bleak picture painted by the ABA report. In 1987 and 1988, newspaper reports from Florida described deaths of elderly clients that were related to the deficiencies in home health care, as well as both physical and financial abuse. Similarly, the California Auditor-General surveyed home care providers in 3 counties and found 709 providers with criminal convictions (Harrington, *1988*).

These complaints and problems have largely been dismissed by the National Association for Home Care (NAHC), the largest trade association representing home health agencies. NAHC sees these problems as episodic and occurring mostly in unlicensed agencies, rather than Medicare-certified agencies.* Nevertheless, some of the abuse in Florida was committed by home health aides employed by Medicare-certified agencies. And other evidence points to potentially serious deficiencies among even the Medicare-certified agencies.

Leader (1986) reports the results from 1985 HCFA surveys of Medicare-certified home health care providers in New Jersey and Region 2 (New York, the Virgin Islands, and Puerto Rico). These surveys found widespread and serious deficiencies in significant aspects of the current standards affecting patient care (HCFA, 1984). For example:

- "coordination of patient services": 40% of New Jersey certified providers and 22% of Region 2 providers were deficient;
- "plan of treatment": 60% of New Jersey providers and 25% of Region 2 agencies failed to meet the standard;
- "conformance with physician orders": 70% of agencies in New Jersey and 26% of Region 2 providers were deficient; and
- "clinical record review": 48% of New Jersey Medicare-certified agencies and 24% of Region 2 agencies were deficient.

Other studies tend to substantiate the finding of potential problems with quality of care in home health agencies (HHAs). For example, Shaughnessy and colleagues (1987) report that in several dimensions of care in HHAs, quality was roughly the same in both the pre-PPS and post-PPS periods. However, selective declines were found among free-standing providers. For example, declines occurred in assessment and documentation and in teaching medication administration.

The National League for Nursing (NLN) is also concerned about the adequacy of home health aide services. The NLN provides accreditation for agencies that meet their standards, and as part of their efforts NLN undertook a study in 1987 to assess aides' skills. Among a group of 265 home nursing aides who had completed a special aide training course,

- 4% could not read a thermometer;
- 1% did not know how to take a patient's pulse;
- 30% did not know what to do if a patient stops breathing;
- 45% did not know proper care for a diabetic;
- 30% could not identify low salt foods;
- 40% did not know how to safely help a stroke victim to walk; and
- 46% did not know how to properly monitor a patient's fluid intake.

*For the elderly in general, this is not a trivial issue. Some estimates place the number of unlicensed agencies—which are set up as "pools" or employment agencies—at nearly equal in number to the approximately 5700 Medicare-certified agencies.

The ABA report (1986) also argued that aides were poorly trained or untrained, were frequently hired by subcontractors, and were often not supervised by home health agency personnel. Reportedly, a forthcoming analysis from the DHHS Inspector-General identifies similar problems with the training and supervision of aides and the quality of home health aide services.

Such findings are disturbing, particularly given the increasing acuity among patients and the more sophisticated array of services and medical technology that are now being used in the home (American College of Physicians, 1986). Thus, the performance of normal duties has become an even more complex task for home health agency personnel. As Harrington (1988) notes,

> The use of intravenous feedings and medication, ventilators, oxygen, special prosthetic equipment and devices, and other high technologies has made patient care mangement by agencies more complex and challenging. The appropriate use of technology, the training and skill levels needed by agency personnel, emergency back-up procedures, training and supervision of family and other informal caregivers, all become problems which derive from the use of high technology in the home and which represent significant quality of care challenges for home health care agencies and personnel.

The provision of such critical services to frail consumers warrants monitoring in any setting. The issue is especially critical when the services are provided at some distance from the clinical "back-up" provided in a clinic or hospital, when supervision and quality review are distant, and when care providers may not be sufficiently or appropriately trained to provide such care (McAllister et al., 1986). Moreover, while aides do not typically provide the same proportion of care in home health that they do in nursing homes, they still provide a significant portion of care, even in Medicare-certified agencies. Indeed, the ABA study (1986) found an increasing trend to use aides for tasks formerly handled by nurses.

Given the findings discussed above and the increasing use of aides in home health care, one's inclination is to regard the NLN findings as exceptionally disturbing. Yet the question remains whether, given their duties and responsibilities, the kind of knowledge represented in the NLN study is critical for an aide and whether the lack of such knowledge translates into poor patient care and "bad" outcomes.

While these findings are troubling, they do not present a clear picture of the general level of quality in the Medicare-certified home health agencies sector. The problems identified by Medicare certification surveys represent deficiencies in the agency's performance on paper. The surveys focused on written documents and agency records in reaching a determination of deficiencies. However, studies in the nursing home sector reveal that homes can achieve a high level of paper compliance while providing abysmal patient care on a daily basis. We do not know, with the home health agencies in question, whether the deficiencies that exist in their paper work reflect deficiencies in patient care or whether even more serious patient care problems exist that are not identified in surveys.

While it is difficult to generalize about the overall quality of home health care, the available information suggests cause for concern and the need for improved measures of quality. Yet given current regulatory practices and standards, there is, as the ABA notes, little chance of knowing what the quality of home health care is across the nation. As noted, the growing demand for services, the apparent increase in patient acuity, and the pressure to contain costs make the issue of quality a significant public policy concern.

Rising Costs and Interest in Containing Expenditures

Rapidly growing expenditures on home health care are a source of concern to policymakers; however, efforts to contain these costs may have the effect of reducing needed access and impairing quality.

Expenditures on home health care have been growing for the last 20 years and are expected to continue expanding well into the future. In recent years, these expenditures have risen at an average annual rate of between 20 and 25%, with total costs of home health products and services expected to grow to more than $16 billion by 1990 (Frost & Sullivan, 1983). While expenditures on home health care were only 3% of the Medicare budget in 1984, it has been the fastest growing segment of the Medicare budget in each of the past several years. For example home health's recent average annual growth rate of 25% contrasts sharply with the 3% increase in Medicare SNF expenditures (Gornick et al., 1985).

The policy response among Medicare policymakers to such rapidly increasing expenditures—and the prospect of future growth of this magnitude—has been twofold: utilization and cost controls, both of which have implications for quality and the need for improved quality assurance.

Utilization Controls

Although some health utilization is increasing rapidly, expenditures have not kept pace with the growth rates projected by both the Congressional Budget Office (CBO) and HCFA (CBO, 1983). From Medicare's perspective, as a result, there have been some cost-savings legislative changes in the program since 1980. Such changes include reimbursement ceilings, eliminating need for occupational therapy (OT) as a basis for beneficiary entitlement to home health care, and requiring some copayments on durable medical equipment. However, these legislative changes are generally not considered sufficient to explain the marked slowdown in home health utilization and expenditure relative to the projected growth rates (Leader, 1986).

Bishop and Stassen (1986) note that the primary way to control home health costs is to reduce utilization by limiting access to home health benefits. HCFA appears to have adopted such a strategy and has developed a policy of administratively induced reductions. This policy is manifested in increased denial rates for claims, the elimination of the waiver of liability (which waived repayment of Medicare payments for subsequently denied visits if the percent of denied visits did not exceed 2.5% of the total annual claims for visits), and tightening eligibility by using more stringent definitions of the basic criteria (that a client be "home-bound," need "skilled" services and need only "part-time" or "intermittent" care) (Leader, 1986; Harrington, 1988).

Cost Controls

Since 1979 HCFA has set reimbursement limits on home health visits, based on its definition of "reasonable" costs—that is, those necessary for the efficient delivery of needed services. The limits are based on a percentage of the mean costs reported by more than 2800 HHAs for each discipline, adjusted for inflation and geographic wage variations. (Whether the limit applies to an aggregate or to specific disciplinary services has been a topic of some debate, with each method having been tried.) Over a 3-year period beginning in 1985/1986, HCFA announced that the percentage would move from 120% of the mean costs down to 112% (Liu, Manton, & Liu, 1985).

In HCFA's view the limits on per visit costs give home health agencies an incentive to closely monitor and contain their costs. Yet as with nursing home reimbursement, there is concern that such incentives may be inimical to good quality of care (Cotterill, 1983). There is some concern that agencies with costs above 112% of the mean are not inefficient but have a patient case mix that requires more intensive services than is captured by the average visit in a particular discipline. In addition, there is concern that there are real differences in quality that are reflected in cost differences.[*] For example, providers argue that these cost containment measures (including a prohibition against aggregating their costs) will injure beneficiaries in a variety of ways. They argue that small and rural agencies will be bankrupted, costly services curtailed, and heavy care patients avoided (Leader, 1986).

---

[*]Patient case mix measures explain between 40 and 60% of the variation in nursing home costs (Schneider et al., 1987; Arling et al., 1987; Fries & Cooney, 1985; Cameron & Knauf, 1982; and Schlenker, Shaughnessy, & Yslas, 1983). In home health, such studies are just beginning, but Manton and Hausner (1987) found 6 distinct health and functional status dimensions, combined with informal care resources and local market conditions to explain significant proportions of the variance in individual differences in Medicare home reimbursement and number of visits. The relationship of quality to cost is more complex, although nursing home research suggests a generally weak relationship (Schlenker, 1986).

Other critics of the current system argue that its cost constraints are fairly weak, particularly since the limits apply only to cost per visit, while the number of visits is not financially constrained by the reimbursement limits.[*] As a result, both the number of visits per patient and the charge per user vary significantly by agency type (Callahan, 1985). Again, the extent to which these variations are attributable to differences in patient characteristics (case mix), quality of care, and/or efficiency is unknown. And the existing reimbursement limits do little to assure that such cost variations are related to "policy-acceptable" differences in agency operations.

As a result of such perceived weaknesses in the current reimbursement system, HCFA contracted with Abt Associates for analytic work on prospective payment systems and with the Center for Health Policy Studies for study of competitive bidding approaches to reimbursing HHAs (Curtiss, 1986a; see also GAO, 1985). Others at HCFA and elsewhere have expressed interest in the possibility of developing case mix reimbursement for home health (Foley, 1987; Manton & Hausner, 1987). And there is also interest in per episode reimbursement and capitated systems (Eggers & Prihoda, 1982), with new authorization for risk-sharing contracts between Medicare and HMOs for Competitive Medical Plans (CMPs), as defined by the Tax Equity and Fiscal Responsibility Act (TEFRA) of 1982 (Ginsburg & Hackbarth, 1986). Approximately 70 HMOs had enrolled nearly 500,000 Medicare patients by December 1985 (Iversen & Plick, 1986).

Each of these alternative methods of paying for Medicare beneficiaries home health care has strengths and weaknesses from a quality of care perspective. Thus, reimbursement issues contribute to the need for appropriate, effective, and feasible ways of measuring quality—which could be used to evaluate the impact of these different reimbursement options—as well as improved quality assurance mechanisms that are capable of responding appropriately to any perverse or negative quality incentives embodied in reimbursement methods.

QUALITY ASSURANCE IN HOME HEALTH CARE

State and federal quality assurance activities in home health have been widely criticized for many of the same failings as those that have plagued the nursing home sector; yet the task of monitoring agency performance is more daunting.

There are four basic mechanisms for external quality assurance currently in place for home health care: accreditation by various professional organizations; state licensure; and Medicare and Medicaid certification. Oversight by

[*]However eligibility and coverage determinations often effectively limit the number of visits.

PROs will be added to this, as they assume more responsibility for post-acute care of Medicare beneficiaries. These mechanisms will be considerably altered as a result of OBRA '87.

Accreditation

Three voluntary accreditation programs are now in place for home health agencies. *The National League for Nursing* (NLN) has offered accreditation to home health care providers since 1961. In conjunction with the American Public Health Association, the NLN has been working recently to develop improved structural and process quality standards for home health—covering staffing, programs, strategic planning, marketing, organization and management, and internal evaluation. The revised process includes more extensive process quality measures (e.g., evaluations and discussions of patient assessment and the adequacy of the individual care plan). Other new features include adding client home visits to the accreditation surveys and shortening the period of accreditation (from 5 to 3 years). Approximately 100 providers, primarily Visiting Nurse Associations (VNAs) are accredited by the NLN. In addition, individual VNAs have been active in discussing and developing internal standards and quality review mechanisms (VNA of Texas in Rinke and Wilson, 1987a; VNA of metropolitan Detroit in Rinke and Wilson, 1987b).

The *National Home Caring Council* (NHCC), which is now part of the Foundation for Hospice and Home Care, has accredited both home health aide and homemaker services since 1972. NHCC's standards address training, qualifications, and supervision of aide and homemaker services. The approximately 150 agencies accredited by NHCC are surveyed every 5 years. In addition, both the Foundation and the National Association for Home Care (NAHC), a trade association representing most of the Medicare-certified agencies, are working on the development of voluntary quality of care standards for home health agencies.

In 1986 the *Joint Commission on Accreditation of Healthcare Organizations* (JCAHO) began a 2-year process aimed at developing extensive new standards for home health agencies seeking JCAHO accreditation. The goal was to expand the accreditation process to community-based home care agencies, as well as to serve JCAHO's current predominantly hospital-based HHA clientele, and to expand the present JCAHO standards to more accurately capture process quality for both "health" and "support" services (McCann & Hill, 1986). The JCAHO standards address more than structural features (e.g., staffing). They also address critical elements of process quality, such as patients receiving care in a timely manner, the adequacy of instruction and supervision of staff on equipment use, patients' rights, care planning and provision, internal quality assurance, and so on. JCAHO is currently involved in training its surveyors in the use of the new standards. Currently agencies are surveyed once every 3 years. Finally, it is worth noting that JCAHO is using a new method of providing feedback to the agencies it surveys, one that is discussed at greater length in "State of the Art in Measuring and Assuring Quality," below.

While these voluntary programs may be quite useful for the agencies seeking them—and while deemed status is being proposed by HCFA for NLN and JCAH-accredited agencies *(Federal Register*, December 31, 1987)— they do not employ outcome-based measures in conjunction with structure and process measures. In addition, too little attention is given to significant measures of patient and family care giver satisfaction with home health care. Moreover, unless deemed status is granted, agencies have little reason to seek such accreditation. Further, from the perspective of consumers, accreditation is of limited utility. Records regarding the agency's performance are not public; JCAHO has no mechanisms for receiving or responding to consumer complaints; and JCAHO has neither the power (nor the inclination) to sanction agencies that fail to meet accreditation standards or that, though in minimal compliance, nevertheless provide deficient care in some areas (see IOM, 1986 critique on "deemed status" for nursing homes).

Licensure

Many observers argue that government has a critical responsibility to protect frail, dependent persons receiving services supported by government funds. They also argue that this responsibility may be especially critical when individuals receive services in their own homes, at some distance from professional supervision and oversight. Despite this, many observers note that the home health sector is relatively free from external monitoring (Harrington, 1988; Leader, 1986). Certainly, this argument can be made with respect to the effectiveness of state licensure as a quality assurance mechanism.

According to the ABA's (1986) recent study of home health licensure nationwide, several problems arise with home health licensure as a quality assurance system. Some 35 states require licensure for home health agencies, and some states license only proprietary agencies (ABA, 1986; Leader, 1986). In addition even in states that do license agencies, a vast number of entities providing home care escape licensure altogether. Many agencies—the number ranges from 15% of the total one that is equal to the number of licensed agencies—operate as nurse "pools" or employment agencies and escape licensure requirements (Harrington, 1988).

Second, even in states that license home health agencies, the mechanisms of licensure leaves much to be desired in terms of effective quality assurance. Licensure gives home health agencies the authority to organize and operate but does not necessarily ensure quality (ABA, 1986). The licensure standards are typically very general and weak, seldom exceeding or even reaching Medicare certification standards. Even according to the National Association for Home Care, such standards fail to ensure a financial stability in agencies, adequate staffing, training and supervision, and adequate internal quality assurance (Hawes & Powers, 1987). The state efforts at quality asurance are similarly inadequate in terms of assuring home health quality.

The review of state quality assurance programs for home care conducted by Macro Systems (1988) highlighted the very underdeveloped nature of standards, inspections, and enforcement mechanisms.

- Of the 19 states studied only 3 had objective outcome criteria (Minnesota and South Carolina for Title XX and Wyoming for Title III–funded case management).
- Efforts are mainly structural with worker training, training requirements for aides, licensure of home health agencies based on Medicare Conditions of Participation, some other standards including bills of client rights, codes of ethics, but there is wide variation in these beyond the Conditions of Participation core.
- Agency monitoring of home care was usually required but requirements for supervision vary widely.
- Supervisory home visits are required for home health care but the nature and frequency varies.
- Client assessment and evaluation or case management varies in type and frequency.
- Provider surveys are primarily tied to Medicaid certification, state licensure, and accreditation review activities.

Medicare and Medicaid Certification

As with other areas in which it is a major payor, the federal government has established standards for the type and quality of home health services provided to Medicare beneficiaries (Hawes & Powers, 1987). A provider who wishes to be reimbursed by either Medicare or Medicaid must be certified as in substantial compliance with federal standards before being authorized to receive such payments. With Medicare, agencies must actually be certified. For Medicaid, agencies must merely meet the requirements for certification—but need not actually be certified. As with nursing homes, the responsibility for regulating agencies is shared. The federal government sets the standards, while the states are responsible for monitoring/surveying the agencies and determining whether they are in compliance with the standards (although the cost is paid for by the federal government).

When surveying home health agencies for certification, state health department staff use a survey instrument developed by HCFA that measures basic compliance with the federal Conditions of Participation. These conditions address:

- compliance with state and local laws;
- organization of services and administration;
- requirements for professional staff;
- acceptance of patients, plan of treatment, and medical supervision;
- provision of skilled nursing services;
- provision of therapy services;
- requirements for medical social services;
- availability of home health aide services;
- maintenance of clinical records; and
- ongoing evaluation.

These standards and the survey instrument designed to measure agency compliance with them are subject to many of the criticisms that have been leveled against the old system of standards and surveys for nursing homes (IOM, 1986). First, the standards are largely structural, with some process requirements. Even so, they do not contain such structural items as basic as requirements for the training and competency of aides. In addition, the process quality standards are poorly specified. Further, the standards do not include outcome measures. Thus most of the deficiencies reported for home health care agencies reflect structure and to a lesser extent process deficiencies that have not been related to outcomes of care for home health recipients. While the structure and process problems reported could result in serious problems for clients, generally the surveys did not report such negative consequences. This dearth of outcome measures and information about consequences is not merely the result of inadequate outcome criteria for the surveyors to evaluate. It is also a result of the method of data collection/ surveying conducted under federal guidelines.

The second criticism of home health quality assurance is that it deals largely with "paper compliance." The certification survey instrument consists basically of a checklist of procedural and structural requirements, and a surveyor can audit the agency primarily from agency records. While federal survey procedures require the surveyor conduct a minimum of three home health care visits to clients as part of the survey process, preliminary results of a study of home health regulation in California and Missouri reveals that home visits are frequently not done (Harrington, 1988). Thus, as a practical matter, interviews with patients and their families and observation of care provision are often not part of the survey. In addition, there is no independent assessment of the accuracy and completeness of the agency's initial patient assessment and care plan, nor, as noted, is there any regulatory attention to patient outcomes.

In addition, the procedure for home health survey/certification visits to clients' homes is faulted on grounds similar to the criticisms of nursing home survey process. Nursing home inspections/surveys were often criticized for being announced in advance to providers—or timed so predictably as to be easily anticipated. Critics argue that such a process allows "bad" providers to dramatically change their performance for the brief period around a survey date and therefore does not yield an accurate picture of the care provided (IOM, 1986). The survey process for visits to home health clients receives similar criticism. When conducted as part of survey/certification activities, home visits are scheduled in conjunction with the regular delivery of a home health agency visit to a client. While this may facilitate observation of care, there is some legitimate question as to whether the care provided under observation will accurately replicate care provision that occurs on a routine basis. Further, few observers believe such a process would facilitate an open exchange with the client or a family care giver about any problems with the agency (Harrington, 1988).

More recently, home health surveys have become even more circumscribed. As a result of a number of factors, including federal budget reductions, state licensing and certification agencies appear to be limiting the number of surveys primarily to those agencies about which they receive complaints. While federal guidelines allow a "yearly" survey for less than 100% of HHA, even a goal of annually surveying 53% of all agencies appears to be falling by the wayside. Reports from California indicate that in 1987/88, only about 10% of the Medicare-certified home health agencies actually face yearly surveys (Harrington, 1988).

While standards and surveys come in for criticism, enforcement is also considered a notably weak part of home health quality assurance. Having no intermediate sanctions, HCFA's options are limited. As was the case with Medicare and Medicaid-certified nursing homes prior to OBRA, HCFA's only option for dealing with poor quality providers is termination of the provider agreement. And as with nursing homes, this is a penalty often too severe for mild and moderate deficiencies but seldom used even for serious deficiencies (Leader, 1986; Harrington, 1988). As a result, even if standards and inspections were models of effectiveness, the government would have difficulty enforcing these.

Peer Review

Another group that will become involved in the monitoring of home health agencies is the Peer Review Organization. OBRA 1986 required that PROs, as their contracts were renewed during 1988, begin reviewing the quality of post-acute care for Medicare patients readmitted to the hospital within 31 days of discharge (so called "intervening care"). In addition, PROs are required to investigate any complaints they receive about quality of care in SNFs, home health agencies, and hospital outpatient departments. As yet, however, the PROs have not had an opportunity to demonstrate their effectiveness in assuring high quality of care.

In summary, existing mechanisms for assuring the quality of home health care are inadequate. While developments in the standards and approaches of the NLN and JCAHO are promising, both have serious deficiencies as regulatory mechanisms. Existing regulatory systems suffer from inadequate standards, ineffective surveys/inspections, and insufficient enforcement remedies. Thus, there has been substantial interest among federal policymakers in improving the regulation of home health quality—efforts that have culminated in the "Home Health Quality Improvement" bill enacted by Congress in 1987.

1987 OBRA Mandates on Home Health Quality and Regulation

The Omnibus Budget Reconciliation Act (OBRA) of 1987 (P.L. 100-203) made sweeping revisions of both nursing home and home health conditions of participation (now called requirements) for Medicare and Medicaid, the survey process, and enforcement mechanisms. Indeed, much of the new home health survey process and enforcement remedies are similar to the changes in nursing home regulation, which in turn derive from the recommendations of the Institute of Medicine Committee on Nursing Home Regulation (IOM, 1986).

The new home health conditions of participation create a patients' bill of rights, specify notification/disclosure of agency ownership, require that home health agency personnel be either licensed or trained in a program that meets standards specified by the Secretary of DHHS, include some requirements for the content of the training, and require that the agency include each patient's plan of care in their clinical record.

The new law also sets up a process of "standard" and "extended" surveys for home health agencies, requiring annual surveys without prior notice and scheduled in such a way as to minimize the ability of the provider to predict the timing of the survey. In terms of content, the standard survey, to which each agency is to be subject, calls for visits to the homes of clients, selected on the basis of a "case-mix stratified" sample of the agency's clients, to evaluate the quality of care provided by the agency. The home visits appear to be directed at gathering outcome-based measures of quality, particularly in the areas of physical functioning. In addition, the plan of care and clinical record must be in accord with a "standardized assessment instrument." Finally, the standard survey must be based on a protocol that is developed, tested and validated by the Secretary no later than October 1, 1989.

Extended surveys, which are triggered by negative findings on the standard survey (but can occur for other reasons), will focus on more extensive review of policies and procedures in order to determine whether the apparent negative performance recorded in the standard survey is, in fact, a product of noncompliance with federal conditions of participation. Enforcement remedies are expanded to include intermediate sanctions, such as civil fines, and suspension of payments, and to require what is in effect, temporary "health care receivership" for agencies with serious violations.

In conclusion, enhancing our ability to accurately measure quality of care in home health and to incorporate such measures in quality assurance and reimbursement systems is an issue of national significance. The new regulations, particularly the new survey process, will depend on uniform assessment information on clients (baseline and over time) and the development and use of improved process and outcome quality measures. This development is critical for 4 fundamental reasons:

- The demand for home health care is growing with the aging of the population; moreover, not only is there increasing need for services, there is growing acuity of need among health patients. These factors make the quality of services especially critical.
- Although home health care has not suffered from the scandals and disrepute of the nursing home sector, quality of care nonetheless appears to be a problem. In addition, the pressure to contain costs and utilization, as well as the changing structure of the provider industry, may exacerbate existing quality problems.
- The current quality assurance systems—whether private and voluntary or public and mandatory—appear to have serious limitations in terms of ensuring the provision of adequate home health quality. As providers face greater cost containment pressures, their commitment to maintaining high levels of quality will be severely tested, while cost constraints on government regulatory agencies appear to have left their systems sorely wanting. Given the direction of the home health regulations embodied in OBRA 1987, in terms of uniform patient assessment, an emphasis on outcome-based measures, key indicators of quality, and targeted reviews, the proposed research is critical.
- Finally, the desire of policymakers to improve the provision of home health care to Medicare beneficiaries in other ways, including keeping the program solvent, will lead to experimentation with both new regulatory mechanisms, such as sanctions and incentives, and new reimbursement experiments.

For these reasons, it is essential both to develop new and improved ways of measuring quality and to understand the relationship among various aspects of structural, process, and outcome quality. Such an understanding will contribute to improved standards, enhanced ability to monitor quality (and evaluate the effects of new policies), and more effective use of compliance mechanisms.

STATE OF THE ART IN MEASURING AND ASSURING QUALITY

There is a tendency in long-term care to view quality of care in the same way that one justice of the U.S. Supreme Court reputedly viewed cinematic pornography. The jurist noted that "I can't define it, but I know it when I see it." Whatever the merits of this approach to identifying pornography, such subjectivity and individuality is unworkable in any but the most rudimentary (and small) system aimed at assuring adequate quality of long-term care. Hence the emphasis we find on the search for appropriate and workable definitions and measures of quality.

Defining Quality

As Wyszewianski (1988) notes, there is a tendency to avoid the difficult task of assessing and assuring quality by asserting that no one really knows or can adequately define what quality is. In fact, however, considerable time and attention, much of it fruitful, has been devoted to defining and developing measures in the areas of acute and long-term care.

Home Health Care in Context

Quality assurance has typically been built on the techniques or approaches developed in the acute care sector, including admission and continuing stay reviews and medical care evaluations (Kane et al., 1979; Kane, 1981). However, these approaches must be adapted and supplemented for post-acute care because of the different goals and situations involved. While home health care often shares the objectives of acute care—in terms of patient recovery and rehabilitation—it is, at some level, much more complicated. In home health care, the determinants of need for service include not only the patient's medical condition but also cognitive and functional status. In addition, home health service episodes are typically longer and more difficult to define, and the location of service is the patient's home, where many needs must be met by a combination of formal and informal care providers. Thus, quality in home health care must be defined in multidimensional terms, covering health, functional and social needs of patients. These fundamental differences have implications for how we define and measure home health quality, as well as how we assure it.

These differences between home health care and acute care can be more systematically thought of in terms of five features; time, technology, site, goals, and links to the acute care system (Kane & Kane, 1988).

Time. Home health care typically involves care provided over a longer time period than acute care. Where the latter typically involves a length of stay given in days, and a decreasing number at that, home health care usually occurs over a period of weeks, and sometimes longer (Gornick et al., 1985; Manton & Hausner, 1987; Gornick & Hall, 1988).

Technology. While all patients receiving Medicare-reimbursed home health care require skilled nursing care and/or therapies, and while their plan of care is physician-certified, many also have lost some capacity for self-care and require education to regain self-care abilities and/or some assistance in the activities of daily living (Manton & Hausner, 1987). Thus, home health care often involves what is typically termed "low technology" care, that is help with basic personal care and mobility or the tasks associated with a household (Kane & Kane, 1988). Such assistance may be provided by Medicare-certified home health aides in conjunction with skilled care or by families. But whoever the provider, such care is an essential contributor to the patient's well-being and outcomes.

Site. Home health care is precisely that, health care provided not in an institution (hospital, nursing home) but in a home and at some distance from the initiator of the care, the patient's physician. Moreover, the formal care provider may be present only for short, discrete periods of time. Thus, like ambulatory care, the patient's care and outcome is partly dependent on the patient's and family's ability and willingness to comply with the processes of care specified by the physician and home health provider. This reliance on patient and family compliance can have a significant effect on outcomes. For example, one study finds that home health clients do more poorly than nursing home patients when the "outcome" being considered is continence (Shaughnessy, Kramer, & Schlenker, 1987). Interviews with home health personnel and families reveal that bladder continence programs, such as timed voiding, are difficult for families to accomplish. Additionally, the site (the client's home) makes monitoring quality, whether in terms of process or outcome, more complex.

Goals. The goals of home health care, which in part, define the processes and outcomes of interest, are affected by the nature of the clients, the multiplicity of their care needs, and the different modalities or functions of home health care, which are a response both to patient needs and third party payment criteria. In general, however, home health care goals encompass patient well-being in such aspects as physical health and functioning, including maximizing the ability for self-care, psychological well-being, increasing knowledge about self-care and monitoring, alleviating unmet care needs, and responding to client preferences.

Relationship to Acute Care.   Neither the process of home health care nor the outcomes for patients can be neatly separated from acute care, the setting in which most patients begin their course of treatment, nor from the physician who prescribed home health care. To some significant degree, the quality of each is likely to affect both the course of home health care and the patient's outcomes. Yet little is known about the relationship between the adequacy of acute hospital care and physician care and home health care process and outcomes.

Baumann and her colleagues (1988) have added to this list of unique aspects of home health care several more factors:

- The limited nature of physician participation removes a further opportunity for supervision.
- The large number of unlicensed personnel creates special challenges for assuring that problems are recognized and dealt with.
- The increased use of sophisticated technology (e.g., renal dialysis, total parenteral nutrition, ventilators) stands in stark contrast to the lack of sophistication in the preparation of the workers or the information base available to support them.

Kramer and his colleagues (February 1989) identified as major issues standing in the way of an effective home care quality assessment system:

- the limited ability of home care providers to influence the patient care environment;
- patients often receive other types of care at the same time, both at home and in places like physicians' offices;
- patient goals differ considerably across the spectrum of patients and may differ between those giving and receiving the care; and
- data for quality measurement are more difficult to acquire than in the acute sector, especially the hospital.

Indicators of Quality

In one of the best known and most useful approaches to defining and measuring quality, Donabedian (1966; 1978) suggested classifying measures by whether they evaluate structure, process, or outcome.

Structural measures are both factors that characterize the provider (e.g., ownership, size, location) and various resource inputs (e.g., policies, staffing levels and staff qualifications/credentials, available services such as therapies, equipment). As with nursing homes (IOM, 1986), and for both private (JCAHO, NLN, NHHC) and public agencies, home health licensure accreditation and certification standards are heavily weighted toward structural measures and criteria for them.

Process measures refer to the activities or procedures involved in providing care, such as procedures for patient assessment, services that should be provided given patient care needs, and the manner (service provider, frequency and length of visits) in which care is provided. The evaluation of process quality is typically defined in terms of whether the care meets commonly accepted professional norms or criteria regarding the types of procedures a patient requires and whether the manner in which care is provided meets professional standards. As noted previously, both the NLN and JCAHO have developed more detailed process criteria for home health care (NLN, 1986a; McCann, & Hill 1986). In addition, there has been substantial work in the field of community health nursing on the development of process criteria in home health care (e.g., Januska, Engle, & Wood, 1976; American Nurses Association, 1986; Baer et al., 1984; Daubert, 1977; Griffith, 1986; Sorgen, 1986; Rinke & Wilson, 1987a; 1987b). Further, several of the federal certification standards, such as "conformance with physician's orders" represent types of process criteria.

In addition, Abt Associates has developed a "HomePACS" survey form and protocol designed to measure some process quality aspects of home health care, focusing in particular on the completeness of the initial patient assessment, the content of the plan of care, whether there is evidence in the clinical record that the patient's needs have been reevaluated, and whether the record indicates that prescribed/ordered services and care have been delivered.

The Abt process quality evaluation form also involves respondent/surveyor observation of the home health care giver and is designed to measure process quality. For example, it asks the respondent to determine the appropriateness of care relative to the patient's condition, whether it corresponds to the plan of treatment and plan of care, and to evaluate the care giver's capabilities based on observation. While we have reviewed only the June 1987 draft of this instrument, we regard it as having useful components; however, the lack of definition in several response categories, particularly in the observation form, is troubling in terms of potential reliability problems. Moreover, the apparent inability of the survey to distinguish between "undelivered" services and "unrecorded but delivered" services is troubling. Thus, this form and the protocols suffer from some of the same limitations as the nursing home PACS process, while also representing a tremendous step forward from the traditional home health certification survey (IOM, 1986).

A detailed manual on process quality has also been developed for nursing home patients by Woodson et al. (1981). For a variety of patient conditions it specifies the care required, with appropriate exceptions for particular medical complications. While none of the developers are still with the University of Colorado Center for Health Services Research (CHSR), this manual and its process quality criteria for nursing home patients form the basis for that CHSR's subsequent development of assessment instruments used in the evaluation of hospital-based swing-beds, the National Long-Term Care Study, the Teaching Nursing Home Evaluation, and more recently, the adaptation of these instruments for the HCFA-funded study of home health care through the Center for Health Policy Research.

In summary, there has been substantial work in developing both process criteria and measures for home health quality, and much of it in the nursing literature which has largely been ignored by most long-term care researchers. Moreover, existing criteria and instruments provide a good basis for the development of more focused, case mix–adjusted measures of process quality.

Outcomes. Recently, attention has been focused on the potential for developing outcome-based measures of patient status as the cornerstone of a quality assurance system—in nursing homes, hospitals, and home health. However, the question of whether this is feasible, much less desirable, has not been adequately addressed in home health. Outcome measures are the "end results" of health care, that is what has happened to the patient in terms of cure, rehabilitation, control of illness, and palliation (Brook, Williams, & Avery, 1976). While the strictest definition of outcomes refers to changes in patient status over time that is directly attributable to the care received, some more "intermediate" outcomes are also considered useful in evaluating acute and long-term care (Brook, 1979; Kane et al., 1982; Hawes, 1983). For example, positive outcomes might include improved function and discharge, as well as participation in enjoyable activities and satisfaction. Negative outcomes might be death, bedsores, and urinary tract infections.

Selecting appropriate indicators of outcome quality is a challenging task throughout the health care sector. The classic measures, as Lohr (1988) notes, are "the five Ds": death, disease, disability, discomfort, and dissatisfaction. Although it is possible to conceive of these in the more positive aspects of survival, states of physiologic, physical, and emotional health, and satisfaction, it is at some level easier to define what is clearly a "bad" outcome than to presume that some alternative set constitutes or are proxies for the whole of good quality. This is the rationale in nursing home regulation in New York, for example, in which "sentinel health events" or SHEs represent negative outcomes (decubitus ulcers, urinary tract infections) which, if appropriate care were provided, should have been avoided (Schneider,

Hatcher, & O'Sullivan, 1980). Those measures traditionally used to investigate outcome quality are discussed in greater detail below.

Death. In the acute care sector, premature, avoidable, or unexpected death is often used as a "sentinel" event which raises the possibility of poor quality of care (Rustein et al., 1976). HCFA, for example, in its first contracts with PROs, attempted to operationalize this concept, and the release of hospital-specific mortality rates indicates the prominence HCFA gives to the objective of preventing avoidable deaths. Some long-term care researchers believe premature death, along with discharge and rehabilitation, are good indicators of quality and can be used to compare the performance of nursing homes, and it has been used in a variety of studies (Weissert et al., 1983; Meiners et al., 1985; Chekryn & Roos, 1979; Linn, Gurel & Linn, 1977). Its value as a measure may chiefly be in its nonintrusive nature, its reliability, and the relative ease of collecting it from existing data sources, such as Medicare claims files, if the patient dies in a hospital, nursing home, or home health agency as Medicare patient (Hawes, 1983; Lohr, 1988). Thus, in theory, differences in patient mortality rates, aggregated to an agency-level measure, may be attributable to variations in quality (Lohr, 1988; DuBois, Brook, & Rogers, 1987). However, it is critical to first understand the relationship of individual patient characteristics to this outcome and to adjust comparisons among agencies on the basis of such variations in patient characteristics (DuBois, Brook, & Rogers, 1987; Mitchell, 1978). For example, in adjusting crude death rate for hospitals, DuBois, Brook, and Rogers (1987) used age, origin of patient from the ER or nursing home, and a hospital case mix index based on DRGs. And, based on the large differences in observed versus predicted adjusted death rates, they argue that important differences in hospital performance may exist.

Moreover, it may be important to identify and measure the effect of other factors (such as the quality of prior hospital care and discharge status) that may affect premature mortality if there is any reason to expect such factors would differentially affect the home health agencies in the comparison. In addition, it is necessary to assess mortality, as well as other outcomes, over a time period for which it is reasonable to assume a "home health effect." Finally, it is important to determine whether such an outcome should serve as a "screen" that triggers a more in-depth review of an outlier agency or whether it alone serves as a definitive conclusion about the quality of care.

Discharge from home health care (for example differences in the timing of discharge or the patient's discharge location or status) is also a potential indicator of quality and has been used in a number of studies (e.g., Linn, Gurel, & Linn, 1977). However, this measure is heavily compromised by factors other than the quality of home health services. According to preliminary findings from the Washington State Home Care Project, home health agency discharge records are notably inaccurate, with "discharge to patient's home" connoting everything from full recovery to imminent death. Moreover, variations among patients in payment sources and among agencies in the fiscal intermediary's eligibility and coverage decisions may affect observed discharge and use rates more than differences in the quality of an agency's performance (e.g., Benjamin, 1986a). In addition, there is the difficulty of interpreting discharge data. For example, in an era of "sicker and quicker" hospital discharges to the community, the movement of an individual from the community with part-time/intermittent home health care to a nursing home may signify an accurate assessment and referral on the part of the agency rather than poor quality of care. Thus, "discharge status" as a trigger that generates further review would be appropriate if an agency's pattern makes it an "outlier." Four types of discharge are potentially troublesome: discharge to hospital; discharge home with no referral; death at home; and discharge to a nursing home.

Disability/Rehabilitation.   Unlike traditional long-stay nursing home residents, many Medicare home health patients can be expected to improve and to regain lost functioning (Smits, 1982). And indeed, both general measures of rehabilitation, such as functioning in ADLs and IADLs, and problem-specific measures, such as recovery from aphasia for stroke patients, have been widely used in health services research and are features of current home health studies and post-acute care studies, including well-developed measures in the *University of Minnesota Study of Post Acute Care*. Other relevant work on developing statistical norms for expected rates of decline/improvement in certain areas, such as physical functioning, was done by Spector and his colleagues at Brown University in the HCFA-funded "Longitudinal Study of Case Mix, Outcomes and Resource Use in Nursing Homes."

Discomfort,   particularly in terms of alleviation of pain, is often recommended as a measure of home health quality. For the Washington Home Care Association Project, Lalonde developed a "general symptom distress" scale that includes the following:

- pain
- bowel problems
- nausea/vomiting
- urinary/bladder problems
- cough
- respiratory difficulties
- skin problems
- swelling/fluid retention
- speech problems
- mood
- activity level

Health care professionals argue that these symptoms occur frequently in the client population served by home care or, if they occur infrequently, they are very distressing to clients and families and are important to monitor for all or the majority of home health clients.

The Aftercare study conducted by Mathematica Policy Research was designed to look at the adequacy of home health care under Medicare in the immediate 2 weeks after hospital discharge. It made extensive use of specific (process quality) guidelines designed to link services to client problems or conditions. This same condition-specific approach was then used to develop outcomes (generally adverse) for these conditions. These were complemented by more general outcomes such as functioning, rehospitalization, and death.

The data were collected primarily by telephone interviews with clients or their proxies. The interviewing required a sophisticated branching aproach to identify candidate conditions for the appropriate guidelines; this was supported by the use of computer-assisted interviewing techniques. Data from the interviews were supplemented by abstracts of the patients' hospital charts to ascertain their condition on discharge. In a number of cases these independent information sources revealed a serious problem of patient underreporting. Patients seemed unaware that they had some conditions or even that they were taking medications for them (Phillips, 1989).

Dissatisfaction or satisfaction with home health services is a mildly controversial indicator of quality, and there is no consensus within the medical profession about the role satisfaction should play in the assessment of quality (Cleary & McNeil, 1988). On the one hand, providers fear that patients who are ill will be unfairly negative, influenced not so much by the actual quality of services as by their preexisting health status, or other sociodemographic characteristics (Lebow, 1974; Cleary & McNeil, 1988). On the other hand, researchers recognize that satisfaction may be an adequate indicator of quality if patients lack the knowledge to evaluate the technical aspects of care, if they feel intimidated in expressing their opinion, or if they have become habituated to lowered expectations (Kane & Kane, 1988). However, research suggests that satisfaction can be a valid indicator of the characteristics and performance of providers and their services (Pascoe, 1983; Ware, Davies-Avery, & Stewart, 1978; Lebow, 1974). Based on research in public welfare and social services, we know that there is a tendency for recipients of any service or assistance to express satisfaction. Thus, we recommend the development of very service-specific measures of satisfaction which also offer respondents a range of responses, rather than simply yes/no. Work on developing measures of patient and family/caregiver satisfaction has been done by a variety of providers and researchers, including Mumma (1987), Hawes and Spencer (1987) and Reif (1987).

Client Knowledge and Self-Care Ability. One of the critical dimensions of home health care involves its role in patient education (Rinke & Wilson,

1987). In the System Sciences/Mathematica pilot study of the adequacy of post-hospital care (Phillips, 1989), the University of Minnesota (Kane, 1988), the Washington Home Care Association project, the University of California–San Francisco (Reif, 1987) and the University of Colorado (Hawes & Spencer, 1988) significant work has been done on developing measures of client knowledge about warning signs and symptoms, monitoring their status, taking prescribed medications, and following prescribed care processes.

Care-giver Burden. Homecare is not delivered solely, or even primarily, by paid workers. Part of its goal is to relieve at least some of the burden borne by family and others, who form the bulwark of the client-support system. Measures of care giver burden are important aspects of the assessment of the overall quality of home care services. Many of these measures have been developed in the area of dementia (Zarit, Orr, & Zarit, 1984). Others are more generic and can be applied to the gamut of home care. The Post-Acute Care study, for example, uses a modification of the care giver burden scale developed by Montgomery (1982).

In summary, substantial prior work has been done in the area of home health quality, on defining quality along a variety of dimensions, on measuring quality and assessing provider performance, and on developing criteria for evaluating process of care and patient outcomes. The proposed project recognizes this work and can effectively use it in developing model measures and survey protocols.

The Relationship Between Process Quality and Patient Outcome

One of the puzzling phenomena in long-term care has been the apparent confusion about the relationship among structural and process quality measures and patient outcomes (see summary in Kurowski & Breed, 1981; Hawes, 1983). Several studies have found links between certain structural characteristics (e.g., RN/patient ratios; spending of food) and outcomes such as survival, improvement, and discharge rehabilitation (Linn, Gurel, & Linn, 1977) and between higher levels of resource inputs and superior performance by nursing homes (Ohio, 1979), including process quality measures. However, other studies have found no association between outcome quality and process and structure (Chekryn & Roos, 1979: Levey et al., 1973; Lee, 1984). For example in one study of ambulatory care, process quality in 7 conditions was evaluated for both patients with "good" outcomes and those with "poor" outcomes, but the study found only minor differences in process quality scores (Kane et al., 1977).

On the face of it, such a lack of correlation leads one to mistrust one or both sides of the equation. If the outcome-based measures are appropriate and achievable but not associated with process quality, then, the argument goes, the process measures are of no value, since they apparently do not contribute to the desired end result. Alternatively, if the process criteria are well established and uniformly accepted as the best-known intervention/ treatment for a given condition, one then questions whether the outcome as defined is appropriate or achievable (Kane & Kane, 1988).

It is important to note that some of the studies that found weak or nonexistent associations between process and outcome examined the effect of very general process quality measures on problem-specific outcomes (e.g, initial assessment and its association with mobility). However, the appropriate relationship to examine is between parallel measures, for example problem-specific measures of process quality (e.g., for PT) and problem-specific outcomes (e.g., range-of-motion) (Kurowski & Breed, 1981; Hawes, 1983; McAuliffe, 1978).

The Role of Case Mix in Assessing Quality of Care

Initially when one mentioned "patient case mix," the idea connoted a general summary of characteristics of patients in an agency or facility. For example, a "heavy care case mix" in a nursing home typically described in general terms a facility with a preponderance of patients who required significant amounts of either fairly constant hands-on care and supervision or, more recently, highly skilled care and technologies. More recently, patient "case mix" has denoted characteristics of patients that are associated with variations in resource use, and there has been been substantial research on hospital and nursing home patients to identify the particular characteristics or sets of characteristics that best predict resource use. Much of this grew out of interest in various reimbursement options, such as the development of a prospective payment system for hospitals that recognized differential costs among institutions based on variations based on diagnostic-related-groupings or DRGs for Medicare patients (Fetter et al., 1980).

In the late 1970s state Medicaid agencies in Illinois, West Virginia, and Ohio began basing payment for certain categories of costs on patient characteristics, but these early "case mix" systems evolved clinically without the methodological rigor that arose with the development of classifications of patients into resource utilization groups or RUGs. This system, developed for the New York Medicaid program, sorts nursing home residents into one of 16 categories based on dependencies in ADLs, the need for skilled, clinically complex or rehabilitative care, and the presence of severe behavior problems. These groupings, and others developed for other states (e.g., Texas and Minnesota), are associated with different levels of resource use, and such case mix measures are predictive of between 45 and 58% of the variance in use of nursing resources (Fries & Cooney, 1985; Deane & Cella,

1982; Arling et al., 1987; Schlenker, 1984). Research on patient case mix, that is, the characteristics of home health patients associated with variations in resource use (e.g., duration and intensity of services), is also underway, given interest in the development of prospective payment systems for home health and in capitated payment systems (Foley, 1987; Manton & Hausner, 1987).

Effective assessment and monitoring of quality, particularly in a system using outcome-based measures, also depends on understanding the relationship between patient characteristics and outcomes. In such a system, the quality assurance goal is to identify those specific aspects of a given outcome that are attributable to the care the patient received. In order to do so, one must be able to determine the independent effects of other variables.

Case mix can be used as an independent variable to address the following related questions:

- What is the relationship of patient characteristics to specific patient outcomes?
- What patient characteristics place them at particular risk of adverse outcomes?

Substantial research demonstrates that a variety of individual patient characteristics affect patient outcomes. For example:

- Initial health and functional status are a powerful predictor of status at discharge (Mitchell, 1978);
- social isolation and cognitive decline have been linked to premature death;
- health status is associated with morale and behavior (Keeler, Kane, & Solomon, 1981; Morris & Granger, 1982); and
- discharge location is affected by marital status, climate, and source of payment for charges (Weissert & Scanlon, 1985).

When the effects of such characteristics on outcomes are known and understood, the task of evaluating the care given by a provider—or a group of providers—is much simpler and the results more accurate. Otherwise, one might end up in the unenviable position of comparing two agencies on their reported crude mortality rates and concluding that an excellent hospice-oriented home health agency was in fact providing worse care than a mediocre free-standing nursing "pool" agency that served patients with chronic impairments but not acute or terminal illnesses.

Another important quality assurance issue is whether and how to "target" surveys. As previously noted, the IOM (1986) suggested the use of "case mix adjusted" standard surveys for nursing homes, and such surveys were enacted in the 1987 OBRA. The IOM (1986) suggested several "key indicators" or "tracer" conditions that could be used in the standard survey. Because the 1987 OBRA requirements for home health agency certification surveys are very similar, this nursing home development is directly relevant.

For some time state licensure and survey agencies have been using patient-specific, outcome-oriented measures to evaluate the performance of nursing homes. New York's SHEs (sentinel health events), Illinois' QUIP (Quality Incentive Program), Iowa's licensure survey (Lee, 1984) and parts of the new federal PACS survey are examples. In addition, in response to a HCFA demonstration, several states experimented with focused reviews, screening surveys, survey by exception and the aforementioned SHE system (Schneider, Hatcher, & O'Sullivan, 1980; New York, 1984; Connelly et al., 1983; Lee & Braun, 1981; IOM, 1986). Each involved, to a greater or lesser degree, an attempt to focus some attention on outcome-based indicators of quality problems and some form of case-mix adjustment, either in the targeting of patient samples to be surveyed or in the interpretation of the facility-level measures of quality.

Understanding patient case mix is clearly critical to evaluations of quality in long-term care. The inherent challenge in approaching quality of home care has been to abstract the problem sufficiently to make it manageable without distorting it altogether. In part, one seeks to capture a moving picture (both the process of care and changes in patient status) in a series of snapshots. Much of the dynamic character of this care will never be recognized in the measures used, many of which capture only cross-sections of the process. The interactions among the various conditions make examining them indepently an abstract exercise. But associated with the patient, the provider, the family and the payor quality assurance systems must attempt such an examination.

The difficulty of the task has spawned several responses. In evaluating the performance of providers some method of case-mix or risk adjustment of both process and outcome measures of quality is needed. Essentially, one can either adjust for risk factors in the analysis of patient outcomes, treating them as covariates (as was done in the Minnesota Post-acute Care Study) or one can group the patients by risk factors and use stratified analytic approaches. A dominant form of the latter has been to divide the care process into discrete units of behavior around which standards for good care can be created. This was essentially the approach followed in the After-care study, where a list of conditions was developed, for each of which minimal standards of performance were created by a clinical panel and for most of which specific outcomes were identified. CHPR has developed a similar approach by which they use clusters of problems selected because they suggest a common treatment approach and similar measures of successful care. Kramer and his colleagues (July, 1988; February, 1989) have proposed 16 such clusters, which they term quality indicator groups (QUIGS). Although the current list still needs refinement because several of the clusters are, in fact, defined by treatments rather than problems, the strategy represents a useful and promising approach for simplifying a very complicated process.

In addition to the studies and demonstrations noted above, a few other attempts have been made to link case mix and quality. For example, Kane introduced the concept of a "prognosis adjustment factor" (PAF) in his project designed to link payment to nursing home resident outcomes (Kane et al., 1983). The PAF reflects the extent to which the actual outcome of care exceeds or falls short of an expected level. The system is based on resident functioning in 6 domains and generates a predicted outcome for the resident based on the experience of similar residents.

Morris and his colleagues (1987) also monitored outcomes and established statistical norms for certain outcomes (e.g., decubitus ulcers, ADLs, communication, behaviors). Data on patients in more than 100 facilities, including new admissions, were collected over a year, with a focus on changes in measures of quality of life, controlling for case mix.

Other significant research in case mix adjusted measures of quality is being undertaken in states that have developed nursing home case mix reimbursement systems or demonstrations. For example, New York is currently involved in a demonstration (NYQAS) to link the data generated by their case mix reimbursement system with the health department's survey process.

In summary, there has been substantial work on measuring the effects of patient case mix on costs and utilization. Less systematic attention has been devoted to case mix and outcomes, although research and demonstrations in the nursing home sector can inform the proposed research.

Assuring Quality and the Role of Feedback

For the first 20 years of Medicare and Medicaid, the predominant feature of the long-term care quality assurance system has been "feedback." In home health certification surveys and in nursing home surveys, state surveyors make yearly visits (or fewer in the case of HHAs), evaluate the facility/agency in terms of absolute standards for structure and process quality, and report back to the facility/agency on its performance relative to these fixed standards. The JCAHO and NLN surveys are much the same. The provider is evaluated in relation to absolute standards, with no reference to the performance of peer provider agencies. Each agency surveyed receives feedback on how it did relative to the established performance criteria.

While it is true that state and federal agencies have the threat of licensure revocation or termination of the provider agreement ("decertification"), and agencies accredited by JCAHO and the NLN could lose their accreditation, these remedies have been so seldom used that even providers acknowledge that such a threat was viewed as largely "symbolic" (IOM, 1986). De-certification and loss of accreditation are so severe that they are not used for "minor" problems and in fact seldom used even for major problems or deficiencies. This failure of the enforcement remedies, documented most effectively in the nursing home sector (IOM, 1986) has meant that regulatory personnel have had to rely on various forms of persuasion in attempting to ensure compliance with standards.

In effect, then feedback, and to some degree, consultation, have been the major methods used by survey agencies to assure quality in nursing homes and Medicare-certified home health agencies in this country for some time. Surveyors reported to the providers about the problems, that is provide retrospective feedback, and hope for improvement. However, this approach has had only limited success.

As Daubert (1977) notes, "The test of any quality assurance program is its impact on patient care, especially its ultimate effect in dealing with areas identified as problems or deficiencies." By this standard, quality assurance, at least in nursing homes, has been a failure. One of the severest criticisms leveled against the regulatory system is that it failed to ensure even minimal compliance from facilities that had repeated serious violations of the same type, year after year. (IOM, 1986).

There is no reason to believe that results will differ in home health unless major strategic changes are made in the nature of the feedback to agencies. It is critical to consider the fundamental nature of a regulatory QA system. Such a system must at the minimum achieve the following (IOM, 1986).

- Include standards that are precise and clear, clinically relevant, and adequate to assure (or at least promote) desirable patient outcomes;
- generate a monitoring/inspection system that accurately identifies the level of an agency's compliance with the standards;
- be enforceable, ideally in such a way that the severity of any violations or deficiencies (or conversely the relative excellence of performance) can be tied to various levels of sanctions or positive incentives; and
- be fair, resistant to provider "gaming," not burdensome to consumers, and feasible/affordable in terms of regulatory agency staffing requirements, timeliness, reliability, and cost.

In addition, it is desirable to have a system in which the data that are routinely collected for quality assurance purposes are compatible with the best practices in provider assessment of patients and care planning. Moreover-er, it would be helpful if such data could also be used either for reimburse-ment (e.g., as in case mix reimbursement for nursing homes) or for assessing the effect of various other policy interventions, such as reimbursement experiments. Finally, it is desirable for a quality assurance system to be proactive in the sense of offering valuable information to providers on an ongoing basis. Such information can then be used for internal quality monitoring and to generate improvements in performance. This is particularly critical in a field such as home health, where the service or care is of relatively short duration but of real importance to the well-being of the client. While receiving reactive evaluations of performance problems may assist providers in avoiding similar problems or deficiencies in the future, it does little good to the patients who received inadequate care. Thus, a system with proactive features holds more promise for improving quality of care.

Research suggests several innovations that might enhance the effectiveness of feedback/consultations:

- *The feedback should not simply report how the agency performed relative to some abstract criteria*, which may or may not be considered relevant by the agency; instead, *the agency's performance should be compared to that of its peers* and, as appropriate, the measures adjusted to account for differences in patient case mix and variables other than the quality of care the agency provides. Research suggests that feedback involving an assessment of performance coupled with direct comparison to the performance of one's peers is more influential than if the comparison is to an abstract set of criteria, no matter how widely accepted the criteria are (Fairbank & Prue, 1984).
- *The feedback should also include information on how the agency can improve its self-monitoring capacity.* This is in line with substantial work in the health care field that argues for a regulatory process that intervenes by creating expectations for the process of internal quality assurance (Vladeck, 1988). Moreover, it is in line with the call for proactive rather than reactive quality assurance processes (IOM, 1986; Kane & Kane, 1988). Finally, this feedback mechanism is in line with research in organizational psychology and organizational behavior management which finds that feedback on performance should take place quickly after the performance and that the process of feedback should be more continuous (Fairbank & Prue, 1984).
- *The feedback should be precise.* Long-term care providers frequently complain that the survey and certification standards and criteria are unclear, and that the survey report does not convey sufficient information to explain the deficiency or to suggest how performance might be improved (IOM, 1986; Ohio, 1979). To be effective, feedback must be precise in its content and it must convey specific performance goals expected of the recipient (Kim & Hamner, 1976; Nemeroff & Cosentino, 1979). With an improved patient assessment and monitoring system, providers can be given immediate and precise information about process and outcome quality measures, and indeed, can generate evaluative reports for them-

- selves. Moreover, processes of self-monitoring have proven successful in a variety of clinical settings (Komaki, Blood, & Holder, 1980; Prue et al., 1980).
- *The most effective source of feedback is unclear.* Research indicates effective feedback can come from a variety of sources including supervisors (Chandler, 1977), subordinates (Hegarty, 1974) and outside consultants (Komaki, Waddell, & Pearce, 1977). Apparently the content and timing of feedback are most significant in affecting performance than the source.

Developing Better Information Systems to Support Home Health Care and Assure Quality

Any effort to assess quality must rely on an information source. In long-term care, both in the nursing home and home care, records have been a special problem. There is little uniformity about what is charted or the extent to which a standardized set of information is recorded, even though regulatory efforts have mandated certain elements within the records of each care source. For example, precise medication records are required including a careful record of what was dispensed and when. Similarly, physicians' orders, progress notes, and other basic components are expected, but the depth and accuracy of these items varies widely.

Some new standards are being developed as a result of requirements in OBRA, 1987. HCFA has mandated a uniform assessment system for nursing home residents, which will include a method for translating the assessment information into a care plan. HCFA has likewise contracted to develop a home assessment system and improved ways of measuring home health quality but the extent to which this will involve improving the client records is unclear.

A pilot effort to develop standards for home health care under Medicare and to assess the extent to which they were met has been conducted by Mathematica. In conjunction with investigators at Boston University, they developed process quality guidelines for 46 distinct types of care (37 types of skilled care and 9 types of semi/unskilled care). Each guidelines identifies a minimal level of care adequate for a patient with defined characteristics. Applying these to a sample of 299 hospital discharges screened to represent high risk cases, they found 183 instances of inadequate care, 49 adverse outcomes among 428 applications for the skilled guidelines, and 36 instances of inadequate care and 41 adverse outcomes among 870 applications of the unskilled care guidelines (Phillips, 1989).

Several difficulties stand in the way of developing a better information system for long-term care. One barrier is the difference in language used by the different parties involved. Because long-term is interdisciplinary, the languages used by the various participants may provide a barrier to communication. Although one might argue that "function" is the lingua franca of long-term care, different professions involved in this care have very strong interests in the way ideas are expressed. For example, nursing has been developing a nursing minimum data set, which reflects its own conceptual framework and terminology (Werly & Long, 1988). At the same time, the minimum data set for nursing home resident assessment is being commissioned by the federal government, which is also simultaneously commissioning another minimum data set for hospital discharge planning. It is not at all clear whether any single information system will satisfy all users and allow for meaningful information transmission across the increasingly dynamic system of long-term and post-acute care, both of which are remarkable for the numbers of transitions they involve and hence the need to track patients' status over time and across settings.

The second major obstacle confronting long-term information systems is the volume of information involved. Not only is it important to collect comprehensive data on consumers of care, that information must be placed into a format that will facilitate its use and will permit comparisons over time in client status. Especially in long-term care, where the very term connotes duration, changes in status over time are a critical element in patient management. Any data system must encourage and simplify the presentation of information in a fashion that permits temporal analysis, by users as well as assessors.

The inevitable conclusion is that data management in LTC seems to involve the computer. Microcomputer systems to facilitate data collection and manipulation in LTC are now becoming avaliable. Some are quite sophisticated. Although many began as billing and accounting systems, there is now a growing appreciation among providers and software companies of the need to develop systems to support care applications, especially assessment, care planning, and tracking client progress.

The nursing home industry is slowly beginning to recognize the need for more sophisticated, computer-driven information (*Provider*, January 1989). But there will continue to be a very limited market for such products until regulations compel their adoption.

A recent compilation of available software to support LTC applications listed almost 100 products or firms, of which only 47 had a system that claimed some ability in medical records or patient care (*Contemporary LTC*, February 1989). It is not clear how many of these applications include a comprehensive assessment and its translation into a care plan. Several products being actively marketed use some variant of fixed screens or forced choices. These rely on relatively simple recall programs to bring forward a standard set of items for a given problem or when a particular response is made.

The computer provides the most reasonable way to collect structured information within a complex branching logic set and to facilitate the development and monitoring of care plans. Early experience with computerized information systems for long-term care suggests that they also reduce redundancy of information collection among various disciplines and hence promote efficiency.

Not everyone welcomes a structured approach to data collection. The more professionalized the group, the greater is the expected resistance to external programming guiding their actions. However, the external pressures for greater structure in data collection are already evident in the requirements for standardized data collection at discharge from hospital and uniform resident assessment on admission to nursing homes. Similar demands on home health are already being formulated. The issue for the future is how to increase this information collection without its becoming burdensome and stealing time from patient care. Computers seem the likely answer. Not only can they be effectively used to structure collecting information, they can display it narratively and graphically. The latter is especially important in encouraging care givers to think in terms of changing client status over time and to develop a basis for comparing progress against goals and norms. These goals and norms can come from either clinical prognosis based on professional judgment or statistical analysis of how similar clients have fared under circumstances of good care.

Because the natural course of most long-term clients is toward deteriorating status, positive feedback and a sense of accomplishment come only from comparing the results of good care with those from more typical care. The difference in the 2 lines generated shows the effects of greater effort and serves as a reward for those efforts.

Information technology can also be used to address one of the most perplexing problems in monitoring home care—namely, the ability to supervise those who act independently. Much of home care goes on without any accessible on-site supervision. In the extreme case, it may not even be possible to ascertain with certainty whether a worker showed up and stayed the full allotted time. It is more difficult to determine just what services were done and whether they were done correctly.

One device to assist in this task is a portable, relatively inexpensive laser bar code reader. This reader, about the size of a credit card, contains a microchip that can be programmed as well as a built in clock/timing device. By simply reading the client's bar code identifier and the care giver's the machine will determine when services began and ended. Many services can be organized to take advantage of this technology, which requires only minimal reading skills. For example, basic questions about the client's status can be recorded. Also, By creating a program that automatically checks the name and dose of medications with the time of scheduled administration, one can develop an almost foolproof system of dispensing drugs and preventing errors. Similarly, behavioral conditioning for problems like toileting can be managed by using this device to record what was done and what was found at precise intervals. This information can then be later transferred into a larger system as part of the recharging process for the laser reader.

Once entered, the data can be manipulated to show the patterns of performance for the individual client over time, differences across clients treated by different firms, or changes within the same client over time. This display provides both subtle and overt feedback to those on the firing line and encourages them to think in more dynamic terms about the changes that are possible in their clientele.

Quality Assurance and Home Health Care

Developing and implementing an effective quality assurance system is both important and, given improvements as information technology, increasingly feasible. This section of the chapter sets out general principals for such a QA system.

a. *The imminent and paramount need is to develop feasible approaches to measuring quality of home care.*

b. *The ideal properties of measures to study quality do not mirror ideal measures for a regulatory system.*

For a study of quality, one might wish to measure the full range of constructs. A quality assurance system for home health, by contrast, will rely on key indicators to reflect adequacy of Medicare home health care, and both the clinical relevance of indicators and ease of collection are important considerations.

c. *Medicare home care is multidimensional in its intent and function, and a QA system must develop distinctive approaches for each identifiable "modality" of home care*

Many studies of home care have been flawed by inattention to the differences in goals among home health agencies and to the variety of goals that can exist for clients within a single agency.

d. *There are at least 6 modalities for Medicare home health: (1) rehabilitation; (2) subacute post-hospital care; (3) terminal care; (4) patient education; (5) case management; and (6) personal care associated with skilled home health care.*

Rehabilitation is a classic goal of Medicare home health and is reflected in the coverage of physical therapy (PT), speech therapy, and occupational therapy (OT), as well as skilled nursing. In recent years, the delivery of skilled, subacute post-hospital care has become more prominent; in this modality, the home health agency continues care begun in the hospital, with the goal of promoting full recovery and minimizing complications. Similarly home health agencies report that providing care to patients who are terminally ill is a significant part of their mission. The case management function of Medicare home health comes into play with the initial assessment and the effort to assist the patient in locating necessary services not covered by Medicare. Similarly, home health agency personnel indicate that when they close a case (often because Medicare coverage is no longer available), they perceive their role as including arrangements for any necessary continuance of care. Finally the provision of supportive personal services to patients is often critical to their ability to function at home while receiving skilled home health services. Different measures of quality can be developed for each modality.

e. *The outcomes for persons receiving home health care could potentially be influenced by a variety of factors, including the quality of acute care the patient received prior to referral (e.g. in hospital), the quality of non-Medicare home care, patient and family compliance, and eligibility and coverage decisions.*

Home health patients may receive a variety of other services that can affect their outcomes. Quality assurance in home health care is considerably more complex than in other settings, such as hospitals or nursing homes, in part because of the level of patient (and family care giver) compliance involved and in part because of the difficulty of adequately assessing or monitoring agency performance in so many noncentralized care settings. In addition, home health agencies and the care they provide are profoundly influenced by Medicare hospital and home health eligibility and coverage decisions, rules that may affect patient care and agency practice patterns. As a result of these factors, the outcome and process measures used to assess the quality of care in skilled nursing facilities (SNFs), and hospital swing-beds may be inadequate or inappropriate in a home health setting. In effect, we argue that the measures of quality must emerge from the nature of home health and the particular responsibilities of home health agencies.

Non-Medicare assistance could include home care paid for privately by the patient or by a third party such as Medicaid or private insurance. Often patients simultaneously receive home care with more than one payment source, and indeed a single agency and even the home health provider team may be combining payment sources to render care. Similarly, a patient may be discharged from Medicare home health care to home care under a different payment source and perhaps delivered by a different provider.

Finally, assessing the "quality" of Medicare home health care is made more complex by the time period typically covered. The length of stay (LOS) for Medicare home care is quite short—The Visiting Nurse Association of Los Angeles, for example has reported a mean LOS of only 12 days. Thus, sorting out the effects of Medicare home health care is complex, and we must take into account that some forms of improvement are unlikely to be observable after 12 or even 20 days.

f. *It is possible and desirable to develop meaningful, reliable, and valid outcome measures for home health care and to place such outcome measures at the heart of a QA system.*

Despite the caveats already mentioned, we are convinced that outcome-based quality assurance is feasible.

g. *Structure and process measures also have an important place in a QA system.*

When we are confident that certain processes are related to certain outcomes, it is sensible to use the regulatory system to ensure those processes take place. Moreover, a strong argument can be independently made for the utility and importance of process quality measured in a regulatory system.

h. *Measures of quality—whether measures of outcome, process, or structure—vary in type: they may be disease-specific (e.g. organized around stroke); problem-specific or symptom specific (e.g. organized around aphasia); service specific (e.g. organzied around PT for stroke); or general outcomes (e.g. general functioning, general satisfaction).*

Each may be useful in assessing various aspects or dimensions of home health quality.

i. *A parallel approach across outcome, process, and structural measures of quality is necessary.*

If the outcomes examined are specific and disease-related, so too, should be the measures. If the outcomes are general—for example, satisfaction with care—the processes examined in relation to that outcome should measure, in a parallel way, the general procedures for working with patients. Too often in QA efforts, processes of care are measured in specific detail and then related to very general, global, or nonequivalent outcomes.

j. *Case mix—i.e., characteristics of the patients—are relevant for QA, but the case mix groupings relevant to QA may not be identical to case mix groupings associated with resource consumption.*

It is important to consider the relationship between patient characteristics and outcomes. In monitoring agency performance, it is also important to consider critical patient characteristics and to identify those patients at particular risk for receiving inadequate care. Case mix groupings could also be used to sample care in a QA system—a principle built into the Institute of Medicine's 1986 recommendations for nursing homes—and to compare performance among different providers.

k. *Home health care is particularly difficult to monitor for quality.*

Home care QA efforts must contend with a large number of providers and clients, the relatively short length of stay for many beneficiaries of Medicare home health, the large number of disciplines involved, the invisibility of the encounters between home care providers and the clients, and the rudimentary state of home health care information systems. Relatively few home health agencies have automated patient assessment and care planning records; there may be little consistency from agency to agency about how client status is measured in the initial assessment; and there appears to be a lack of consistency in the continuing records and the closing summary.

l. *Computers can be usefully incorporated into effective information systems for home health care.*

Computers can facilitate the collection of information by using branching logic. Once entered, such information can then be displayed in various ways to emphasize changes in client status over time or to compare the effects of one provider's care with another. Similarly, other information technology, like portable laser readers, can make such care more effective and improve monitoring of otherwise unsupervised care givers.

m. *Home health care patient records need to be improved as a prerequisite for an efficient QA system; fortunately, the investment in an improved record system can be expected to also have a payoff in better care.*

Far from robbing time from care, a good patient record is essential to high quality care. The importance of the record is multiple. First, delivering quality care entails making an accurate assessment and delivering the care appropriate to the problem(s). A QA system should be able to evaluate the adequacy of the decisions about care, as well as monitoring the processes and outcomes of the type of care delivered. Improved records would help make those decision paths clearer and auditable. The record also provides the basis for sampling home care clients for QA purposes. One must, for example, be able to trust the reliability and accuracy of the record when sampling cases to include patients with characteristics that put them at risk for poor outcomes. Sampling is also essential to evaluations of such indicators as patient satisfaction or knowledge of self-care, since it will not be feasible in an operational QA system for home care to do very many in-person or even telephone reviews as a proportion of home health visits and clients.

n. *The most desirable QA system is a proactive one that provides regular feedback to providers about the patient's status and their own performance.*

Too often the health care provider being monitored is in a reactive position—finding out well after the fact that its outcomes or processes fell short of expectations. It is more useful to have mechanisms built into the patient record-keeping and care process that give providers regular feedback they can use to evaluate their performance.

REFERENCES

American Association of Retired Persons. (1984, January). Long-term care survey. Washington, DC.

American Bar Association. (1986, August). The 'black box' of home care quality. Report prepared for the House of Representatives, Washington, DC. Comm. Pub. No. 99–573.

American College of Physicians. (1986, September). Home health care. *Annals of Internal Medicine 105*, 454–450.

American Nurses Association. (1986). Standards of home health nursing practice. Kansas City, MO. 1–42.

Arling, G., Nordquist, R. H., Brant, B. A., & Capitman, J. A. (1987). Nursing home case mix: Patient classification by nursing home resource. *Medical Care 25*, 1.

Baer, N., Blakemore, R., Foster, J., Rose, J., & Trafon, J. (1984, July/August). Home health services social work treatment protocol. *Home Healthcare Nurse*, 43–49.

Balinsky, W. (1985, Spring). A comparative analysis of agencies providing home health services. *Home Health Care Services Quarterly 6*(1), 45–64.

Balinsky, W., & Rehman, R. (1984). Home health care: A comparative analysis of hospital-based and community-based agency patients. *Home Health Care Services Quarterly 5*(1), 45–61.

Bauman, M. K., Kramer, A. M., Shaugnessy, P. W., & Schlenker, R. E. (1988). Development of outcome-based quality measures in home health services, Study Paper 1: Literature and program review of quality assurance systems related to home health care. Center for Health Policy Research, Denver (under Contract No. 500-88-0054 from the Health Care Financing Administration).

Beebe, J., Lubitz, J., & Eggers, P. (1985). Using prior utilization to determine payments for Medicare enrollees in HMOs, *Health Care Financing Review 6*(3), 27–38.

Bell, D. (1987, February). Home care in New York City: Providers, payers, and clients. New York: United Hospital Fund of New York, Paper Series 6.

Belsley, D. A., Kuh, E., & Welsch, R. E. (1980). *Regression Diagnostics: Identifying Influential Data and Sources of Collinearity.* New York: Wiley.

Benjamin, A. E. (1986a, June). "Determinants of state variations in home health utilization and expenditures under medicare." *Medical Care 24*, 535–547.

Benjamin, A. E. (1986). State variations in home health expenditures and utilization under Medicare and Medicaid. *Home Health Care Services Quarterly 7*(1), 5–28.

Berk, M. L., & Bernstein, A. (1985). Use of home health services: Some findings from the National Medical Care Expenditure Survey. *Home Health Care Services Quarterly 6*(1), 13–23.

Berry, N. J., & Evans, J. M. (1985–86). Cost effectiveness of home health care as an alternative to inpatient care. *Home Health Care Services Quarterly 6*(4), 11–25.

Birnbaum, H., Bishop, C., Lee, A. J., & Jensen, G. (1981). Why do nursing home costs vary? The determinants of nursing home costs. *Medical Care 19*, 1095–1107.

Birnbaum, H., Bishop, C., Jensen, G., Lee, A. J., & Wilson, D. (1979). Reimbursement strategies for nursing home care: Developmental cost studies. DHEW Contract No. 600-77-0068, Cambridge, MA: Abt Associates.

Bishop, C. (1980). Nursing Home cost studies and reimbursement issues. *Health Care Financing Review 2*, 47–64.

Bishop, C. (1980). Nursing home behavior under cost-related reimbursement. Discussion Paper (DP-9, revised), Waltham, MA: Brandeis University, University Health Policy Consortium.

Bishop, C. (1985, May). *Home Health Agency: Cost and Service Mix in a Changing Environment.* Baltimore, MD: Health Care Financing Administration, Project Summary.

Bishop, C., & Stassen, M. (1986). Prospective reimbursement for home health care. *Pride Institute Journal 5*, 18–19.

Brook, R. H., & Lohr, K. N. (1981). Quality of care assessment: Its role in the 1980s *American Journal of Public Health 71*, 681–682.

Brook, R. H. (1979). Studies of process-outcome correlation in medical care evaluations, *Medical Care 17*, 879–883.

Brook, R. H., Williams, K., & Avery, A. (1976). Quality assurance today and tomorrow: Forecast for the future, *Annals of Internal Medicine 85*, 809–817.

Bulau, J. M. (1986). *Clinical Policies and Procedures for Home Health Care*. Rockville, MD: Aspen Publishers, Inc.

Bunker, J. P. (1988). Is efficacy the gold standard for quality assessment? *Inquiry 25*, 51–58.

Burda, D. (1986, November). Five future areas of liability risks haunt providers. *Hospitals*, 48–53.

California Auditor General. (1987, March). The Department of Social Services could reduce costs and improve compliance with regulations of the in-home supportive services program, 630.

Callahan, W. (1985, Winter). Medicare use of home health services. *Health Care Financing Review 7*(2), 89–91.

Cameron, J. M., & Knauf, R. A. (1982). Case mix and resource use in long-term care. Paper presented at the American Public Health Association Annual Meeting. Montreal, Canada.

Caswell, R. J., Cleverley, W. O. (1983). Cost analysis of Ohio nursing homes. Final report to the Ohio Department of Health, Columbus, OH.

Chandler, A. B. (1977). Decreasing negative comments and increasing performance of a shift supervisor. *Journal of Organizational Behavior Management 1*, 99–103.

Chekryn, J., & Roos, L. L. (1979). Auditing the process of care in a new geriatric unit. *Journal of the American Geriatrics Society 21*, 107–111.

Chromy, J. R. (1981). Variance estimators for a sequential sample selection procedure. In Krewski, D., Platek, R., Rao, J.N.K. (Eds.), *Current Topics in Survey Sampling*. New York: Academic Press.

Cleary, P. D., & McNeil, B. J. (1988). Patient Satisfaction as an Indicator of Quality Care. *Inquiry 25*, 25–36.

Coe, M., Wilkinson, A., & Patterson, P. (1986, May). *Preliminary Evidence on the Impact of DRGs: Dependency at Discharge Study*. Beaverton, OR: Northwest Oregon Health Systems.

Collier, G. (1984, May). Certificate of need requirements for home health services. *Caring*, 19–26.

Congressional Budget Office. (1983, March). *Changing the Structure of Medical Benefits: Issues and Options*. Congress of the United States.

Connelly, K., & Dreyer, P. I. (1983). Targeted inspections of nursing homes. *Quality Review Bulletin 9*, 239–242.

Cook, T. D., & Campbell, D. T. (1979). *Quasi-Experimentation: Design and Analysis Issues for Field Settings*. Chicago, IL: Rand McNally College Publishing.

Cotterill, P. G. (1983). Provider incentives under alternative reimbursement systems. In Vogel, R. J., & Palmer, H. C. *Long-term Care: Perspectives from Research and Demonstrations* (Eds.), Washington, DC: Health Care Financing Administration.

Craig, Heather M. (1985). Accuracy of indirect measures of medication compliance in hypertension, *Research in Nursing and Health 8*, 61–66.

Currie, C. T., Burley, L. E., Doull, C., Ravetz, C., Smith, R. G., & Williamson, J. (1980). A scheme of augmented home care for acutely and sub-acutely ill elderly patients: Report on pilot study. *Age and Aging 8*, 149–151.

Curtiss, F. R. (1986a). Financing home health-care products and services. *American Journal of Hospital Pharmacy 43*, 121–131.

Curtiss, F. R. (1986b). Recent developments in federal reimbursement for home health care. *American Journal of Hospital Pharmacy 43*, 132–139.

Daniels, K. (1986, July). Planning of quality in the home care system. *Quality Review Bulletin*, 2147–2151.

Daubert, E. A. (1977). A system to evaluate home health care services. *Nursing Outlook 25*, 261–268.

Day, S. R. (1984). Measuring utilization and impact of home care services: A systems model approach for cost-effectiveness. *Home Health Care Services Quarterly 5*(2), 5–24.

Deane, R. T., & Cella, M. A. (1982). New concepts in nursing home reimbursement. Paper presented at the American Economic Association Annual Meeting, New York, New York, December 28.

Deniston, O. L., & Jette, A. (1980). A functional status assessment instrument: Validation in an elderly population. *Health Services Research 15*, 21–34.

Division of National Cost Estimates, Office of the Actuary. (1987). National Health Care Expenditures, 1986–2000. *Health Care Financing Review 8*(4), 1–36.

Donabedian, A. (1966). Evaluating the quality of medical care. *Milbank Memorial Fund Quarterly/Health and Society 4*(181), 166–206.

Donabedian, A. (1978, July). *Needed Research in the Assessment and Monitoring of the Quality of Medical Care*. DHEW Publication No. (PHS) 78-3219.

Donabedian, A. (1986). Evaluating the quality of medical care. *Quality Assurance and Utilization Review 1*(1), 6–12.

Donabedian, A. (1988). Quality assessment and assurance: Unit of purpose, diversity of means. *Inquiry 25*(1), 173–192.

Doty, P. (1986). Family care of the elderly: The role of public policy. *The Milbank Quarterly 64*(1), 34–75.

Doty, P., Liu, K., & Weiner, J. (1985, Spring). An overview of long-term care. *Health Care Financing Review 6*(3), 69–78.

Dranove, D. (1985, Spring). An empirical study of a hospital-based home care program. *Inquiry 22*(1), 56–66.

Dubois, R. W., & Brook, R. H. (1988). Assessing clinical decision making: Is the ideal system feasible? *Inquiry 25*(1), 59–64.

Dubois, R. W., Brook, R. H., & Rogers, W. H. (1987). Adjusted hospital death rates: A potential screen for quality of medical care. *American Journal of Public Health 77*(9), 1162–1166.

Eggers, P. W., & Prihoda, R. (1982). Pre enrollment reimbursement patterns of Medicare beneficiaries enrolled in at-risk HMO's. *Health Care Financing Review 4*, 1.

Ellwood, P. M. Jr., & Paul, B. A. (1986). But what about quality? *Health Affairs 5*(1), 135–140.

Evashwick, C. (1985). Home health care: Current trends and future opportunities. *Journal of Ambulatory Care Management 8*(4), 4–17.

Fairbank, J. A., & Prue, D. M. (1984). Developing performance feedback systems. In Williamson, J. N. (Ed.), *The Leader-Manager*, (pp. 331–341). Eden Prairie, MI: Wilson Learning.

Fashimpar, G. A. (1985). A manual for the administration, scoring, and interpretation of the homemaker-home health aide program evaluation questionnaire. *Home Health Care Services Quarterly 6*(1), 65–85.

Fetter, R. B., Youngsoo, S., Freeman, J. L., Averill, R. F., & Thompson, J. D.

(1980). Case mix definitions by diagnosis-related groups, *Medical Care 18*(2), 3–53, Supplement.

Findley, T. W., & Findley, S. E. (1987). Rehabilitation needs in the 1990's: Effects of an aging population. *Medical Care 2*(8), 753–763

Flynn, B. C., & Ray, D. W. (1979, October). Quality assurance in community health nursing. *Nursing Outlook*, 650–653.

Foley, W. (1987). Developing a patient classification system for home health care. *Pride Institute Journal 6*(1), 22–24.

Forgy, L., & Williams, J. (1987, May 27). Preliminary analysis of mediqual data. Unpublished report to the Health Care Financing Administration.

Fries, B. E., & Cooney Jr., L. M. (1985). Resource utilization groups: A patient classification system for long-term care. *Medical Care 23*(2), 110–122.

Fries, J. F., & Crapo, L. M. (1981). Vitality and aging—implications of the rectangular curve. San Francisco: W.H. Freedman.

Frost and Sullivan. (1983). *Home healthcare products and services: Markets in the U.S.* New York: Frost & Sullivan Inc.

Gelder, S. V., & Bernstein, J. (1986). Home health in the era of hospital prospective payment: Some early evidence and thoughts about the future. *Pride Institute Journal 5*(1), 3–26.

Ginsburg, P. B., & Hackbarth, G. M. (1986). Alternative delivery systems and medicare. *Health Affairs, 5*(1), 6–22.

Ginzberg, E., Balinsky, W., & Ostow, M. (1984). *Home Health Care: Its Role in the Changing Health Services Market*. Totowa, NJ: Rowman and Allanheld Publishers.

Glen, K. (1985). Hospital continuing care arrangements. *Washington Report on Medicine and Health 39*(19).

Goodwin, L. D., & Prescott, P. A. (1981). Issues and approaches to estimating interater reliability in nursing research. *Research in Nursing and Health 4*, 323–327.

Gornick, M., Greenberg, J. N., Eggers, P. W., & Dobson, A. (1985, December). Twenty years of Medicare and Medicaid: Covered populations, use of benefits and program expenditures. *Health Care Financing Review*, 1985 annual supplement, 13–59.

Gornick, M., & Hall, M. (1988). Trends in Medicare utilization of SNFs, HHAs, and rehabilitation hospitals. *Health Care Financing Review*, annual supplement, 27–38.

Gould, E. J. (1985, November). Standardized home health nursing care plans: A quality assurance tool. *Quality Review Bulletin*, 334–338.

Granger, C. V., Green, D. S., Liset, E., Coulanbe, J., & O'Brien, E. (1975). Measurement of outcomes of care for stroke patients. *Stroke 6*, 34–41.

Griffith, D. G. (1986). Blending key ingredients to assure quality in home health care. *Nursing and Health Care 5*, 301–302.

Groth-Junker, A., & McCusker, J. (1983). Where do elderly patients prefer to die? *Journal of the American Geriatrics Society 31*, 457–461.

Harlow, K. S., & Wilson, L. B. (1985, July 30). *DRGs and the Community Based Long-Term Care System*, Dallas, TX: Southwest Long Term Care Gerontology Center, University of Texas Health Sciences Center.

Harrington, C. (1988, May 15). Quality, access, and costs: Public policy issues for home health care services. Unpublished paper. Institute for Health and Aging, University of California, San Francisco, CA.

Harris and Associates. (1982). Priorities and expectations for health and living circumstances: A survey of the elderly in five English-speaking countries. A survey conducted for the Commonwealth Fund.

Harris, M. D., Santoferraro, C., & Silva, S., (1985, Sept–Oct). A patient classification system in home health care. *Nursing Economics 3*, 269–281.

Hawes, C. (1987). *Quality Assurance in Swing-Beds.* A monograph published by New York University, Rural Hospital Program.

Hawes, C. (1983). *Public Policy and Long-Term Care: Defining, Measuring and Assuring Quality.* Final report for the Robert Wood Johnson Foundation, Princeton, NJ.

Hawes, C., & Powers, L. (1987). Quality assurance in long-term care: Special issues for patients with dementia. In Cook-Deegan R. (Ed.), *Losing a Million Minds.* Washington, DC: Office of Technology Assessment.

Hawes, C., & Spencer, (1988). Research Triangle Institute and University of Colorado Center for Health Services Research. Part of instrument development conducted at CHSR on a HCFA-funded study of home health quality.

Hay, J. W., & Mandes, G. (1984). Home health care cost-function analysis. *Health Care Financing Review 5*(3), 1111–1116.

Health Care Financing Administration. (1984). Intermediary Workload Report.

Hedrick, S. C., & Inui, T. S. (1986). The effectiveness and cost of home care: An information synthesis. *Health Services Research*, Part II *20*(6), 851–880.

Hegarty, W. H. (1974). Using subordinate ratings to elicit behavioral changes in supervisors. *Journal of Applied Psychology 59*, 746–766.

Holahan, J. F., & Cohen, J. W. (1985). How should Medicaid programs pay for nursing home care? Washington, DC: The Urban Institute, Report, 3172-12.

Holahan, J. F., & Cohen, J. W. (1986). *Medicaid: The Trade-Off Between Cost Containment and Access to Care.* Washington, DC: National Academy Press.

Horn, B. J., & Swain, M. A. (1978, August). Criterion measures of nursing care quality. Hyattsville, MD: National Center for Health Services Research.

Hughes, S. L. (1985). Apples and Oranges? A review of evaluations of community-based long-term care. *Health Services Research 20*(4), 461–488.

Hughes, S. L. (1986, November 1). Home Health Monitoring: Ensuring Quality in home care services. *Hospitals 74*–80.

Hughes, S. L. (1987) Impact of Long-term home care on hospital and nursing home use and cost. *Health Services Research 22*(1), 19–47.

Institute for Health and Aging and Institute for Health Policy Studies, University of California, San Francisco. (1985, October). *Organizational and Community Responses to Medicare Policy: Consequences for Health and Social Services for the Elderly.* San Francisco, CA.

Institute of Medicine, Committee on Nursing Home Regulation. (1986). *Improving Quality of Care in Nursing Homes.* Washington, DC: National Academy Press.

Inui, T. S., Stevenson, M., Plorde, D., & Murphy, I. (1980). Needs assessment for hospital-based home care services. *Research in Nursing Health 3*, 101–106.

Iversen, L. H., & Plich, C. L. (1986, June). State pre-admission screening programs. *Coordinator*, 28–31.

Januska, C., Engle, J., & Wood, J. (1976). Status of quality assurance in public health nursing. Annual Meeting of the American Public Health Association, Public Health Section, December, New Orleans, LA.

Jeejeebhoy, K. N., Langer, B., Tsallas, G., Chu, R. C., Kuksis, A., & Anderson, G. H. (1976). Total parenteral nutrition at home: Studies in patients surviving 4 month to 5 years. *Gastroenterology 71*(6), 943–953.

Joint Commission for Accreditation of Hospitals. (1986). *Evaluation Form: Proposed Home Care Standards.* Chicago, IL.

Kane, R. (1981). Assuring quality of care and quality of life in long-term care. *Quality Review Bulletin 7*, 3–10.

Kane, R. A., & Kane, R. L. (1988). Long-term care: Variations on a quality assurance theme. *Inquiry 25*(1), 132–146.

Kane, R. L. (1983). Predicting the outcomes of nursing home patients. *Gerontologist 23*(2), 200–206.

Kane, R. L., Bell, R. M., Hosek, S. D., Riegler, S. Z., & Kane, R. A. (1983). Outcome-based reimbursement for nursing home care. Prepared for the National Center for Health Services, Research, The Rand Corporation, Santa Monica, CA.

Kane, R. L., Gardner, J., Wright, D. D., Snell, G., Sundevall, D., & Woolley, F. R. (1977). Relationship between process and outcome in ambulatory care. *Medical Care 15*, 961–965.

Kane, R., Kane, R., Kleffel, D., et al. (1979). The PSRO and the nursing home. Vol. I; An assessment of PSRO long-term care review. Report submitted to HCFA, DHEW under contract No. 500-78-0040.

Kane, R. A., & Kane R. L. (1987). *Long-Term Care: Principles, Programs and Policies,*. New York: Springer.

Kane, R., Riegler, S., Bell, R., Potler, R., & Koshland, G. (1982). Predicting the course of nursing home patients. A Rand Note, Santa Monica, CA.

Kaye, L. W. (1985). Setting educational standards for gerontological home care personnel. *Home Health Care Services Quarterly 6*(1), 85–99.

Keeler, E. B., Kane, R. L., & Solomon, D. H. (1981). Short- and long-term residents of nursing homes. *Medical Care XIX* (3), 363–370.

Kim, J. S., & Hamner, W. C. (1976). Effect of performance feedback and goal setting on productivity and satisfaction in an organizational setting. *Journal of Applied Psychology 61*, 48–57.

Kirby, W., Latta, V., & Helbing, C. (1986). Medicare use and cost of home health agency services, 1983–84. *Health Care Financing Review 8*(1), 93–100.

Kish, L. (1965). *Survey Sampling.* New York: Wiley.

Koetting, M. (1980). *Nursing Home Organization and Efficiency.* Lexington, MA: Lexington Books.

Komaki, J., Blood, M. R., Holder, D. (1980). Fostering Friendliness in a fast food franchise. *Journal of Organizational Behavior Management 2*, 151–164.

Komaki, J., Waddell, W. M., & Pearce, J. G. (1977). The applied behavior analysis approach and individual employees: Improving performance in two small businesses. *Organizational Behavior and Human Performance 19*, 337–352.

Koren, M. J. (1986). Home care—Who cares? *The New England Journal of Medicine 314*(14), 917–920.

Kramer, A. (1988). Patient sampling strata. Working Paper 4a: National Home Health Study, Denver, CO.

Kramer, A. M., Bauman, M. K., Crisley, K. S., Schlenker, R. E., & Shaugnessy, P. W. (1989). Development of outcome-based quality measures in home health services. Denver, CO: Center for Health Policy Research.

Kramer, A. M., Shaugnessy, P. W., Bauman, M. K., & Winston, C. L. (1988). A study of home health care quality and cost under capitated and fee-for-service payment systems, study paper 3: Quality measurement and payment classification for home health care. Center for Health Policy Research, Denver, CO (under Cooperative Agreement No. 17-C-99051/8-01 from the Health Care Financing Administration).

Kramer, A., Shaugnessy, P. W., Pettigrew, M. L. (1985). Cost-effectiveness implications based on a comparison of nursing home and home health case mix. *Health Services Research 29*(4), 387–405.

Kunkel, S. A., & Powell, C. K. (1981). The adjusted average per capita cost under risk contracts with providers of health care. *Transactions Society of Actuaries 33*, 221–230.

Kurowski, B., & Breed, L. (1981). A synthesis of research on client needs assessment and quality assurance programs in long-term care. Denver, CO: Center for Health Services Research, University of Colorado Health Sciences Center.

Kurowski, B. T., Schlenker, R. E., & Tricarico, G. (1979, March). *Applied Research in Home Health Services, Vol. II: Cost per Episode.* Denver, CO: Center for Health Services Research, University of Colorado Health Sciences Center.

Lave, J. (1985). Cost containment policies in long-term care. *Inquiry 22*, 7–23.

Lawton, M. P., Moss, M., Fulcomer, M., & Kleban, M. (1982). A research and service oriented multi-level assessment instrument. *Journal of Gerontology 37*, 91–99.

Laxton, C. (1988). Editorial introduction. *Caring 7*, 3.

Leader, S. (1986, September). *Home Health Benefits Under Medicare.* American Association of Retired Persons, Washington, D. C.

Lebow, J. L. (1974). Consumer Assessments of the quality of medical care. *Medical Care 12*, 328–337.

Lee, Y. S. (1984). Nursing homes and quality of health care: The first year of result of an outcome-oriented survey. *Journal of Health and Human Resource Administration* 7(1), 32–60.

Lee, Y. S., & Braun, S. (1981). Health care for the elderly: Designing a data system for quality assurance. *Computer, Environment, and Urban Systems 6*, 48–82.

Levey, S., Ruchlin, H. S., Stotsky, B. A., Kinloch, D. R., & Oppenheim, W. (1973). An appraisal of nursing home care. *Journal of Gerontology 28*, 222–228.

Linn, B. S., Linn, M. W., & Gurel, L. (1968). Cumulative illness rating scale. *Journal of the American Geriatrics Society 16*, 622–626.

Linn, B. S., Linn, M. W., Greenwald, S. R., & Gurel, L. (1974) Validity of impairment ratings made from medical records and from personal knowledge. *Medical Care 12*(4), 363–386.

Linn, M. W. (1967). A rapid disability rating scale. *Journal of the American Geriatrics Society 15*, 211.

Linn, M. W., Gurel, L., & Linn, B. S. (1977). Patient outcome as a measure of quality of nursing home care. *American Journal of Public Health 67*, 337–344.

Liu, K., Manton, K. G., & Liu, B. M. (1985). Home care expenses for the disabled elderly. *Health Care Financing Review* 7(2), 51–58.

Livengood, W. (1986). The federal budget: Its impact on home health agencies. *Home Healthcare Nurse* 4(4), 44.

Lochman, J. E. (1983). Factors related to patients' satisfaction with their medical care. *Journal of Community Health 9*, 91–109.

Lohr, K. N. (1988). Outcome measurement: Concepts and questions. *Inquiry 25*(1), 37–50.

Lohr, K. N., Brook, R. H., Goldberg, G. A., Chassin, M. R., & Glennan, T. K. (1985, March). *Impact of Medicare Prospective Payment on the Quality of Medical Care: A Research Agenda.* Santa Monica, CA: The Rand Corporation.

Lyons, M. & Steele, G. A. (1977). Evaluation of a home health aide training program for the elderly. *Evaluation Quarterly 1*(4), 609–621.

Macken, C. (1984, November). 1982 long-term care survey: National estimates of functional impairment among the elderly living in the community. Paper presented at the Gerontological Society of America Annual meeting, San Antonio, TX.

Macro Systems, Inc. (1988). Review of state quality assurance programs for home care. U.S. Department of Health and Human Services, Office of the Assistant Secretary for Planning and Evaluation.

Manton, K. G., & Hausner, T. (1987). A multidimensional approach to case mix for home health services. *Health Care Financing Review 8*(4), 37–54.

Manton, K. G., & Liu, K. (1984). Projecting chronic disease prevalence. *Medical Care 22*, 511–526.

Manton, K. G., Liu, K., & Cornelius, E. (1985). An analysis of the heterogeneity of U.S. nursing home patients. *Journal of Gerontology 40*, 34–46.

Manton, K. G., & Yashin, A. I. (1986). Control issues in stochastic model of national and subnational health service delivery systems. *Research Monograph on the Application of Operation Research Technology to Health Service Issues.* New York: Pergamon Press.

Massachusetts Department of Public Health. (1984). Quality assurance by sampling: First annual report, August 29, 1983–February 14, 1984.

Mathematica Policy Research. (1985, January). *Evaluation of the State Demonstrations in Nursing Home Quality Assurance Processes.* Princeton, NJ.

McAllister, J. C. III., Black, B. L., Griffin, R. E., & Smith, J. E. (1986). Controversial issues in home health care: A roundtable discussion. *American Journal of Hospital Pharmacy 43*, 933–946.

McAuley, W. J., & Blieszner, R. (1985). Selection of long-term arrangements by older community residents. *The Gerontologist 25*, 188–193.

McAuliffe, W. E. (1978). Studies of process-outcome correlations in medical care evaluations: A critique. *Medical Care 16*, 907–930.

McAuliffe, W. E. (1979). Measuring the quality of medical care: Process versus outcome. *Milbank Memorial Fund Quarterly/Health and Society 57*, 118–152.

McCann, B. A., & Hill, K. L. (1986, May). The JCAH home care project. *Quality Review Bulletin*, 191–193.

McFarland, B. H., Freeborn, D. K., Mullooly, J. P., & Pope, C. R. (1986). Utilization patterns and mortality of HMO enrollees. *Medical Care 24*(3), 200–208.

Meiners, M. R., Thorbum, P., Roddy, P. C., & Jones, B. J. (1985, October). A NCHSR Report. *Nursing Home Admissions: The Results of an Incentive Reimbursement Experiment*, U.S. Department of Health and Human Services.

Miller, S. C. (1986). The home care client record project: Model forms and comprehensive guidelines. *Quality Review Bulletin*, 187–190.

Mitchell, J. B. (1978). Patient outcomes in alternative long-term care settings. *Medical Care 16*(6), 439–452.

Montgomery, R. (1982). Impact of institutional care policies on family integration. *The Gerontologist 22*(1), 54–58.

Morris, J. N., & Granger, C. (1982). Assessing and meeting the needs of the long-term care person. In O'Brien, C. (Ed.). *Adult Day Care: A Practical Guide.* Belmont, CA: Wadsworth Health Service Press.

Morris, J. N., Sherwood, S., May, M. M., & Bernstein, E. (1987). FRED: An innovative approach to nursing home level-of-care assignments. *Health Services Research 22*, 17–140.

Morrison, P. et al. (1985, December 31). A study of patient classification for prospective rate-setting for Medicare patients in general hospital psychiatric units and psychiatric hospitals. Final report, Contract No. NIMH-278-84-0011(DB), Macro Systems, Health Economic, Research and the Health Data Institute.

Mumma, N. (1987). Quality and cost of home care services: Coordinated funding. In

Fisher, K., & Gardner, K. (Eds.) *Quality and Home Health Care: Redefining the Tradition* (pp. 105–112). Chicago, IL: Joint Commission on Accreditation of Healthcare Organizations.

Mundinger, M. O. (1983). *Home Care Controversy: Too Little, Too Late, Too Costly.* Rockville, MD: Aspen Systems Corporation.

National Association for Home Care. (1986, January). *Toward a National Home Care Policy: Blueprint for Action,'* 39.

National League for Nursing, Division of Accreditation for Home Care and Community Health. (1986a, July). *Accreditation Program for Home Care and Community Health: Criteria, Standards, and Substantiating Evidences,* New York.

National League for Nursing, Division of Accreditation for Home Care and Community Health. (1986b, July). *Policies and Procedures for the NLN Accreditation Program.* New York.

Nemeroff, W. F., & Cosentino, J. (1979). Utilizing feedback and goal setting to increase performance appraisal interview skills of managers. *Academy of Management Journal 22,* 566–576.

Neter, J., & Wasserman, S. (1974). *Applied Linear Statistical Models.* New York: Wiley.

New York Department of Health, (1984, May). *Report to the Governor and Legislature on the New Surveillance Process for New York State Residential Health Care Facilities.* Albany, NY: Office of Health Systems Management.

Nielsen, M., Blenkner, M., Bloom, M., Down, T., & Beggs, H. (1972). Older persons after hospitalization: A controlled study of home aide service. *American Journal of Public Health 62*(8), 1094–1101.

(1989, January). Computers: A sure bet for quality management. *Provider, 9.*

Office of Inspector General. (1983). Semiannual Report, October 1, 1983–March 31, 1984.

Ohio Nursing Home Commission. (1979). *A Program in Crisis.* Final report to the Governor and Ohio General Assembly, Columbus, OH.

Padilla, G. V., & Grant, M. M. (1985). Qualtiy of life as a cancer nursing outcome variable. *Advances in Nursing Science 8,* 45–58.

Pascoe, G. C. (1983). Patient satisfaction in primary health care: A literature review and analysis. *Evaluation and Program Planning 6,* 185–210.

Peters, D. (1988). Quality care: Quality documentation. *Caring 7,* 30–35.

Pettigrew, M., Kramer, A., Polesovsky, M., & Shaughnessy, P. (1986, March). *Hospital-Based and Freestanding Home Health Case Mix: Implications for Medicare Reimbursement Policy.* Denver, CO: Center for Health Services Research, University of Colorado Health Sciences Center.

Pettingill, J., & Vertrees, J. C. (1982, December). Reliability and validity of hospital case-mix measurement. *Health Care Financing Review.* 4(2), HCFA Pub. No. 03149, Office of Research and Demonstrations, Health Care Financing Administration, Washington, DC: U.S. Government Printing Office.

Phillips, B. R. (1989, January). A pilot study of the adequacy of post-hospital community care of the elderly: Final report. Mathematica Policy Research, draft.

Prue, D. M., Krapfl, J. E., Noah, J. E., Cannon, S., & Maley, R. F. (1980). Managing the treatment activities of state hospital staff. *Journal of Organizational Behavior Management 2,* 165–181.

Reichardt, C. S. (1979). The statistical analysis of data from nonequivalent group designs. In Cook, T. C., & Campbell, D. T. (Eds.), *Quasi-Experimentation Design and Analysis Issues for Field Settings* (pp. 147–206). Chicago, IL: Rand McNally College Publishing.

Reif, L. (1987, November 9–10). Measuring the quality of home care: Assessing providers' performance from a consumers' perspective. Paper presented at *Nursing Leadership in Home Care Research*, an invitational conference sponsored by the National League for Nursing and the National Center for Homecare Education and Research, Chicago, IL.

Riley, P. (1989). University of Southern Maine, Portland, ME. Personal; communication with author about USM's project surveying the elderly about their perceptions of quality of care in home health services.

Rinke, L. T., & Wilson, A. A. (1987a). *Outcome Measures in Home Care: Volume I—Service.* New York: National League for Nursing, pp. 1–283.

Rinke, L. T., & Wilson, A. A. (1987b). *Outcomes Measures in Home Care: Volume II—Service.* New York: National League for Nursing, pp. 1–283.

Rustein, D., Berenberg, W., Chalmers, T., Child, C., Fishman, A., & Perrin, E. (1976). Measuring the quality of medical care: A clinical method. *New England Journal of Medicine 294,* 582–588.

Sabatino, C. P. (1986, August). *The 'Black Box' of Home Care Quality.* Washington, DC: U.S. Printing Office. A report presented by the chairman of the Select. Committee on Aging, House of Representatives, 99th. Cong. 2d. sess., prepared by the American Bar Association.

Schlenker, R. E. (1984). Nursing home reimbursement, quality, and access—A synthesis of research. Prepared for the Institute of Medicine Conference on Reimbursement, Anaheim, CA.

Schlenker, R. E. (1986). Case mix reimbursement for nursing homes. *Journal of Health Politics, Policy, and Law 11*(3), 445–461.

Schlenker, R., Shaughnessy, & Yslas, I. (1983). The effect of case mix and quality on cost differences between hospital-based and freestanding nursing homes. *Inquiry 20,* 361–368.

Schneider, D., & O'Sullivan, A. (1980). *Quality Assurance for Long-Term Care: Revising the Periodic Review.* Troy, NY: Schneider and Associates.

Schneider, D., Hatcher, G., & O'Sullivan, A. (1980). Quality assurance for long-term care: The Sentinel health event system. Final report to New York State Health Planning Commission, Albany, New York. Troy, NY: Rensselaer Polytechnic Institute.

Schneider, D. P., Fries, B. E., & Desmond, M. (1983). *Incentives and Basic Principles for Long-Term Care Patient Classification Development* (Report 1, New York State Case Mix Prospective Reimbursement System for Long-Term Care). Troy, NY: Rensselaer Polytechnic Institute.

Schneider, D., Foley, W., Lefkowich, W. K., et al. (1987, April). New York Quality Assurance System (NYQAS) Report 1: A discussion of the issues, mimeo.

Seidl, F. W., Applebaum, R., Austin, C., & Mahoney, K. (1983). *Delivering In-Home Services to the Aged and Disabled.* Lexington, MA: Lexington Books.

Shaughnessy, P., Kramer, A., & Schlenker, R. (1987). Preliminary findings from the national long-term care study. Presented to HCFA, October, 1987. University of Colorado Center for Health Services Research, Denver, CO.

Shaughnessy, P. W., Kramer, A. M., Schlenker, R. E., & Polesovsky, M. B. (1984). Nursing home case mix differences between Medicare and non-Medicare and between hospital-based and freestanding patients. Denver, CO: Center for Health Services Research, University of Colorado Health Sciences Center.

Shaughnessy, P. W., Kramer, A. M., Schlenker, R. E., & Polesovsky, M. B. (1985). Nursing home case-mix differences between Medicare and non-Medicare and between hospital-based and freestanding patients. *Inquiry 22,* 162–177.

Sivertsen, L., & Fletcher, J. (1982, June). Assisting the elderly with drug therapy in the home. *Nursing Clinics of North America 17*(2), 293–301.

Smith v. Heckler. (1984). 747 F.2nd 583 (10th Cir.).

Smits, H. (1982). Quality assurance of long-term care. *World Hospitals 3*, 37–39.

Soldo, B. J. (1983). *A National Perspective on the Home Care Population*. Washington, DC: Center for Population Research, Kennedy Institute of Ethics, Georgetown University.

Soldo, B. J., & Manton, K. G. (1985). Health status and service needs of the oldest old: Current patterns and future trends. *Milbank Memorial Fund Quarterly 62*, 286–319.

Sorgen, L. M. (1986). The development of a home care quality assurance program in Alberta. *Home Health Care Services Quarterly 7*(2), 13–28.

Stassen, M., & Bishop, C. E. (1983). *Incorporating Case Mix in Prospective Reimbursement for SNF Under Medicare: Critical Review of Relevant Research*. Waltham, MA: Center for Health Policy Analysis and Research, Brandeis University.

Stiver, H. G., Trosky, S. K., Cote, D. D., & Oruck, J. L. (1982). Self-administration of intravenous antibiotics: An efficient, cost-effective home care program. *Canadian Medical Association Journal 127*, 207–211.

Swan, J. E., & Carroll, M. G. (1980). Patient satisfaction: An overview of research—1965 to 1978. In Hunt, E. K., & Day, R. L. (Eds). *Refining Concepts and Measures of Consumer Satisfaction and Complaining Behavior*. Bloomington, IN: Indiana University Press.

Taylor, M. B. (1986, Summer). Contradictions in federal policies put elderly at risk of health care neglect. *Home Health Care Services Quarterly 7*, 5–12.

U.S. Congress, Senate Special Committee on Aging. (1986). *Aging America: Trends and Projections*. 99th. Cong. 2d sess.

U.S. Department of Health and Human Services, Health Care Financing Administration, Bureau of Data Management and Strategy. (1983, September). *Medicare Statistical Files Manual*. Baltimore, MD.

U. S. Department of Health and Human Services, Health Care Financing Administration, Bureau of Data Management and Strategy. (1985a, October). Conditions of participation: Home health agencies. *Federal Regulations*. 405.1201-405.1227, Chap. 4.

U. S. Department of Health and Human Services, Health Care Financing Administration, Bureau of Data Management and Strategy. (1985b, November). Conditions of participation. *Home Health Agency Manual*. Baltimore, MD, Interpretive Guidelines, Appendix B.

U. S. Department of Health and Human Services, Health Care Financing Administration, Bureau of Data Management and Strategy. (1986a, September). Development of a patient-oriented approach for surveying home health agencies. *Request for Proposal*, HCFA-87-003/JD, Baltimore, MD.

U.S. Department of Health and Human Services, Public Health Service, National Center for Health Statistics. (1986). Americans needing home care. *Vital and Health Statistics 10*, 153.

U.S. General Accounting Office. (1981, September 25). *Medicare Home Health Services: A Difficult Program to Control*. GAO/HRD-81-155, pp. 10–17.

U.S. General Accounting Office. (1982, December). *The Elderly Should Benefit from Expanded Home Health Care but Increasing These Services Will Not Insure Cost Reductions*. Washington, DC.

U.S. General Accounting Office. (1983). *Medicaid and Nursing Home Care: Cost Increases and the Need for Services Are Creating Problems for the States and the Elderly*. Washington, DC.

U.S. General Accounting Office. (1985, September 30). *Simulations of a Medicare Prospective Payment System for Home Health Care*. GAO/HRD-85-110.

U.S. General Accounting Office. (1986, June 30). *Post-Hospital Care: Efforts to Evaluate Medicare Prospective Payment Effects Are Insufficient.* Report to the Special Committee on Aging, U.S. Senate.

Vibbert, S. (1986). Report charges HCFA with unfair restrictions on home health benefits. *Long Term Care Management* 15(19), 5–6.

Vladeck, B. (1988). Quality assurance through external controls. *Inquiry* 25(1), 100–107.

Ware, J. E., Davies-Avery, A., & Stewart, A. L. (1978). The measurement and meaning of patient satisfaction. *A Review of the Recent Literature: Health and Medical Care Services Review* 1(1), 1–15.

Weisbrod, B. A., & Schlesinger, M. (1983). *Public, Private, Nonprofit Ownership and the Response to Asymmetric Information: The Case of Nursing Homes.* Discussion paper #209, Center for Health Economics and Law, University of Wisconsin–Madison, WI, Weissert, W. G.

Weisbrod, B. A., & Schlesinger, M. (1985). Estimating the long-term care population: Prevalence rates and selected characteristics. *Health Care Financing Review* 6(4), 83–91.

Weissert, W. G., & W. J. Scanlon (1985). Determinants of nursing home discharge status. *Medical Care* 23(4), 333–342.

Weissert, W. G., Scanlon, W. J., Wan, T. H., & Skinner, D. (1983). Care for the chronically ill: Nursing home incentive payment experiment. *Health Care Financing Review* 5(3), 41–49.

Werley, H. H., & Long, N. M. (1988). *Identification of the Nursing Minimum Data Set.* New York: Springer.

Williamson, J. W. (1988). Future policy directions for quality assurance: Lessons from the health accounting experience. *Inquiry* 25(1), 67–77.

Wood, J. B. (1985). The effects of cost-containment on home health agencies. *Home Health Care Services Quarterly* 6(4), 59–78.

Wood, J. B. (1984). Public policies and current effect on home health agencies. *Home Health Services Quarterly* 5(2), 75–86.

Woodbury, M. A., & Manton, K. G. (1982). A new procedure for analysis of medical classification. *Methods of Information in Medicine* 21, 210–220.

Woodson, A. S., Foley, S. M., Daniels, P. J., Landes, D. P., & Kurowski, B. T. (1981). *Long-Term Care Guidelines for Quality.* Denver, CO: Center for Health Services, Research, University of Colorado Health Sciences Center.

Wolf, R. (1983, Winter). Medicare policy and regulatory control. *Pride Institute Journal of Long Term Care Health Care.*

Wyszewianski, L. (1988). Quality of care: Past achievements and future challenges. *Inquiry* 25(1), 13–22.

Zarit, S., Orr, N., & Zarit, J. (1984). *Working with Families of Dementia Victims: A Treatment Manual.* UCLA/UCS Long-Term Care Gerontology Center.

Zimmer, J. G., Growth-Juncker, A., & McCusker, J. (1985). A randomized controlled study of a home health care team. *American Journal of Public Health* 75(2), 134–141.

Zimmer, J. G. (1979). Medical care evaluation studies in long-term care facilities. *Journal of the American Geriatrics Society* 27, 62–72.

Zimmer, J. G., Growth-Juncker, A., & McCusker, J. (1983). Effects of a physician-led home care team on terminal care. *Journal of the American Geriatrics Society* 32(4), 288–292.

Zimmer, J. G., & Williams, T. F. (1978). Spectrum of severity and control of diabetes mellitus in skilled nursing facilities. *Journal of the American Geriatrics Society* 26, 443–452.

Index

Index

Staff
 education of, on law, 121–122
 impact of psychosocial interventions
  on, 19–20
 responses and beliefs of, regarding
  restraints, 91
 selection and training of, for SCUs,
  45–46
Standards, compliance with, 160–161
State hospital, SCUs in, 54–55
State surveyors, 117–121
Stress incontinence, 68–69
Structural measures, of home health
  care, 220–221
Strumpf, N. E., 89–90, 95–96
Sunnybrook Medical Centre, 97
Surveyors, state, 117–121
System Sciences, 226

Targeting, 140–142
Tax Equity and Fiscal Responsibility
  Act (TEFRA), of 1982, 210
Teaching Nursing Home Program
  (TNHP) Study, 172–174, 176–
  177, 178, 180, 222
Technology, in home health care, 219
Teteberg, B., 172–174
Therapeutic effects, specific and
  nonspecific, of psychosocial in-
  terventions, 17–18
Therapy; see also Interventions; Treat-
  ment interference
 medical, falls and, 37–38
 reminiscence, 11–12
 validation, 10–11
Title III, 125, 126, 213
Title 5, United States Code, Chapter
  5, 111
Title XX, 125, 213
Todd, S., 51
Training
 behaviorally oriented, for urinary incontinence, 70–71
 of NP, 181–182
 in SCUs, 45–46, 56–57
Travelers Insurance Company, 194

Treatment interference, restraints and,
  97–98; see also Interventions;
  Therapy
Turemark, U., 85

USDA, 152
U.S. Public Health Service, 29
U.S. Senate Special Committee on Ag-
  ing, 3, 148, 195, 196, 203
U.S. Supreme Court, 218
University of California—San Francis-
  co, 203, 204, 226
University of Colorado, 204, 222
University of Miami, 137
University of Michigan, 158
University of Minnesota Study of Post
  Acute Care, 224, 226, 229
University of Utah College of Medi-
  cine, 172
Urban Medical Group, 174, 177
Urge incontinence, 72–73
Urinary incontinence, see Incontinence
Urinary tract infections (UTIs), 61, 62
Utilization, service, 129
 controls of, in home care, 208–209

Validation therapy, 10–11
Validity, of study of psychosocial interventions, 16–17
Veterans Administration, 137, 139,
  178, 183, 193
 study of NPs by, 172–175
Visiting Nurse Associations (VNAs),
  211, 237

Wandering, restraints and, 98
Washington State Home Care Project,
  223–224, 226
Waxman bill, 156
Weissert, W. G., 189
Wieland, D., 172–175
Wilson, K., 53–54

Yee, D., 127, 128, 129